# DRAMATIZING GREEK MYTHOLOGY

TO MY LATE COUSIN ANNE SEWARD TOWNSEND,
WHO DEVOTED HER LIFE TO HELPING PEOPLE.

Published by Smith and Kraus, Inc.
177 Lyme Road, Hanover, NH 03766
Copyright ©2002 by Louise Thistle
Manufactured in the United States of America

*Cover and Text Design by Julia Hill Gignoux*
*Illustrations by Susan Corey*

First Edition: June 2002
10 9 8 7 6 5 4 3 2 1

The Library of Congress Cataloging-In-Publication Data
Thistle, Louise.
Dramatizing Greek mythology / Louise Thistle. —1st ed.
p. cm. — (Young actors series)
Includes bibliographical references (p.  ).
ISBN 1-57525-293-7 (pbk.)
1. Children's plays—presentation, etc. 2. Mythology, Greek—Juvenile drama. I. Title. II. Series.

PN3157 .T48 2002
792'.0226—dc21
2002070500

# DRAMATIZING GREEK MYTHOLOGY

## Louise Thistle

YOUNG ACTORS SERIES

A Smith and Kraus Book

# CONTENTS

## PART II: DRAMATIZATIONS

# INTRODUCTION

*There's a little of wanting to perform in all of us. No one wants to be ordinary. Everyone wants someone else's attention.*

Virginia Welch, retired teacher

*I would like to do another drama project because I think it's very wonderful to be in a play.*

Diana Ramirez, student

This book fulfills several teacher needs. First, it provides a method for putting on simple, quick, effective plays and gives all students in classes of up to thirty-five students significant roles; second, it provides dramatizations of Greek myths—an important part of our cultural literary heritage; third, it provides a method for developing language, literature appreciation, and performance skills in a meaningful, memorable way; finally, it provides activities in which students of all levels can succeed and learn to work together as a team and, at the same time, grow and develop individually.

In a sense, I started this book when I was a child. My father put a platform in our backyard as a stage. There I put on plays with my neighborhood friends. I made up these plays and dictated them to my father who typed them on his typewriter using carbon paper, so I could have scripts for my friends. I still thank my father for nurturing in me this early love of acting and theater that has stayed with me throughout my life and has become my lifework.

I went to elementary school when educational-philosopher John Dewey's "learn by doing" approach was popular. I had a teacher who loved drama and involved the class in both informal and stage acting. The experience was exhilarating. It was liberating to act out the strong emotions and lively actions of characters and situations, especially in the classroom where expression of these strong feelings and boisterous actions was not the norm. From then on, drama became my favorite school activity.

Later, as a teacher, I found that students shared this excitement when performing on stage or acting in class. They looked forward to plans, practices, and performances. Everyone could succeed and feel part of the team. Indeed, before performances, teachers, parents, the actors, and other students shared a little of the excitement. They were all eager to see the play. There is something celebratory, magical, and memorable about theater that brings the whole school community together and produces memories and commentaries for years to come.

As a freelance drama teacher, I know from experience both the joys and problems teachers encounter when trying to stage a class play using traditional scripts and production styles. I had to solve the problem of line memorization—when students do not learn their lines until the last moment, if at all; the problems of backstage fooling around; the problem of uneven roles, with three or four major roles and numerous insignificant walk-ons; and the problem of needing to create elaborate costumes and scenery. I also realized the problem of lengthy rehearsal periods in which students lose interest and focus until the last week or so before the opening of the play. Eliminating these problems enables teachers to focus on student enjoyment and participation, and to concentrate on the development of students' imagination and their theater and performance skills. The solution to these problems is *narrative mime theater*.

## Eliminating Lengthy Line Memorization

Most scripts require that students memorize lines—sometimes quite a few of them. However, students often do not learn these lines until the last moment, and some are still shaky on performance day. Sometimes too an actor with many lines is absent on performance day, and the teacher must put in a student who has to read the part from a script.

The essence of good acting is to get inside the characters and portray them truthfully—rather than simply memorizing lines. Students who pursue acting will certainly need to memorize lines, but this should not be the emphasis for beginners. Development of the imagination, voice skills, and characterization skills are of greater concern at the beginning level.

Line memorization is at a minimum with narrative mime theater (in these plays only the leading roles require some moderate memorization). Instead, the plays use storytellers (the chorus), who read from scripts. Most of the actors' lines spring directly from strong cues given by the chorus. For example, chorus members read, "Persephone called to Zeus to help her," and Persephone's line is, "Zeus, king of the gods, help me." Using a chorus also has an immediate creative benefit—actors never hold a script and can move freely, using their whole bodies beginning on the first day of rehearsals.

If actors don't know a line during rehearsals, the director can tell it to them. If actors forget during the performance, the chorus can whisper it.

## Eliminating Backstage Fooling Around

A teacher who has directed one play may never want to direct another because of the problem of backstage fooling around. Most plays require that actors enter and exit from backstage, so the problem is virtually unavoidable. Lecturing students to pipe down backstage is time-consuming—and exhausting. In addition students who are goofing around backstage are not out front listening and learning to act by watching other students during rehearsal.

In narrative mime, the solution is to have all actors sit on the stage at all times, in chairs arranged in a semicircle in view of the audience and director. The costumes and props they use for their parts are under their chairs. The chorus members stand on either side of the stage, and the sound crew are at a table to one side of the stage with their rhythm instruments for sound effects laid out before them.

Having the performers out front enables the audience to see the theatrics. The audience watches a student in the sound crew tap a wood block as a dog trots along; then they see students wiggle blue fabric and shake a tambourine to create the rippling sea. Actors, sitting out front at all times, learn the movements and lines of the other actors, so they are able to step in at the last moment if someone is absent during rehearsals.

## Eliminating the Star System and Becoming a Team

Most scripts feature a few leading roles and relegate the rest of the participants to walk-ons as villagers or to props, such as trees. Naturally the trees and villagers often become bored and restless. The goal in narrative mime presentations is for all students to have significant roles in order to feel involved and to learn performance skills. Not all students want leading roles, of course, and some prefer not to act at all. The non-actors comprise a sound crew of six. Each member is assigned several, rhythm instruments to create sound effects that enhance the action and help the actors act with more conviction. For example, a sound crew member strikes a drum to create the majestic pomp of Hades proceeding to his throne, and another sound crew member rings bells to help actors fly lightly like Hermes, the messenger god.

Students in narrative mime theater who want to act but do not want a major role portray many inanimate objects, such as dancing flames, mountain peaks, and swirling mist, using props and movement. Students playing these roles are assigned several parts, keeping them active and involved throughout the play. These roles are often played in pairs or threes to loosen inhibitions and increase the fluidity of creative expression. Directors often discover that those at-first-reluctant actors want to play more roles—and sometimes even speaking roles as they gain confidence playing many small parts. Casting in these plays is flexible. Directors can add or subtract parts as necessary. For example there can always be a few more sailors, or a few less. Amazons, mountains, flowers, birds, servants, nymphs, and other collective parts can be expanded as needed.

A bonus of incorporating sound effects and inanimate objects is that it guarantees the success of a production. So much activity is occurring onstage in a narrative mime performance—with so much visual and auditory stimuli—that imperfections are overlooked.

## Eliminating Elaborate Costumes and Scenery

Sets and elaborate costumes can be time-consuming to create, and they can detract from what is most important—developing the imagination and learning acting and performance skills. So much time and emphasis is placed on the sets and costumes in traditional productions that the central acting skills, which are the essence of good theater, suffer. Students should realize that acting is created by performers through the use of their imaginations, voices, and movements rather than by elaborate costumes and technological effects. It is better to play a part with conviction but without a costume than to play it limply in an elaborate costume.

In narrative mime theater, performers wear all-black clothing to create uniformity. Costume pieces (mostly headpieces), fabrics for scenery, and simple props are kept under the actors' chairs. The needed prop can be popped on or picked up when needed to act out a part. Scenery can continually move and change. Students comprise the set, and their simple costumes and props transform them from one piece of scenery into another, challenging the imagination of the performers and audience alike. If teachers decide to use tunics for major characters in these plays, the same set of tunics can be worn over and over again for all of the myths in this book.

## Teaching Acting Skills

Teachers often find that students act woodenly when they perform on stage. Drama comes from the Greek word *dran*, "to do or to act." To eliminate wooden acting, characters in narrative mime presentations are given specific actions to do in almost every sentence: "A lion prowled in front of the house," "Odysseus thrust his arms up, and Circe kneeled to him," "The Sirens glided into the field of flowers." These actions require the participation of students—they give students something to do.

## The Value of Dramatizing Greek Mythology

I began this project to fulfill teachers needs and provide them with ways to dramatize Greek myths.

As I field-tested the material, I grew more and more excited. I discovered that students of all backgrounds reacted with such enthusiasm to these powerful stories and vivid characters that every American should know, as E.D. Hirsch Jr. says in *The Dictionary of Cultural Literacy*. Their involvement reinforced my appreciation for the genius of the ancient Greeks—the first to invent theater as we know it today, with actors performing plays.

Psychologists talk about two kinds of knowledge: One kind of knowledge is intellectual knowledge, gained through activities such as reading and discussion; another kind is knowledge gained through direct experience. Knowledge about Greek mythology, their characters, and stories may be best gained by coupling direct experience of the characters and their actions with reading, writing, and discussion.

Students cannot be passive and uninvolved as they stride with the majestic bearing of a god or goddess, swirl like a menacing whirlpool, or row like sailors escaping sea monsters. These acting experiences develop the imagination, teach students new ways of expressing themselves as actors, while expanding and enriching their appreciation of Greek mythology. Dramatization also tests comprehension in a very direct way—the job of an actor or storyteller is to communicate the meaning of the play to the audience. If the meaning is clear, they understand the literature. No one understands the characters in a play better than the actors who act them.

Acting also develops public speaking skills. A recent article in the *San Diego Union* said that employers in professional occupations most often seek qualified employees who are able to make an effective speech. Dramatization develops speaking skills and teaches students how to present themselves courageously to the public.

This book also has several writing components. The students are asked to write about why they want a particular part, and later they are asked to write a reflection on their experience in the play. The last chapter of the book describes how students can write and produce their own narrative mime scripts and TV interviews.

## *Using Dramatizing Greek Mythology*

Part I, Getting Started, describes how to train students in speaking and acting skills and how to produce and direct the plays presented in this book. Some of the information in these chapters are repeated in my other books, but are necessary to the material in this book. Part I has the following chapters:

**Chapter 1** describes how to develop the four principles of effective speech and other speaking techniques.

**Chapter 2** explains how to develop the three principles of good acting.

**Chapter 3** tells how to produce the plays presented in this book—with detailed information on the mechanics of directing these and other plays. It includes casting, stage blocking, acting techniques, methods to train the audience in theater appreciation, and techniques for training the sound crew.

**Chapter 4** describes Greek costumes and provides guidelines for making or obtaining simple, generic costumes and props that can be used for a variety of different plays.

**Chapter 5** explains how to use rhythm instruments and create them from objects found around home or school and how to teach students a simple Greek dance.

**Chapter 6** suggests a model step-by-step rehearsal schedule, from introducing the play through after-performance follow-ups.

**Part II** presents scripts for five Greek myths. They are:
- *The Creation and the Birth of the Olympian Gods*
- *The Myth of Demeter and Persephone or The Origin of the Seasons*

- *The Labors of Hercules*
- *The Odyssey*
- *The Myth of Orpheus and Eurydice or Descent into the Underworld*

These plays have been field-tested and performed with success. The scripts are set off from the rest of the book by a decorative border. The scripts may be photocopied and distributed to each student participating in a production. Please note that permission is granted for productions in which an admission fee is not charged. For all other uses, written permission must be obtained from the author.

Each play includes a synopsis, a TV interview with the characters telling their stories to plunge students immediately into dramatization while giving them background on the characters and the plot. Scripts also have acting activities to get all students involved quickly and to teach them acting skills. Production Notes for each play include costume and props suggestions. Finally, there is a section with critical-thinking questions, research, and art activities, including a "Classical Connections" (developing language) section with questions on words in the myths that have entered the English language.

Your experience with narrative mime theater should not be limited to the scripts presented in this book. Chapter 12 describes how to write your own dramatized narrative mime scripts and TV interviews based on stories chosen for their relevance to your specific teaching situation. Students can write, direct, and produce their own narrative mime scripts and instructions for guiding such activities are provided as well.

There is a Glossary of drama and literature terminology and an explanation of words and phrases from Greek mythology. Also included is a Selected Bibliography.

Now more than ever students need a creative vent for strong feelings. They crave ways to develop and use their imaginations—the source of all creativity. They need and want to enact the powerful characters and situations that lurk in their imaginations.

Some of my most pleasurable experiences are when students who were at first reluctant to participate at all after a few rehearsals asked if they might play more parts, or if they might have a speaking role next time, and when teachers tell me that students who were never recognized got positive regard and new respect as actors.

It takes extra effort to produce a play, but it is well worth the effort to see the students get excited and involved in developing their imaginations. The student-actors, their teachers, and their relatives are so grateful and enthusiastic. When teachers produce a play, something significant happens—something the teacher, students, and their relatives will remember all of their lives.

# PART I: GETTING STARTED

# 1

## The Four Stage-Speaking Principles

*Great actors make ordinary words exciting surprises.*
Stanley Kauffman, theater critic, author

*What I want most from actors performing my plays is clarity of utterance.*
Tom Stoppard, playwright

*Actors need verbal relish. They should taste, feel, and see the language.*
John Barton, acting teacher

The most important attribute of a good actor is a strong expressive voice. In fact, lack of projection and speaking too rapidly are the major flaws of many amateur productions. Other common speaking flaws are letting the voice trail off at the end of sentences and not emphasizing important words.

Beginning actors need continual training on speaking clearly right from the start because speaking well is the most essential requirement of a successful performance. Actors who speak so that every word is easily understood by the audience in the back row perform a great service to the audience.

Four speaking principles are the foundation of a good acting program. This chapter describes the four principles and how to teach them. (A detailed description of how to introduce and teach the principles in rehearsals is in chapter 6, "A Model Step-by-Step Rehearsal Schedule.")

The four principles are:
   **Projection:** speaking loudly enough so that every word is heard
   **Articulation:** saying every consonant distinctly so that the word is clearly identifiable
   **Colorization:** coloring speech so that words sound like what they describe and adding gestures to enhance the meaning
   **Slowing the pace:** slowing the rate of speech to focus on important words and phrases

List these principles on the board, or a chart, and refer to them throughout each lesson. Begin the lesson by asking students why acting teachers and directors agree that the most important quality of a good actor is a strong expressive voice.

# PROJECTION

Projection is the first and most important speaking principle. Projection means throwing your voice out to the back of a space so that everyone can hear what you're saying. If students project well, the other principles that we'll discuss will likely follow. Good projection promotes involvement in the material. It is hard to be passive and lackadaisical if you project when you speak. Another plus is that speaking rapidly becomes more difficult.

To instill good projection:

- Model good and poor projection. Invite a student to the front of the room and carry on a brief conversation about the weather—first using poor projection and then good projection. Then ask which conversation would be more interesting to an audience and why.

- Ask what happens to an audience when performers or speakers don't project. Then have students define projection.

- Explain that a microphone-free, projected voice is the most expressive voice.

- Practice projection with students. Make sure students understand that projection requires using a strong voice but not shouting, which would annoy an audience. Then, have students stand and chant "PROJECTION" four times while throwing an arm outward as if throwing a ball. Encourage them to aim to the farthest reaches of the room.

- Push for better projection right from the beginning by interrupting students and saying "louder," when necessary. Always reject poor projection, but be sure to praise improvement. As you praise, you can coax students to attain a higher level of projection.

- Help students emphasize important words that need "to be hit" with more projection by telling them which words to hit. It helps to explain why that particular word is a significant word for the audience to know. (In the scripts many words that need emphasis are capitalized.)

# ARTICULATION

Articulation means saying every consonant in words distinctly so the exact word is understood. For example, say "cat," so that it sounds like "cat," not like "cab" or "can."

Good articulation requires active use of the articulators—teeth, tongue, lips, and gum ridges. The best speakers energetically use their articulators—vigorously moving the jaw, lips, and tongue. Good articulation helps participants experience the language fully and sensually on the lips, teeth, tongue, and palate, which makes every word clear to the audience. To instill good articulation:

- Model poor and then good articulation. For example, say "dog" swallowing the *g*. Then say it again emphasizing the *g*. Ask students to describe the difference between the first and the second time you said it.

- Practice using good articulation with students. Write *articulation* on the board. Have them rise and chant AR-TIC-U-LA-TION four times pointing emphatically at each syllable—to dramatize enunciating each syllable clearly.

- Before dramatizing a myth, read the pronunciation guide in the cast list, and then articulate each mythological character's name, so that students can hear the names pronounced correctly. Have them practice saying the names with you with good articulation. You might pronounce Scylla, Charybdis, Odysseus, Hippolyta, Eurystheus, Sisyphus, Augeas, and then have students say the names with you.

- Recite limericks, particularly tongue-twister limericks such as "The tutor who tooted the flute" and "A flea and a fly in a flue." These demand good articulation. (For some dramatized limericks, see my book *Dramatizing Classic Poetry* listed in the Bibliography.)

# COLORIZATION

Colorization means saying words so they sound like what they describe. For example, say "joy" in a bright light voice and thrust your arms up exuberantly. Then say "gloom" in a dark, deep, heavy voice and slump depressingly. Colorization is used by storytellers to help audiences experience the action and imagery.

To develop the use of colorization:

- Ask students what it means when you say that speakers should speak colorfully when reciting poetry. Make a big colorful gesture as you say "colorfully," speaking in a colorful voice.

- Have students rise and chant "colorization" four times, each time opening their arms up and out in a big, wide, colorful gesture and opening their eyes as if enlivened.

- Recite a rhyme focusing on using colorful speech to express the meaning of the words. For example, recite "Humpty Dumpty" in a big, full voice. Say, "Sat on a wall," heavily. Stretch out "F-A-L-L" as he plummets off a high wall. Add excitement and speed up the pace as the horsemen prance during "All the king's horses, and all the king's men." Slow down your speech and shrug hopelessly on "Couldn't put Humpty together again."

- Let students choose rhymes to recite line by line making each word as colorful as possible.

- Recite the alphabet letter by letter giving each letter a personality and a gesture. For example, say "A" explosively and excitedly thrusting your arms up because it begins the alphabet. Say "B" belligerently and punch a fist while puffing up your lips.

# SLOWING THE PACE

Drama, speech making, or the recitation of literature should never be rushed. In our speeded-up society it requires discipline to slow the pace. Although some scenes call for a quickening pace, this must be done purposively. In most cases, it is best to slow the pace so that the audience can enjoy and understand. In these Greek plays, the members of the chorus particularly need to speak slowly so that the audience can understand the story. Projection and speaking slowly and distinctly are the two speech techniques that students need the most work on.

Speakers are often struck at how attentively audiences respond when the speakers consciously slow down their speech and gestures. People in power, such as the queen of England, never rush. They speak and move slowly to show they are in complete command.

To instill slowing the pace:

- Model speaking and moving slowly yourself. For example, when introducing a lesson, slow the rate of your motions as you hold a triangle high; strike it three times, taking time to turn and face the left, right, and center of the room; make a leisurely, large, welcoming gesture with your arms; and freeze demonstrating slow, artistic control.

- Ask students why it's important for the chorus to speak slowly.

- Model a too-speedy delivery of a Mother Goose rhyme and then a slowed-down version. Ask students which an audience would prefer and why.

- Have students stand and chant with you, "SLOW THE PACE" four times, each time slowly opening your arms out to your sides and pausing after each word to emphasize a slow rate of speech and gesture.

- Have students echo you as you recite the prologue from the play you are dramatizing. Be sure to speak slowly, so your students learn by your example.

# GESTURING AND FACIAL EXPRESSION

Ancient Greek plays demand a grand acting style—with strong dramatic speech and enlarged gestures to communicate the powerful feelings and emotions to the audience. Gestures heighten the feeling and open up the voice. This often helps actors speak and act with more conviction. For example, assume a posture of extreme grief, and you will begin to feel grief in your body and it will come into your voice too.

Most students don't gesture naturally, so give them gestures to do. For example, tell Persephone to hold her hands high prayerfully as she begs Zeus to save her. Suggest that Uranus point aggressively at his children as he banishes them underground. Ask the Cyclopes to spread their feet wide and put their hands on their hips, showing aggression.

Gestures may not always spring from the play's narration, so help your actors create appropriate gestures. For example, for the play's introduction, when the chorus members say "Good morning students, adults too," you might suggest that chorus members wave as they speak this line. Tell Chorus 2 to gesture to the audience on "Today we'll act a myth for you." These gestures may seem overdone, but they enliven the audience and let them know the actors care.

Model gesturing slowly. Slow stylized gestures, like a dance, can be beautiful. It is usually best to gesture with the upstage arm (the arm away from the audience), so that the gesture doesn't cover the actor's face.

Facial expressions further vitalize the gesture. For example, Cerberus narrows his eyes and bares his teeth; Charon, the boat man, scowls as he leans forward menacingly; Zeus opens his eyes wide in shock when Demeter lets the crops die. You'll find suggestions for many actions and choreographed gestures in the scripts.

Other speaking techniques are:

**EMPHASIS** is stress on important words through variation in volume, pitch, pause, gesture, and facial expression. Students often need help knowing which word to emphasize. This helps them make the meaning clear. The scripts in this book have important words written in capital letters. You might ask students to underline other words you think need emphasis.

**INFLECTION** is a vocal technique in which the voice rises or falls. Rising inflection carries thoughts and ideas forward. A falling inflection indicates the end of a thought or idea. People tend to let the voice fall and trail off at the end of sentences—but the most important words are often there. Even though it feels unnatural, they need to pay attention and make their voices rise on these final words.

**PAUSE** means stopping after a word or phrase. Most beginners don't hold a pause long enough.

**PITCH** is how low or high your voice is.

**RATE** is how fast or slowly you speak. In scenes of excitement, quicken the pace. In these Greek plays, chorus members may need a reminder to pick up the cues quickly for scenes in which events happen rapidly one after another.

**VOCAL QUALITY** is whether the voice is shrill, raspy, lilting, simpering, barking, or booming.

**VOLUME** is loudness or softness of voice. For a whisper, use a stage whisper that communicates to an audience.

## Vocal Rehearsal Warm-up

It is beneficial to begin each rehearsal with a vocal warm-up. This helps students prepare to use their stage-speaking voices. The prologue of each play is good to use because it opens the play and speakers must use all their speaking skills to grab the audience's attention. It is also short and peppy, and there are suggested gestures for each line. Have students echo you as you recite each line of the prologue modeling good projection, articulation, and colorization at a slow pace. Later, a student with excellent speaking skills could lead this exercise. You might also warm up using dialogue from the scene that you are rehearsing that day.

# 2

## *The Three Acting Principles*

*The actor's ultimate goal is to make the audience believe what is happening.*

William McNulty, actor

*Classic acting is larger than life . . .*

Stanley Kauffman, theater critic, author

Three simple principles are the foundation of a good acting program:

**Believe** you are the part you are playing.
Exercise **control** over your actions and emotions.
Use **voice and movement** expressively to portray characters thoughts, actions, and emotions.

These principles are followed by all good actors. If students practice them, their acting will be successful and will interest an audience. Involvement with the characters, the language, and the story will be deep and satisfying. If these principles are not followed, the acting will lack conviction and not be worthwhile.

To train students in these principles, it helps to list them on a chart and discuss each one individually. You might also use my book *Dramatizing Aesop's Fables* with fables scripted to act in the classroom (see Bibliography). Specific guidelines are given below.

## BELIEVING

Believing is the most important principle. The more students are willing and able to make believe that they are inside the shoes of the character, the fur or feathers of an animal, or even the spirit of an inanimate object, the more involved they will be and the more convincing their acting will be to an audience. For example, an actor playing Zeus must imagine that his power and actions can rule the world. The actor playing the grain goddess Demeter must imagine she can cause crops to grow and die at her command. Actors playing oak trees need to think of their legs as trunks rooted in the ground and their arms as branches reaching to the sun.

To inspire belief:

- Discuss with students the need to believe in the parts they are playing to make the drama real. You might refer to the film, *The Wizard of Oz*, pointing out how seventeen-year-old Judy Garland imagined she was a little girl, and how other actors imagined they were a wicked witch, a man of tin, a cowardly lion, and a man of straw.

- A number of acting activities accompany each play. Be sure to allow time to do these acting activities. These activities help students get involved with the characters and learn how to believe.

- Show the dramatic action pictures of the characters with each script to help students visualize the characters and the action.

- Model limp, ineffective, uncommitted acting to let students see objectively what doesn't work.

- Model belief. When asking students to become Odysseus determined to rescue his sailors, you too "climb into the shoes of Odysseus" who is ready to rescue. Your playfulness and willingness to imagine will help your students believe too.

- Reinforce students' believable acting each time you see it. Compliment a student who has wholeheartedly become a ruthless Uranus determined to banish his children. Reinforce the actor playing Penelope who is moving with majestic graciousness and speaking with sincere kindness to befriend the beggar.

- After each rehearsal, ask students which characters they believed in. Then lead students to figure out what those actors did to make the acting believable.

# CONTROL

A good definition of art is giving form and focus to strong feelings and emotions. Control gives drama artistry and purpose. Dionysus, the Greek god of the theater, abounds with enthusiasm, emotion, and excitement. These are all important qualities for an actor, but this dynamic energy must be tempered by clarity, form, and order—qualities represented by the god Apollo. Greek myths are full of powerful actions and emotions that require stylized choreographed movements. These choreographed movements help give them artistry and form. Choreographed movements also are very pleasing to observe. As students gain artistic control and are able to exercise it, they begin to have a feeling of accomplishment and self-esteem.

To instill control:

- Ask students why a large group of dancers can leap and spin in a small area and not bump into each other.

- Discuss the need to exercise control to give the drama style and artistry. Point out the drawbacks of "over the top" acting—which create a mess. You might ask, for example, what would be wrong if an actor playing an angry king tore the scenery apart in his rage.

- When directing scenes with strong emotion and action, use such devices as slow-motion movement, traveling in place, the creation of frozen pictures, and repetitive choreographed actions. Choreographed movement suggestions are in the scripts.

- Practice one of the script's control activities.

- Reinforce artistic control and style when you see it, by mentioning how effective it looks.

# VOICE AND MOVEMENT

Voice and movement are the actor's tools. Many artists—painters, sculptors, writers and musicians—need equipment to practice their art, but actors rely almost entirely on the use of their voices and movement to communicate who their characters are and what they are doing. Indeed, dramas are sometimes played not in costumes, but in ordinary street clothes.

Characters in Greek mythology are universal types and require clear movement styles and vocal qualities to communicate effectively who they are to the audience. A cruel master uses a strong aggressive voice, posture, and gestures to dominate. A muse moves lightly and gracefully, speaking with an uplifting voice to create beauty and harmony in the world.

To teach voice and movement:

- Ask what it means to say that voice and movement are the actor's tools.

- Ask students whether they would prefer to see an actor as a king in an elaborate outfit but playing a king weakly or a king speaking with majesty and authority, but without the fancy outfit.

- Demonstrate a weak king's stance and voice—then become a majestic monarch.

- Have students practice using the voice and movements of two contrasting characters. For example, say "Go away," first as a fierce lion, and then as a frightened mouse. Then include some of voice and movement exercises you'll find in the script.

# 3

## *The Mechanics of Producing and Directing a Play*

*Talk little. Do much.*

Francis Hodge, director, author

*I enjoyed performing the play because everyone played their parts diligently, beautifully, and wonderfully. At the end when Hercules was elevated to a god, everyone acted their parts with their souls shining.*

Melissa Klose, student

The plays in this book can be produced in two weeks. Schedule daily rehearsals of about an hour for up to thirty-five students. No drama experience is necessary. Each script takes about twenty-five to thirty minutes to perform. Students playing minor roles or inanimate objects can play more than one part as long as the roles don't overlap.

The scripts can be copied from this book and distributed to each performer. During the onstage rehearsals and the performance, only the chorus and the sound crew need scripts. Most of the actors' lines and actions (except for a few for the leading players) follow direct cues given by the chorus.

The plays in this book use the narrative mime approach. In narrative mime theater, four chorus-storytellers position themselves on or at the front of the stage (two on each side), and read from the script. The actors, dressed in black, sit in a semicircle on stage. They will use the costume pieces, props, and fabrics (to create scenery) that are under their chairs or on their laps.

When the chorus read the story, the actors have their props ready and step forward onto the stage to act their parts. For example, when a chorus member recites, "Suddenly, a sad old dog trotted along," an actor wearing dog ears attached to a baseball cap stands and trots onto the stage.

The sound crew sits at long tables beside the stage. These six students, who are dressed in black, have their instruments and other homemade instruments laid out before them. The crew might also use a piano for effects. (Piano players need not know how to play the piano.) The tables and piano are placed so that the crew can see the actors, and so the audience can watch the sound effects being made. (See diagram.) All of the sound cues are in the script.

10

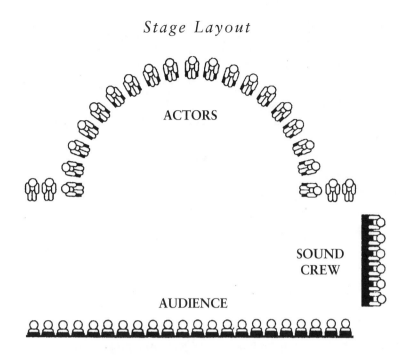

At the beginning of each script you'll find self-explanatory speaking and acting activities. The activities help students develop stage speech and acting skills. They also encourage students to use their imaginations and become involved with the characters and the action of the play. Play chapters also include questions on the story, art activities, and a "classical connections" section with words and ideas in the myth that have entered our modern English vocabulary and culture.

Production Notes for each script suggest costume pieces and props. Steps for an optional simple Greek dance to begin and end each play are given in chapter 5, page 39.

This chapter describes techniques to cast, direct, and produce the scripts with students of varying academic and English-language abilities. It also outlines ways to train the audience in theater techniques, so they can provide feedback for the performers. Part of our aim is to develop the audience's appreciation and understanding of theater-performance skills, and to inspire some to want to perform too.

The following techniques may be used to train performers and direct the plays in this book, as well as any narrative mime script you develop on your own. A step-by-step rehearsal schedule incorporating these techniques is outlined in chapter 6.

# THE STYLE OF THESE PLAYS

The characters in these plays are types—the graceful spring-maiden, Persephone; the forceful god of the underworld, Hades; the mysterious Priestess of Delphi; the bold heroic Hercules.

Actors' movements must be clear and enlarged so the audience can immediately identify the type. Each character needs to have his or her own distinctive vocal and movement style. For example, Persephone's voice needs to be light and lilting, her movements, lithe and graceful; Hades needs to speak in a forceful voice and with movements that are direct and strong. The Priestess speaks hypnotically, moving slowly and regally, using flowing, sweeping gestures. Hercules speaks with bold determination and moves briskly with shoulders back, chest out—ready for action.

The style of a narrative mime performance is *presentational*, meaning the performers present the material directly to the audience. It differs from *realism*, in which actors frequently turn and talk to other characters, pretending they are in their own world and the audience doesn't exist.

In presentational theater, actors open up their bodies and share their movements, expressions, and thoughts with the audience, frequently pantomiming actions and exaggerating facial expressions and gestures. Ancient Greek plays are full of powerful actions and emotions. Movements are often choreographed or frozen in tableaux to create artistry and style. Staging techniques to achieve these effects are in the script.

## Theater of the Imagination

The plays in this book emphasize the development of the imagination. Visual and audio interpretations of characters and objects are presented as they are described by the chorus or other actors. Filmy, sea-blue fabric rippled by two actors across the front of the stage represents the sea; actors hunched over become rocks; characters sitting in a row of chairs and pulling their arms are sailors rowing a boat.

Sound effects are executed in full view of the audience. These effects help the actors act with purpose, punctuate the action, and stimulate the audience. This type of presentation demands that both the actors and the audience use their imaginations to fill in the details and bring the characters and action to life.

# THE DIRECTOR'S ROLES

## The Director as Leader

The director's first job is to "direct"—so directors must be very organized and know what their goals are for each rehearsal. It is useful to communicate the goals and how you plan to go about meeting them at the beginning of each rehearsal. This will help make it so that everyone is clear on what will happen. This also helps everyone feel a sense of security and purpose if they know what they are aiming for. The step-by-step rehearsal guide suggests goals for each session.

Beginning artists learn by imitating. Thus, the director should continually model the behavior desired—such as using an expressive, projected voice and clear enlarged gestures during rehearsals. If students don't understand your directions, act the role yourself, doing an exaggerated demonstration of it. For example, to help them act a prowling lion, leap onto the stage, crouch, and paw along strongly. Your enjoyment of playing and your use of imagination will transfer to them, developing and stimulating their imaginations, creating confidence and an eagerness to jump in and play the part.

## The Director as Inspirer and Confidence-Builder

Everyone needs praise. Beginning performers need a lot of encouragement to reinforce their efforts. Director William Ball in his book, *A Sense of Direction: Some Observations on the Art of Directing* (see Bibliography) says, "Praise is like food to an actor. The actor cannot live without praise, cannot flourish without it. Directors must discipline themselves to praise ceaselessly."

Most people understandably feel vulnerable when they expose their imaginations and themselves in such a conspicuous, physical way. The experience for students is a new one, and the creative process is delicate. It isn't necessary for the actor to have done anything extraordinary to be praised. Comments such as "Your voice is getting stronger and clearer every day," or "It's a real pleasure to work with you" will suffice.

Support, encouragement, and appreciation will help beginning artists develop their talents and gain confidence so that they will hunger to do more. Also when a director praises what actors do well, they'll feel stimulated to do more of it.

General reinforcement, such as "I am so enthusiastic about this group. You are putting this play together so well in such a short time," creates a generalized feeling that they all are a successful, creative, artistic team. The group becomes committed to the production and will more and more love to play. Your job becomes much easier and more enjoyable. Everyone feels reinforced, confident, and eager to push to achieve more.

Another effective way to involve students and to improve the playing is to ask what they thought was done effectively during the rehearsal and what more might be done to enhance the production. Encouraging them to articulate their thoughts on the production shows them that you appreciate their insights, and it forges a creative bond between the performers and director.

Perhaps most importantly, students tend to be eager and willing to push for improvements that are their own ideas. Students often listen to each others' ideas with more interest than to ideas expressed by the director. For example, when students begin coaxing other students to "speak louder" or to "put more emotion into their performance," the projection and emotional commitment of the whole group invariably improves.

## The Director as Coach

While reinforcing students, the director must also act like an athletic coach, pushing students to improve. Performers respond well to an assertive director just as athletes do to a coach who buoys them up and pushes them to achieve their best. This direct exhortation is essential in getting students to fulfill such technical requirements as speaking with projection, creating clear enlarged gestures, speaking slowly, and staying "in character" from the moment they enter until they sit down in their chairs.

Training students to project cannot be overemphasized. Good projection and speaking slowly are essential and must be stressed from the beginning. Few students naturally speak clearly and slowly enough. Speech coaching must begin immediately.

If emphasis on projection and speaking slowly and distinctly is not continual and does not begin immediately, the habit of soft, rapid, stage speech becomes too firmly ingrained. Audiences quickly lose interest if they can't understand the story.

Thus, if actors or chorus speak rapidly with poor projection, stop and say, "LOUD and SLOW," modeling the projection and rate of speech desired. It helps too if the director says the line emphasizing the loud, clear speech required. Then have the student echo your voice.

You may have to continually coach students to project because speaking in this way isn't a habit, but this coaching pays off in a performance that will be alive and audible. Of course, don't hammer away at one individual to improve at any one rehearsal—this would weaken confidence and dampen enthusiasm. After a couple of attempts, praise any improvement or effort made, and then move on. Work on even-better projection the next day.

## The Director as Artistic Collaborator

Perhaps the most productive and fulfilling aspect of directing a student play is to reinforce, encourage, and use students' input and imaginative ideas whenever possible. Theater is a collaborative art. The director depends on the actors' involvement and input to put on an effective production. Students become very involved in a production when their ideas are highlighted, honored, and used.

Students' fresh ideas can inspire a production and help solve difficult blocking problems that may have stumped the director. For example, a director didn't know how to create the River Styx so that it appeared that the boatman Charon was ferrying along it. A student suggested holding up the long black River Styx fabric taut vertically along the front of the stage with Charon behind it and walking slowly from one side of the stage to simulate his ferrying the boat. Another director didn't know how to create an effective boat for *The Odyssey*. A student suggested placing two chairs side by side in rows with a single chair in front for Odysseus as leader. By suggesting blocking and staging ideas, students are also learning the job of the director.

Naturally the director has the final say on what to include, and not all ideas are feasible or beneficial. If an idea cannot be used, show appreciation for the contribution and explain why it is not right for this production. If, for example, someone suggests pulling down the curtain and having the actors enter and exit backstage, explain this is theater of the imagination and the audience likes to observe the actors executing their effects.

## Finding Creative Solutions to Performance Problems

Directors can become frustrated if performers do not do what the part requires. It is tempting to hammer away at the actor to get him or her to "do it right." This, of course, can be counterproductive. Performances do not improve under tense pressure, and both the director and students may lose enthusiasm for the project.

Creative solutions can be found for acting or performance problems. If a performer is not doing what you request after several tries, it is usually best just to skip it and continue with the rehearsal. A solution may be found later, or the problem may resolve itself. The student may not really want to play the part, a possibility that can be discussed later. If an actor cannot speak loudly enough, for example, you might have another student speak the line with him (or even several others).

## *Avoiding the Burden of Perfectionism*

Many directors of beginners feel hassled, especially as the performance time nears. The production method for the plays in this book is designed to avoid much of the harried-director syndrome. There is limited line memorization, and so much action and visual and auditory stimulation are included that if one thing does not work perfectly or is off cue, something else immediately takes over for it.

A way to avoid the burden of perfectionism is to keep your primary goal in mind at all times. If you can keep in mind that the goal for these students is that they first and foremost enjoy the experience so that they will want to do more, the burden of perfectionism is lifted.

Perfection is not possible or even desired. After all, perfection can be stultifying—hindering spontaneity and the creative process. Instead, give students two goals. First, tell them to focus on playing their roles fully. For example, if playing a vicious dragon, tell them to concentrate on looking dragonlike, baring their teeth, showing their claws, and roaring to guard their territory; if playing a chorus member, they must speak in a way to tell the story clearly and to excite the audience; if they are a sound crew member, they must play instruments crisply and on cue to enhance the action. Second, suggest that students work as a team, being ready to help each other when problems arise. Giving students these two clear goals helps reduce self-consciousness and stage fright by giving them things to do to focus their attention.

# STAGE-ACTING TECHNIQUES

Several acting techniques will enhance the quality of your production.

## *Choosing a Character or Neutral Stance*

Each character needs a stance that communicates clearly to the audience who that character is and what he or she is doing. For example, the goddess Athena stands and moves with authority and regal dignity, her chin slightly up, and uses slow, clear graceful gestures. The snarling guard dog Cerberus would crouch with fierce eyes, baring his teeth and ready to attack with a paw outstretched. The graceful muses would move lightly and perhaps stand in a ballet pose. Beginners are greatly helped by being given expressive gestures and postures to help them experience and communicate the feeling and quality of a character.

Students should assume their character stance—or a neutral stance—whenever they are not in the action. Actors must maintain their character—or a neutral stance. They need to do this from the moment they rise from their chairs until they return to their chairs and are seated.

A neutral stance is standing still in a dignified posture. When not acting, actors standing in neutral should be attentive and alert. Train students to use the neutral stance by modeling posture faults like slouching, putting hands in pockets, fidgeting, and shifting from one foot to another. Then, ask what was wrong with the way you were standing. Chorus members always use the neutral stance.

## Miming

Narrative mime theater uses few props and virtually no scenery. The audience depends on actors using their imaginations and pantomiming objects they are using. They show by their movements or actions the different environments they are in. Thus, actors must pretend that plates of food, a crossbow, or a door are there, or that they are traveling through a forest, entering the underworld, or rowing on the sea. The goal of mime is not to create the exact object or situation but an exaggerated essence of it. Thus, the actor might move in the stylized slinking of a wolf or make exaggerated motions of stirring when mixing ingredients in a bowl.

The following skills help actors mime with believability:

- The actor must visualize and imagine the weight, size, and circumference of the object and its tension or resistance when using it. For example, a crossbow must be held imagining its dimensions and weight. The actor must also show that there is resistance and tension in the arms when pulling back the arrow.

- The size of the object must stay consistent—for example, when picking up a glass, be sure it is the size and weight of a glass and always hold it so that it has the same dimensions.

- Objects cannot be dropped in the air. They must be set down or disposed of in a believable way.

- The mimed action should be exaggerated to communicate effectively and artistically, such as the exaggerated resistance of pulling oars through water, the plucking of a grape from its stem, the tying of a knot, the turn of the hand opening a door.

- Facial expressions and gestures expressing emotions such as of joy, fear, laughter, worry, sorrow, and fright must be enlarged. For example, Zeus opens his eyes wide in shock. Demeter stamps her foot firmly in anger at Zeus. Hercules walks in an exaggeratedly brisk fashion as he sets forth to do his labors.

- The director can help actors mime convincingly by using vivid sensual details to describe the situation such as "Imagine you are chewing thick crusty bread and drinking sweet cool orange punch."

## *Choreographing Movements and Gestures*

Choreographed movements are pleasant to see and do. A fundamental concept of drama is that it contains what is or can be chaotic in life. In life, movement is random. Choreographed movements give the performers a sense of security and are very pleasant for an audience to observe.

The scripts in this book choreograph aggressive actions. For example, the punching of the hundred-handed Hecatonchires is synchronized with each Hecatonchire punching five times and freezing on the final punch.

## *Playing Scenery and Inanimate Objects*

Playing scenery and inanimate objects develops the imagination. Scenery can be acted in pairs or small groups, giving shy students non-threatening yet stimulating roles. It is always possible to add one more tree, rock, swirling mist, or flower to give more students opportunities to play roles.

The following tips will help students play objects.

- Students should have props or fabrics ready to use, so they can create the object instantaneously.

- Students should portray the object's quality. For example, to create swirling mist, students must manipulate long white ribbons on dowels with flowing motions to create the illusion of airy mist.

- Students should act only when the chorus cues them to. For example, when a chorus says, "Each night, Demeter lay the boy in the fire to burn away his mortality," the fire-actors create a flickering fire with filmy orange fabric when they are thus prompted by the chorus. Actors stop the flickering when the narration begins again.

- Students should return to their chairs or freeze when their action is over and wait for their next cue.

## Motivation

Drama is action. The Greek word *drama* means "a thing done." Actions are done for a purpose. Understanding a character's motivation (why a character behaves in a certain way) helps actors act with purpose. Characters in Greek myths have strong motivations. For example, the goddess Demeter wills the crops to die to force Zeus to return her daughter to her. Persephone begs Hades to let her remain on Earth because she wants to stay with her mother and her friends. Hades wants to take Persephone to the underworld because he is lonely and desires her as his queen.

The stronger and more urgent the purpose, the more the actor feels compelled to do it. For example, the god Uranus banishes his children underground to guarantee that he'll have total power. If an actor knows this motivation, he will play the part with determination. Self-consciousness will be reduced because he has something purposeful to do.

Motivations are not always clear from the script. For example, in scenes of exposition in which one character gives information to another, a motivation may not seem to exist at all. It helps if directors can think of some motivation to help the actor act with conviction. Thus, Circe warns Odysseus of three deadly sea perils he will face on his journey. If Circe says these lines to help save Odysseus's life, the dialogue will be said with urgency. Give the motivation as an active verb. For example, a character may want *to help, convince, encourage, enlighten, destroy, belittle, seduce, hurt, inspire, seize power, persuade, warn.*

The chorus and the sound crew have motivations for what they do too. The motivation of the chorus is to assure the audience understands the story and to interest them in the action throughout. The sound crew's motivation is to follow cues and create effects that are clear and crisp to heighten the action and to help the actors act with conviction.

## Putting Yourself in the Shoes, Fur, or Feathers of a Character—The "Magic If"

The great Russian director Stanislavski created and developed an acting method called the "magic if." An actor considers "what if" I were in this character's circumstance, what would I do? The more students can make believe that they are the character they are playing, the more authentic their acting will be. The director can help by creating a vivid picture of the character and the situation.

For example, a student becoming a lion would try to imagine he was covered with a thick coat of golden fur, that he walked on padded paws, and that he had strong powerful legs and shoulders with which to pounce forcefully on prey. Actors becoming stormy winds might experience their bodies as mighty winds—making ships and trees toss and sway in their power.

# TRAINING THE SOUND CREW

A highlight of a narrative mime dramatization is the sound effects created by rhythm instruments. Sound effects punctuate the action and help the actors act with conviction. Sound effects also highlight certain actions and make them significant. Creating sound effects also helps students develop musical intelligence.

To create effective sound effects:

- Come in on cue. The crew should highlight their parts, follow their scripts carefully, and get instruments ready ahead of time.

- Coordinate the sound effect with the actors' actions so that the sound effect punctuates the action. Thus, the sound crew must have a clear view of the action.

- Create the quality of the sound imitated. For example, shake a tambourine vigorously and slap it in the center to create the energy of whirling chaos. Strike a wood block rhythmically and briskly to simulate galloping horses. Some students instinctively create precise sound qualities. Others need modeling.

- Capture the theatrical clarity and brightness of the effects by playing them emphatically but not so vigorously that they overpower. Limp effects don't communicate. For example, strike a triangle crisply to highlight the title and author of a play. Ring jingle bells brightly to create the happy feeling of flowers about to bloom.

  Of course, the instruments might be shaken or struck too vigorously or emphatically. For example, a sound crew member might shake rattles too energetically for stirring ingredients in a bowl or strike a wood block too strongly for walking briskly.

### Incorporating Classical Music

A musical overture to a performance can set the tone and help the audience and the performers get in the spirit of the play to come. Finding just the right classical music can enhance your production. For example, *The Creation and the Birth of the Olympian Gods* script suggests using the beginning of the first movement of Beethoven's Fifth Symphony to set the tone of the powerful dramatic material to come. As Director David Grote says, it is important that "the music evokes a feeling or attitude about the play to come."

Other effective selections might be used to introduce other scripts. Ask for advice from music teachers, or perhaps someone from your local symphony organization might have ideas.

# CASTING

There are many ways to cast a play. Many agree a good script and thoughtful casting are the most important elements of a successful production. For example, a confident, animated Chorus 1 with good projection and lively gestures will begin the performance with vitality, inspire the other chorus members, and pull the audience in. Minimal line memorization greatly enhances the possibility of getting the right student in the right part. For if someone doesn't work out, the director can always try another actor.

Three methods of casting a play are given below. Using more than one method is a good idea so that you can see students in different situations and gauge their ability and commitment. Regardless of what method is used, keep the casting flexible, so that students' parts may be changed. Having the right student in the right part enhances the production and inspires the performance of the other students.

## The Preliminary Tryout

For a preliminary tryout, have students read aloud the TV Interviews that precede each script. The interview also acquaints students with the story of the play. You might have students do some of the acting activities included with each script and observe how they respond. This will help you see who has the most natural acting ability, the best voice, and who is most interested and involved. Those who perform limply or with little confidence or commitment may need to build confidence by first playing smaller parts. They could also start as part of the sound crew.

## The Written Tryout

A written tryout helps students articulate what the role requires and shows their commitment to and involvement in the production.

For the written tryout, follow these steps:

- Have students list three roles they want to play in order of preference (roles include acting, storytelling, and sound crew).

- Have students describe what the characters are like or, in the case of chorus or sound crew, what is required to play the role effectively.

- Have students explain why they should be chosen to play the role and what they would try to do to play their part well.

- Consider and evaluate these responses.

## The Formal Tryout

For the formal tryout, choose parts of the script for students. Have them go to the front of the room or stage and try out for the roles they want. It is best to try out in the space where you'll perform because projection and movement ability are more obvious. The formal tryout allows you to focus on each individual, perhaps giving some directions and pointers to see how students respond and compare with each other. Rate chorus members on vocal projection and gesturing, and on their ability to take directions.

## Spotting the Born Actor

There is such a thing as a born actor. Born actors are hungry to act and will do so at any opportunity. The born actor is able to jump inside a character and is able to express the feelings of many characters. The born actor has stage presence and commands the attention of an audience. The best of them will listen eagerly to, and even solicit, the director's ideas. They don't forget directions because they are very involved and the directions seem natural to them. Such born actors elevate the production and inspire a better performance from the others.

Born actors also come up with many ideas for parts and do them spontaneously during rehearsals. They contribute to the direction of the play through their enthusiasm, intuition, imagination, and natural skills. These students have strong voices, and they often have expressive bodies with good kinesthetic skills. They are comfortable on stage and love to play. Not all born actors will have all of these traits in equal degree, but they will have most of them.

For a performance to please an audience, it is often helpful to put the most competent actors in leading roles. The chorus, gods and goddesses, heroes and heroines in these Greek myths benefit from students with stage presence and commitment. Some might argue that leading roles should be spread out democratically; and for classroom dramatization, this is a good idea. When performing before an audience, however, the students, audience, and director will feel more comfortable if a strong actor who is able and eager to handle the part is in the biggest role.

This is essential for Chorus 1 who leads the proceedings and sets the tone for the others. Encourage the strong actors to work with other students to help give them confidence, while creating an atmosphere of teamwork.

Occasionally two or three students seem to be equally good actors. If in doubt, choose the most responsible student with the strongest voice for the most important role. In leading roles particularly, it is essential an actor be heard. A student who is reliable, follows directions, and gives 100 percent effort will improve over time.

If all contenders fit these criteria, then you will have to choose one. Mention that at one time or another every excellent actor has had the experience of not getting a desired role. Indeed, success in acting is due to hard work, willingness to play a less-desired role for the experience, and persistence despite adversity.

# BLOCKING

One of the director's most important functions is to give actors their blocking. Good blocking enables the audience to see what is going on and focuses attention on the important action of the moment. Good blocking has flow and a variety of movement. It combines movement and frozen pictures or still shots. Good blocking creates interesting dramatic stage pictures. Director David Grote believes blocking is the director's primary form of expression.

To help describe the blocking to actors, the stage is divided into areas (see diagram). Some areas get more attention than others. For example, standing down center stage is the strongest position. Upstage left is the weakest. Downstage areas are strong because they are close to the audience. Characters usually talk to the audience from downstage.

*Stage Areas Diagram*

| Upstage Right | Upstage Center | Upstage Left |
|---|---|---|
| Center Stage Right | Center Stage | Center Stage Left |
| Downstage Right | Downstage Center | Downstage Left |

The term *upstage* dates back to a time when stages were *raked* or sloped upward. The area opposite upstage is downstage. Stage right and left are identified from the actors' point of view. As mentioned, some areas are stronger than others, though it is best to use every stage area, even the corners, to open up the full potential of the stage and to keep the action from looking confined or cluttered.

To help students learn the areas, draw the diagram on chart paper or the board, discuss it, and have students practice moving to the various areas in the front of the classroom or on stage. To teach them the areas, perhaps use the nursery rhyme, "Jack and Jill." Choose two students to play Jack and Jill, and tell them they will go to different stage areas on each line. Have them begin by standing downstage center. Tell them on "Jack and Jill went up the hill," to go to upstage center; on "To fetch a pail of water," to go to upstage left. Tell Jack on "Jack fell down and broke his crown," to go to center stage left. Tell Jill on "Jill came tumbling after," to go to downstage center. The term *stage* might not be used when giving the directions, and you might just say, "Go up right" or "Move down left."

There are four blocking techniques students must use to share a performance with an audience:

1. Open up to the audience.
2. Don't get blocked and don't block or crowd other actors.
3. Use all of the stage.
4. Maintain stillness, with no fidgeting, when you are not acting.

To practice these techniques, invite a student to the front of the room. While facing the student in profile, discuss a topic such as the weather. Then, describe the weather again, this time opening up your body in a three-quarter position, so that most of your face and body is visible to the students in the class. Ask which position is better for sharing the dialogue with the audience.

Show how the open position must be adjusted to open up the action to all three sides of the audience and not just the center of the audience. You might compare body position during a conversation in life to that used during a dialogue or mime interaction in the theater.

Ask another student to the front of the room. This time, stand in front of the student while you talk about another topic. Ask what actors might do if they find themselves "blocked" like this on stage. An obvious answer is to step into another position, so that you are not blocked.

Ask a third student to the front and ask them to recite "Humpty Dumpty" while you fidget and shift your feet back and forth. Ask what you did that would distract an audience. Then ask what you might do instead to keep the audience's focus on the speaker. The obvious answer is to stand still, keeping your hands quietly by your side, while looking at the other actor to get the audience to focus there too.

## Check the Sight Lines

Sometimes at performances, directors go to a side of the auditorium and realize that the audience cannot see what is going on from that viewpoint. To prevent this from happening, view the whole performance from all parts of the audience—or have an assistant do this during rehearsals. If some important action is obscured, then naturally you'll have to change the blocking or the stage arrangement somehow.

## Focus on the Important Action

The blocking must help tell the story accurately, so the audience focuses its attention on the most important action occurring on the stage at any given time. An entering character should be a focus—so, entrances and exits of characters must be strong. A good character entrance establishes immediately who the character is and tells the audience exactly what the character is doing.

Use the following guidelines and techniques to help focus attention.

- Place important characters or objects in prominent positions such as center stage or down right. Important characters might stand on chairs or boxes to elevate them from the others, or they might stand alone while the others are grouped together.

- Create strong entrances and exits for characters by having them use clear gestures and movement that draw attention to them. Then have them move into the center stage or to another strong area.

- Create *frozen pictures* to accentuate important images, moments, and actions.

- Have characters turn (perhaps with their backs to the audience), look at a new entering character, freeze, and gesture toward the character.

- Focus on the new character by having the other actors look directly at them.

- Have students turn their bodies directly toward the speaking or prominent actor or action. Emphasize this by pointing with arms, legs, torso, or all three.

- Maintain stillness. No fidgeting, hands in pocket, or other distractions that will shift the focus of attention.

## Create Spectacle, Variety, and Dramatic Interest

Blocking should be varied and have dramatic and theatrical interest. Variety holds the interest of the audience. Use every area of the stage to open up the action and use the full potential of the stage. The spectacle and dramatic power of full stage use can be great. This is necessary in crowd scenes and when many are moving at once. Spectacle scenes or scenes of pageantry such as the displaying of all of the Olympian gods are heightened by using all stage areas.

Students on their own will not usually use the corners of the stage, so just send them there. This is especially necessary in scenes with group actions, such as birds flying. Students tend to cluster together, perhaps due to nervousness.

The following techniques help to create varied blocking.

- "Spike the set" placing white or glow-in-the-dark tape in the spots where you want actors to go.

- Use chairs, boxes, and benches, and place students at different levels by having some lie down, some sit, some kneel on one or both knees, some stand bent over, some stand erect with hands up, and so on. Use sturdy chairs or boxes to create varieties of elevation.

- Have actors move on different levels—high, middle, and low. For example, the whirlpool Charybdis might swirl in a high, middle, and low position. Lions crouch and paw in middle level; Odysseus as a beggar bends low and when triumphant, reaches high. Different types of movement also lend variety.

- Have actors enter from the audience.

- Use the audience area for dramatic entrances and exits. For example, Hermes might fly in from the back of the auditorium. A flute player might introduce the drama by entering down the aisle.

### *Blocking Tips*

Choreographed movements in which one or more performers repeat an action in a stylized way are satisfying and pleasing for the performers and the audience. As mentioned, the scripts suggest choreographed movements.

After working out first blocking, have actors run through the whole act uninterrupted, so that they get the flow. This also helps with line memorization.

With young actors, it's best not to labor over awkward blocking but to figure it out later because they lose the flow and get frustrated. They may even get worse with too much detailed repetition.

If an action is too awkward, such as using rope to tie Odysseus to the mast, find a simpler way to do it. For example, have Odysseus put his hands behind his back and a sailor mime tying him.

For the most part, animal characters, even snakes, should be played on two feet rather than on hands and knees because the actors maneuver better, are more visible, and can use different postures.

During final rehearsals, teacher Cindy Lail uses four hand signals to cue students on strengths and weaknesses with no verbal interruptions. For speaking too softly, she cups her hand to her ear; for speaking too rapidly, she pushes both hands slowly toward the floor; for opening up the action and not crowding together, she sweeps an arm across her body; for everything is excellent and on target, she gives a thumbs-up.

# THE PROFESSIONAL CURTAIN CALL

The curtain call ends the show and is the last impression the audience has of the performance. It should be professional and have panache. A well-staged curtain call makes students feel professional and can influence their attitude toward the performance. The techniques of presenting oneself in a curtain call can transfer to other public situations in which a confident, professional stance is required. We all need an effective public persona at times in order to be a success.

For the scripts in this book, the four chorus members lead the curtain call. Have the chorus announce each group of performers individually. Begin with the actors, then identify the sound crew, and finally have the chorus take bows.

When each group of performers is called, they stand, step forward, saying in turn their names loudly and clearly, and remain standing. When all are standing, the chorus members step center stage, face the performers, and lift their hands in the air. All performers do this, and when the hands of the chorus members are lowered and they bow, the performers do the same and then sit down quietly.

A frequent flaw is that students say their names too softly. Insist that they project and say their names loudly, like a cheer. This may need continual work with some, but it is worth the effort, introducing them to an important public speaking skill and building confidence and esteem. Point out that they deserve to cheer their names because they have done an excellent job. Practice the curtain call several times, explaining its importance in ensuring that the performance concludes with energy and style.

# INVOLVING THE AUDIENCE

A pre- and post-performance discussion and feedback evaluation of the performance will increase audience enthusiasm, teach the audience theater techniques, and help develop informed theater audiences. Audience discussions also provide the performers and director with helpful feedback, and they show the audience that they have a valued, respected, and necessary role.

Perhaps begin your discussion complimenting the audience on how respectfully they've entered the auditorium ready for the play. Mention that an audience is a necessity for the performance of a play. Add that when the audience gives their full attention to the actors, it inspires the actors and helps them give their best to the audience.

Prior to the performance, give the audience a little information on ancient Greece. Include the fact that theater in which actors performed on a stage began in ancient Greece. Perhaps give background on the gods and goddesses and the powers they wield. Briefly describe the myth they will be seeing, perhaps using the synopsis of the script they are performing.

Tell the audience that the performers want their feedback. Ask them to observe how the actors use their imaginations, their voices, and their movement to become, for example, the graceful muses, the mighty Zeus, the majestic goddess Athena, the vicious guard dog. Ask them to listen to the chorus and pay attention to what they do with their voices to make the story clear and exciting. Finally ask them to listen to how the sound crew makes their effects crisply and on cue to highlight the action of the plays. These cues to the audience also give the performers last minute tips on what they must do to perform well for the audience.

After the performance, ask the audience for comments on what they enjoyed and why. Make sure all performance elements are mentioned by asking the necessary questions. You might also ask how seeing a live play differs from watching TV plays or films, what the advantage is of seeing a live play, and why some say stage acting is the most challenging and the highest form of acting. After hearing the audience's feedback at the end of the play, encourage audience members to draw a picture and write the performers letters describing what they liked.

# PERFORMERS' WRITTEN REFLECTIONS

Teachers often mention that a performance is one of the year's highlights. Students are naturally excited and buoyed up after the experience. A follow-up reflection helps students articulate what the experience meant to them. It's also a helpful, calming transition to the daily routine of the classroom.

Some possible reflection questions include the following:

- What did you enjoy most about doing this performance?

- What was the most difficult part of the performance for you?

- What was your reaction to having an audience?

- Would you like to do another drama project? Why or why not? If yes, what might it be?

- What kind of role would you like to play and why?

# CREATING AN ALBUM

Students might also make an album describing and drawing their favorite part of the performance. The album might include copies of posters or programs of the show. The teacher, aide, or a parent might take photos of all the performers and put them in the album. Include notes or pictures from the principal, relatives, students from other classes, and from the performers themselves.

# 4

## Creating Costume Pieces, Props, and Scenery

*Costume is associated with the moving actor and is the most dynamic and "living" of all the visual images.*

Francis Hodge, director-author

*I liked that each person's costume represented who they were and told the audience a little more about their character's personality.*

Meredith Chin, student

Costume pieces excite the students and make them eager to participate. Costumes help students transform from their ordinary student roles into exotic gods and goddesses, muses, heroes, mythological monsters, and trees with golden apples.

## GREEK COSTUME

Costuming was of strong interest to the ancient Greeks. Information on Greek costuming comes mainly from depictions on ancient Greek pottery. The clothes of ancient Greeks were both simple and splendid.

In the fifth century B.C. whenever grandeur was needed in clothes, it is described in color. Brilliant color had dramatic value. Homer mentions a magnificent range of colors in clothes in *The Odyssey*—particularly blue, red, and purple. They used sea-dyes, like cuttlefish for blue and purple, and the colors of various sea weeds. They also used vegetable dyes.

### The Tunic

The basic costume of the ancient Greeks was the tunic. Made on a loom, it looks like a cross with an opening at the center for the head. Tunics were originally of fine wool. Tunics were ankle-length for women and knee-length for men. Athletic women, such as the goddess Artemis and the Amazons, wore knee-length tunics.

## Hairstyles and Headdresses

Both males and females often wore a small fringe of hair on the forehead and had hair or curls hanging down the cheeks. Women frequently wore a *sakkos,* or little cap, on their head with a bunch of curls left loose to hang over the cheeks. Women also wrapped scarves on top of their heads and sometimes wore elaborately carved combs of olive wood, bone, ivory, and shell.

In the 5th and early 6th centuries B.C., gods and goddesses were depicted with long, crimped, or tightly curled, hair. Their hair was often tinted—blonde was the most popular color. Both men and women wore headbands across the forehead. Royalty wore crowns or ornate headbands sometimes decorated with jewels.

## Jewelry and Belts

Most Greek jewelry was the work of skilled goldsmiths. Queens and great ladies wore bracelets. High-ranking people wore belts of brilliant colors with ornaments and embroidery. The Greeks had a variety of belts that were wide and decorated.

## Cloaks

Cloaks were of many colors—both the color and the fabric depended on the rank of the wearer.

## Shoes

The Greeks often went barefoot. Shoes and sandals were worn on special occasions or as a protection. Sandals were light and tied, or fastened with straps both over the foot and around the ankle.

# USING COSTUMES

The best costume captures the essence of a character. Simple minimal costumes can make a strong dramatic statement. Find a central trait of the character, or inanimate object, and emphasize it. For example, a silver thunderbolt on a tall, blue headdress symbolizes the power of Zeus. Golden horns on a headband create the prized golden-horned deer. A long, black, hooded cape creates a forbidding old Charon, the boatman. Suggested costume pieces for each play are in the Production Notes at the end of the play.

Simple suggestive costumes can be more imaginative than full costumes because they allow the actors and the audience to fill in the gaps. It is also intriguing to see everyday clothing and articles used in a novel way. For example, shiny, blue baseball caps and sunglasses can create evil birds; strips of white, crepe paper attached to dowels make swirling mist; a green, feather boa over the shoulders and gold Christmas balls in the hands makes a magical tree with golden apples.

The following are tips for costumes. Specific costume suggestions for each play are in the Production Notes at the end of each play. The Bibliography suggests additional sources on creating and obtaining simple costumes and props.

- Keep costumes as simple as possible, and easy to store under chairs.

- Use costumes that are easy to put on and take off, that do not restrict the actor's movement, and that are as indestructible as possible.

- Use a wrinkle-free fabric for tunics. Choose very different colors for tunics of individual characters to make each character distinct and set each apart. Chorus or others playing group parts might, of course, wear the same color.

- Keep scenery fabrics light so that they are easy to manipulate and store under chairs.

- Aim for pure colors rather than fabrics with muted colors or a busy design.

- Dress significant characters, such as gods, goddesses, royalty, heroes, and heroines in grander and more striking style. For example, tunics of bright rich colors, tall decorated headdresses, and impressive belts give a grand effect.

- Incorporate costumes and props that help actors act their roles. For example, red gloves with long pointed, green, flexi-foam claws attached help a dragon attack more convincingly. A long pole helps cranky boatman Charon ferry his boat and threaten people by pointing it at them.

- Consider footwear. Ancient Greeks usually went barefoot. Never let a queen, goddess, or dancing wood nymph wear heavy sports shoes. If possible, have the whole cast go shoeless.

- Observe how a fabric, costume piece, or prop looks from a distance.

- Do not repeat the same costume piece twice. For example, if white ribbons on dowels are swirling mist in one scene, use white, nylon netting for fog in the next scene.

- Use everyday objects in a new way. Try a white Styrofoam cup with the bottom cut out as a bird beak or a wooden spoon or wire whisk as a microphone.

- Manage costumes for a performance by categorizing them in sturdy clear plastic bags so you can easily see what you've got.

- Use props that must be put on and taken off quickly. Be sure to use them early in the rehearsal period to acquaint students with how to manipulate them.

- Choose two or three reliable students as costume directors to set out the props and costume pieces at the beginning of rehearsals and to gather them and store them in the bags at the end of the rehearsal.

- Try thrift stores, fabric stores, garage sales, parents, friends, and your own castoffs as sources for fabrics, belts, and other pieces.

- Seek help from parents. This will take the burden off of you and involve the parent in the production. Parents often have imaginative ideas that enrich the production. Be sure to give them credit in the program. You might send the following letter to parents before you begin rehearsing to give them time.


Dear Parent,

Our class will be performing a play based on a Greek myth. I'm looking for parents to help make simple costume pieces and props. If you might be willing to help, please let me know. Your help would be greatly appreciated, and the play would be enhanced by your contributions.

Thank you,

# MAKING NO-SEW COSTUMES

## *Headbands*

It is simple to buy headbands or to make them. For example, fabric trim that can be purchased in fabric stores comes in gold braiding and a variety of patterns and textures. It can be used to create attractive hats by just sewing the ends together. Wear these headbands around the forehead to create a Greek-style headband.

Headband hats or crowns can be made in different widths. Cut a two- to three-inch wide strip of tagboard long enough to go around the head with an overlap of an inch. Tape or staple the ends together. For a Greek laurel wreath, attach leaves. For a floral crown, attach flowers and ribbon streamers. To create crowns, make a notched or spiked band about six inches wide and decorate it with junk jewelry or bits of foil.

*Headband Hats*

## God and Goddess Headpieces

Create a paper-band hat with height for a god or goddess. Use poster board, tagboard, or flexi-foam about ten inches high with two-inch wide elastic band for the headband. Use Velcro on the two ends to fasten the hat.

For a moon goddess, cut a crescent moon about ten inches high of cardboard, cover it with silver foil, and attach to the elastic headband. Decorate other headpieces with pieces of foil, cutouts, ribbons, fabric, or junk jewelry.

*Moon Goddess and Sun God Headdreses*

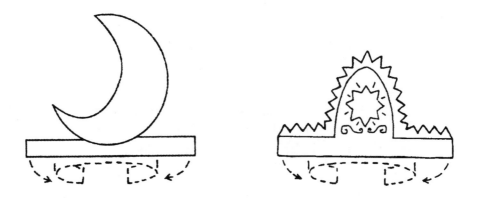

## Tunics

Tunics can be used for the chorus, gods, and goddesses, and significant characters. For the simplest tunic, use part of a sheet, or a piece of lightweight fabric approximately 54"x 54", draped under the right arm and tied on the left shoulder.

For a knee-length tunic for the chorus, male gods and heroes, and female athletic characters, buy two yards of forty-five inch fabric. Fold it in half, and then fold it in half again (quarters). (See diagram.)

Make a three-inch cut for the head. To prevent fraying, apply glue around the opening (fray check, available at fabric stores, is also good for this purpose). For long tunics for goddesses and females, use two-and-one-half yards of fabric. Tunics should be belted. Gods, goddesses, and royalty wear showy belts.

*No-sew Tunic*

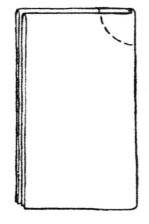

## Atmosphere Sticks

Streamers of ribbon, crepe paper, fabric, or other materials can be attached to dowels and waved to create atmospheric effects such as mist, fog, fire, swirling vapors, and whirlpools. Tape or tie strips of appropriately colored cloth, ribbon, tinsel, or crepe paper to a dowel. Swirling mist needs strips at least two feet long to create the effect, whereas flames for a fire or the sun's beams might be shorter.

## Lyre

To create a lyre, use this or a similar simple lyre design. Use two layers of 18-inch long foam core, inserting seven lyre strings made of wire between the two pieces. Attach a strap or cord so it can be worn over a shoulder.

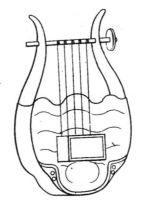

## Wedding Torch

Use this or other simple torch design. Use two layers of 20-inch foam core that is glued together for the torch and for the flame on top.

## Using Fabrics

Fabric can personify nature. Lightweight, black fabric stretched the length of the stage by two students makes an impressive River Styx. White nylon netting held taut becomes fog. Filmy blue or aqua fabric can be sky, rivers, seas, and lakes. Collect lightweight fabric such as nylon netting and other sheer fabrics that are easy to manipulate and store.

## Significant Props

For ease of performance, use only necessary, significant props. For example, Circe needs a lyre to strum and a wand to strike the sailors on the shoulders with—to turn them into pigs. Cronus must have a sickle to commit his evil deed. Charon needs a pole to ferry his boat. Scenes such as eating food or tying Odysseus to the mast can be pantomimed.

## Chairs for Scenery

These plays can be done with minimal scenery. Sturdy chairs can create pedestals for gods. Two chairs together form a couch. A row or double row of chairs can be used to make Odysseus's boat. Gods and goddesses standing on their chairs make a good Mount Olympus.

## Backdrop

To create a simple effective backdrop to use with all of these plays, join sky-blue, king-size sheets together. Paint white, Greek columns on them using white tempera or latex paint. Use a sponge to dab on clouds.

# 5

## Incorporating Musical Instruments and Dance

*The sounds of the first poems I heard were to me as the notes of bells, the sound of musical instruments.*

Dylan Thomas

*I like the instruments because they make the play exciting and musical.*

Bryan Lodahl, student

Students not wanting acting roles invariably want to play musical instruments to make sound effects. Sound effects created by musical instruments are an important ingredient of narrative mime theater. The instruments highlight the action, help the actors act with more conviction, and stimulate the audience. Striking instruments at certain times makes certain actions stand out and seem more significant. For example, striking a wood block firmly when Demeter stamps her foot in anger helps the actress to stamp more convincingly. Shaking jingle bells as Hermes flies elevates his feeling and accentuates his agile flight.

Audiences always mention how much they enjoy hearing the instruments and seeing the sound crew play them.

Music is an important part of Greek life. The Greeks have music, song, and dances to celebrate all social events. In ancient Greece, athletes trained to pipe music, and the lyre accompanied the reciting of poetry.

Tips for incorporating instruments are given below. Specific sound effect suggestions are in the scripts. The Selected Bibliography suggests books on creating instruments and sources for obtaining them.

- Explain that instruments must be played on cue and crisply to communicate to the audience the desired effect. (Students may need some demonstration to learn how to strike an instrument to achieve the effect.)

- Buy good quality instruments. They create a better tone, last longer, are more pleasing to play, and introduce students to the real instrument. West Music Company (see Bibliography) has a variety of instruments at reasonable prices. Also check the Yellow Pages for music supply stores.

- Let students suggest and try other instruments to make the same effect or to add other effects not in the play. They may discover, for example, that striking a drum and then a gong add to the power of a god's anger or that shaking jingle bells and handbells together heightens joyful moments.

- Keep instruments in clear plastic bags labeled for each sound crew member (for example, SC 1 for Sound Crew 1; SC 2 for Sound Crew 2, etc.). The sound crew return their instruments to their bags when rehearsals are over.

- Choose a Sound Director in the crew to set out the bags and collect them at the end of rehearsals.

- Acquire the following basic instruments to create many effects: triangle, wood block, jingle bells, drum, tambourine, rattle, gong, and guiro.

## Sound Effect Qualities

**DRUM:** Powerful, threatening, ceremonial

**JINGLE BELLS AND HANDBELLS:** Light, joyful, celebratory, and to signify flying

**TRIANGLE:** Bright, magical, scintillating, brightly punctuating.

**TAMBOURINE:** Energetic, invigorating, cacophonous if shaken vigorously and slapped in the center.

**WOOD BLOCK:** Perky, punctuating, galloping, trotting, walking briskly, knocking, chopping, growing from seed to full-grown plant.

**GUIRO:** Scraping, rasping, slithering, sneaking, squawking.

## Using the Piano

A piano might make all or some of the effects if used in a creative way. For example, strike high notes successively to create plucking flowers or to indicate flying. Strike middle notes to resemble hoofbeats, brisk walking, or a trotting dog. Strike low notes as Hades proceeds to his throne. Place the heel of your hand on low notes to create a thunderbolt or indicate a character's fall. Two students might sit at the piano to create the effects.

An interesting assignment is to have students create instruments from everyday objects. This develops musical discrimination as they discover that some coffee mugs, for example, make a pleasant clink when tapped with a spoon and others, an undesirable clunk. Ask students to strike, shake, and scrape objects in the classroom or at home to test their sounds.

The following suggests simple instruments to make. The Bibliography lists books on making instruments.

**RATTLES:** Any container with a lid filled with hard objects such as beans, popcorn, or pebbles makes a good rattle. Turn it over, and it's a drum. A large bleach bottle with unpopped corn or beans works well.

**DRUMS:** A metal, wastepaper basket struck with a wooden spoon or with the hand makes a good drum, or use a coffee can or the bottom of gallon plastic bottle. To make a log drum, remove lids from three juice cans, tape the cans together to make a log shape, and cover with brown grocery wrap. Strike with sticks.

**PADDED DRUMSTICK:** A ruler or dowel covered with a sock that has another sock stuffed inside of it makes a good drumstick.

**RHYTHM STICKS:** Use two, one-fourth inch dowels cut one foot long or any two objects of the same size and basic shape, such as a wooden spoon and fork or a metal spoon and fork.

**SILVERWARE TAPPERS:** Use two forks, knives, or spoons struck together.

**GONG:** Strike a pot lid with a metal spoon.

**WOOD BLOCK:** Strike a block of wood or even the table or a wall struck with a pen.

**SAND BLOCK:** Use a piece of sandpaper wrapped around a block of wood and scraped with a plastic or metal fork.

**BELL:** Strike a glass or ceramic coffee cup (with the right bell-like ring to it) with a spoon.

**TRIANGLE:** Tap a glass with the right ping sound by striking back and forth on the inside with a spoon.

## Creating Vocalized Sound Effects or Verbal Exclamations

Greek myths are full of strong emotions and are enriched by the inclusion of vocalized sound effects. Gasping, grunting, whining, cheering, snarling, growling, and moaning are "emotional calls," and probably were the first forms of speech. These calls are often accompanied by strong body movement to express the strong emotion. Vocalized sound effects and verbal exclamations done expressively help actors to act and experience the emotion and action of the characters, animals, mythological monsters, and even some inanimate objects. The scripts include vocalized sound effects, and students might add some of their own.

# GREEK DANCING

The scripts in this book suggest beginning and ending each play with students performing a simple Greek line dance. Dancing has always been important to the Greeks.

The Greeks emphasized the importance of sound mind and sound body. They valued and trained the body to acquire strength, skill, agility, and grace of movement. Socrates spoke of dance as a way to acquire grace.

Most Greek folk dances are line or circle dances. Dancing is an expression of grace, strength, vitality, and joy in living. Men are considered more masculine if they dance well and women more graceful and womanly.

Greek dances are easy enough for all to join in the line. The leader often holds a handkerchief in the free hand, which is used like a flag directing the action. Everyone holds hands. (If doing this with middle school students, perhaps simulate holding hands as suggested in the dance below.) The dance should be graceful dignified and stately. Carriage and posture should be erect.

The following simple Greek folk dance can be taught quickly. There is only one simple step to learn so that everyone can enjoy doing it and have success.

### Teaching a Simplified Greek Dance to Begin and End a Play

**PROCEDURE:** Explain that the Greeks believe a man has more style and is more masculine if he dances well and a woman, more graceful and feminine. Choose one to three of the best dancers to be the front-line dancers. These dancers will stand in the front line, begin the dance, and model the correct posture and steps for the other students. One of these front-line dancers is the lead dancer who will signal when to dance by waving a handkerchief.

**STEP 1:** To open the play, the leader followed by the other front-line dancers walks erectly and faces the audience downstage with the leader on the right. They hold arms up elbows bent as if saying "hello" with both arms. They maintain the "hello" position throughout the dance. They face the audience. When front-line dancers are in position, a Sound Crew plays taped music. (Suggested music is given below.)

**STEP 2:** Leader waves handkerchief. First, the leader and front-line dancers dance across the stage and back once and then circle the stage. They do the following two steps that are always repeated. First, step on left foot and cross right foot in front. Again, step on left foot and then cross right foot in back. When going in the opposite direction, footing is reversed, stepping on right and crossing left in front, and then again stepping on right and crossing left foot in back. Dancers should look up and out—and not at their feet—to give dignity of carriage. They dip as they cross in front or back to accentuate the grace of these actions.

**STEP 3:** The leader and front-line dancers pause down center with arms raised. Leader waves handkerchief to signal the rest of the students to rise. The others rise walking with arms in the "hello" position and form several lines behind the front-line dancers. Those who feel least assured doing the dance can go in the back lines.

**STEP 4:** When all dancers are in position, the leader again waves handkerchief, and dancers do the same steps given above going back and forth across the stage two times. The whole group needn't circle the stage. When the leader stops, they all stop. They then walk, still keeping good carriage, with their arms in the "hello" position to their chairs and sit. SOUND CREW 1 fades the dance music.

**GREEK DANCE MUSIC SUGGESTION:** Authentic *Folk Songs and Dances* (the Royal Greek Festival Company) Compact Disc 318; Legacy International: Track 8: Island Dances and Songs

# 6

## A Model, Step-By-Step, Rehearsal Schedule

*The curtain call demands an element of choreography and control. The curtain call is not simply an acceptance of praise, it is a simple and touching sense of oneness between the actor and audience.*

John Jory, Producing Director of the
Actors Theatre at Louisville, Kentucky

*What I enjoyed most during the production of* The Odyssey *was performing the play for other students because we got to see the appreciation other students had for our performance.*

Stephanie Chin, student

*I want to do another play because I want to try to get as many parts as possible. I want to have that thrill of excitement again.*

Donald Reisig, student

The following is a step-by-step schedule for directing narrative mime plays in a class of thirty-five students or fewer. It uses *The Odyssey* as a model. The approach outlined below has been used with many classes. Of course, all the activities are only suggestions, and you will want to use what you need and modify the plan as you see fit. Chapter 3 describes most of these techniques in more detail, and some methods are repeated here to give a detailed rehearsal schedule.

### Getting Started

Each play in this book runs twenty-five to thirty minutes. Onstage rehearsals should be at least one hour. More than one step of the rehearsal process might be presented in a session. Steps, such as blocking the play, will likely take more than one session. The ongoing study of the culture can extend over several weeks and can be presented before, during, and after the performance. It's best to produce the play itself in two weeks or less. This short time focuses student's enthusiasm, involvement, and commitment.

## Introducing Ancient Greek Culture

**Goal:** To give students background on the achievements of the ancient Greeks, to deepen their understanding of the culture, and to enhance appreciation of the myth they'll perform.

**Materials:** Books on the culture and its myths (see Bibliography).

**Procedure:** Tell students they will study ancient Greek culture and perform a play based on a Greek myth. Explain that ancient Greek civilization is called "the cradle of Western civilization" because so much of our civilizations began with the contributions of the ancient Greeks.

Contributions include democracy, trial by jury, the Olympic Games, philosophy, science, art, sculpture, architecture, and drama. The ancient Greeks were the first to have theater as we know it today with written plays performed with individuals cast in specific roles. Mention that the ancient Greeks had an interesting religious system with not one god but many gods and goddesses all responsible for different domains—Zeus, lord of the skies; Hera, queen of the Skies, Demeter, goddess of all growing things, and Poseidon, god of the sea. Students also might study the ancient Greeks' lifestyle including their clothes, musical instruments, diets, pottery, jewelry, hairstyles, homes, and temples.

## Introducing the Characters and Story of
## The Odyssey *Using the TV Interview*

**Goal:** To introduce the story of the myth and to get students dramatizing immediately. This also helps teach students the pronunciation of the characters' names.

**Materials:** A copy of the TV Interview of *The Odyssey* for each student.

**Procedure:** Explain that they will perform a play based on *The Odyssey*, composed in the 8th century B.C. by the Greek poet Homer. Mention that along with *The Iliad, The Odyssey* is one of the oldest literary works and a masterpiece that is still enjoyed and studied today, more than two thousand years later. Using the phonetic key with the pronunciation of the characters' names in the cast list of the TV Interview, pronounce each of the character's names and then have students repeat each name after you. Using the cast list, assign students their roles.

Mention the importance of speaking loudly and enthusiastically to make the characters come alive. Performers form a line in the front of the room. The TV Interviewer, perhaps holding a wooden spoon or wire whisk as a microphone, stands to one side. (The Interview has 18 characters, and so students might perform it twice to give every student a chance to play a role.)

## Introducing the Play

**Goal:** To introduce the play and discuss the characters so that students can begin thinking how they might play them.

**Materials:** A copy of the play for each class member, or students might share copies.

**Procedure:** Describe the different roles students might play in the production—chorus, major characters, minor characters, inanimate objects, and sound crew. Students read the script together as a class and discuss the characters. Again, emphasize the importance of reading loudly, clearly, and with enthusiasm to "share the play" with the audience. It is beneficial if students read the script several times to be very familiar with it.

## Explaining How the Play Will Be Produced

**Goal:** To give students an overview of how the play will be performed.

**Materials:** Stage-layout diagram, as given in chapter 3.

**Procedure:** Draw the stage layout on the board and describe it. Point out the seating arrangement of the actors, chorus, sound crew, and audience. Mention that everyone wears all black clothing to create an ensemble or team feeling and to help show off the costume pieces and props.

Describe how actors playing both characters and inanimate objects keep their props and costumes pieces under their chairs and pick them up, put them on, or use them according to cues in the script.

Point out how the sound crew's table and piano (if used) are placed so that the crew can see the stage action and can be seen by the audience as they make their effects.

## Training Actors in the Principles of Good Stage Speech

**Goal:** To learn and practice the four speaking principles essential to perform a play effectively.

**Materials:** A chart with PROJECTION, ARTICULATION, COLORIZATION, and SLOW-THE-PACE written on it—or write these words on the board. A bell.

**Procedure:** Ask students why when casting a play, directors look for actors with strong expressive voices. Mention that actors-in-training and professional actors take voice classes to learn and develop effective speaking techniques. Explain that performers should follow the four speaking principles to share a play with an audience.

The following exercises require simultaneously chanting the name of each principle and doing a gesture that dramatizes it. Use a bell to signal the beginning and end of each exercise.

## Discussing and Practicing Projection

**Procedure:** Discuss the meaning of projection: tossing your voice out as if you were throwing your voice to the back of the space so that everyone can hear the story. Demonstrate by saying "Projection" and throwing an arm out strongly as if throwing a ball to the back of the room.

Ask why projection is important. Ask how do you feel if a speaker projects poorly? Model poor projection. Mumble a short sentence. Then ask, "What was wrong with the way I said this if I were performing for an audience?"

Tell students that when you ring the bell, they will stand and pretend to throw or "project" a ball to the front of the room while chanting PROJECTION four times. Mention the importance of having good posture to use the voice fully and of not shouting, which would annoy an audience.

## Discussing and Practicing Articulation

**Procedure:** Discuss articulation, or saying consonants distinctly so that the precise word is understood. Mention that many British actors have excellent articulation so that we know exactly what is being said.

Model poor articulation and then, good articulation. Say "cat," slurring the *t*. Say it again emphatically pronouncing the *t*. Ask students, "What did I do differently the second time to make the word clear?" Ask why good articulation is important.

Tell them to stand on the bell signal and to point emphatically to emphasize each syllable, chant AR TIC U LA TION four times.

## Discussing and Practicing Colorization

**Procedure:** Ask students what it means to say that good actors put color in their voices. Describe the vocal technique of colorization—speaking words colorfully to make them sound like what they describe. Mention that colorization is the actor's favorite tool to make language and literature come alive. Demonstrate colorization, having students say the opposite words: *fiery, icy; high, low; huge, tiny; gloom, joy.* Then, on the bell signal, tell students to stand and chant COLORIZATION four times while opening their arms out in a big colorful gesture.

## Discussing and Practicing Slowing the Pace

**Procedure:** Discuss the importance of slowing the pace to help an audience understand and fully enjoy the story. Recite the prologue's opening line, "Good morning students, adults too" rapidly. Ask what was wrong with your recitation.

On the bell signal, have students stand and slowly stretch their arms across their bodies while chanting "SLOW-THE-PACE" four times focusing on speaking slowly and using slowed-down action.

## Practicing the Four Speaking Principles Using the Script

**Goal:** To practice the stage-speaking skills using introductory verse from the script.

**Procedure:** Explain that the job of the chorus is to immediately grab the attention of the audience and to make sure the audience understands the story of the play. Thus, the chorus must speak particularly slowly and clearly, exaggerating their good speaking skills.

Recite each line of the following introduction, modeling good speaking skills using gestures. Then have the students recite each line with you. (This is a good vocal warm-up to use before any rehearsal. You can also use dialogue in the scene you are rehearsing that day.) You might also use my books *Dramatizing Mother Goose* and *Dramatizing Classic Poetry* (listed in the Bibliography) to train students in the four effective, stage-speaking skills while reciting and dramatizing poetry.

### Chorus Introduction

*(Very energetically.)* Good morning students, adults too,

*(Pointing on "you.")* Today we perform a myth for you.

*(Raising hands up on "new.")* From ancient Greece, it's old yet new.

*(Opening arms up colorfully.)* We'll make it come alive for you.

*(Gesturing to audience.)* So watch our play *The Odyssey.*

*(Opening arms out and freezing.)* And wondrous feats you will see.

### Training Actors in the Three Principles of Good Acting

**Goal:** To learn and practice the Three Acting Principles while dramatizing incidents from the play. You might take this opportunity to observe who might be best to play major roles. It's also beneficial to do acting activities before rehearsals as warm-ups. (Students might practice these acting skills in informal classroom dramatization using my book, *Dramatizing Aesop's Fables*, see Bibliography.

**Materials:** A sign with BELIEF, CONTROL, VOICE, and MOVEMENT written on it, or you can list these words on the board; the acting exercises that accompany the script; and a bell to indicate the beginning and end of each exercise.

**Procedure:** Explain that good actors follow three acting principles to make the drama believable and effective. Discuss each principle separately and then apply it to the acting exercises.

## Belief

**Procedure:** Discuss why it's necessary for actors to believe or pretend to be the character they're portraying to make the characters seem real. Play Odysseus walking casually and acting like yourself. Ask how an audience would feel about your portrayal. Mention that it requires enthusiasm and wholehearted commitment to play a role effectively.

Have students do the "Becoming Odysseus" activity on page 171 and the Scene One: "Miming the Characters' Situations" activities to practice belief. Students evaluate each other's believable acting, describing specifically how voice and movements were used to make their acting believable. (During subsequent rehearsals for scene two and scene three, use the Scene Two and Scene Three "Miming the Characters' Situations" activities on pages 168–169.)

## Control

**Procedure:** Ask what it means for actors to use control over their voices and movements to make the performance artistic. Ask why a group of twenty dancers can leap and spin in a small space without bumping into each other.

Discuss movements that the group might do to portray Charybdis, the Whirlpool, and the Sea Monster, Scylla, in a controlled artistic way. Then, do the "Becoming Charybdis " and "Becoming Scylla" activities on pages 169–170 to practice control.

## Voice and Movement

**Procedure:** Ask what it means for actors to use their voices and movement to show a character's feelings and personality. Demonstrate by asking them to say the word, *voice,* twice—first in the mighty voice of the god Zeus and then in a timorous, mouse voice. Then tell them to say the word *movement* twice—first taking the regal commanding stance of Zeus and then a timid mouse position.

Have students do the Circle Walk Character Transformation on page 168 and the Developing Effective Stage Speech Using the Script and Developing Majestic Bearing activities on pages 210–211 to practice using voice and movement.

## Developing Majestic Bearing

**Goal:** To stand, sit, and move with dignity, nobility, and majesty.
**Acting Principles:** Belief, Movement.
**Materials:** Drum (optional).
**Procedure:** Tell students that Odysseus, Circe, the Sirens, Athena, Telemachus, and Penelope have a royal or commanding stance. Explain that they sit and stand erectly with excellent posture. Model poor posture. First slouch, then lean on

one foot, shift from one foot to another, put your hands in your pocket. As you do these, ask "What was I doing wrong to convey royal stance?" Then, stand with a royal bearing. Have them do the following majestic bearing activity.

Sit with head up, shoulders back, feet together and firmly on the ground.

Place your hands on each side of the chair to help lift you. Then keeping head up, press hands on chair to help lift you and slowly rise.

Walk slowly with head up, shoulders back, and hands by sides perhaps to the accompaniment of steady majestic drumbeat.

Finally, stand with feet planted firmly on the floor, hands by sides, shoulders back, and head looking slightly up to the back wall of the auditorium. Lift arms up and out in a gesture showing you are ready to lead your people.

## Presenting the Written Tryout

**Goal:** To let students express in writing what role they want to play and to involve them in thinking about the characters and how they might portray them.

**Procedure:** Tell students that the first casting step is the written tryout. Explain that the written tryout does not guarantee they'll get the part they want. On the board or a chart, list the following points to include in their written tryout.

1. List three roles you want to play in order of preference—including characters, inanimate objects, chorus, or sound crew.

2. Describe the characteristics of the character or what is required to perform the role. (Mention that students can play more than one inanimate object as long as the parts don't overlap.)

3. Explain why you should be chosen to play that role.

## The Formal Tryout—Flexible Casting

**Goal:** To let students try out for two or three parts they want to play; to determine who's able to use projection, articulation, colorization, and to speak slowly to communicate to an audience.

**Materials:** A copy of the script for each class member.

**Procedure:** Explain that students will now try out for the parts they want and remind them that an essential requirement for chorus and actors with speaking parts is good projection so that the audience can hear and enjoy the play. Explain that those playing a character should concentrate on voice and movement.

Explain that all casting is flexible and that if someone is absent or does not work out for some reason, the part will be reassigned. Mention that unfortunately not everyone will get the part they most want, and that even the best professional actors don't get every role they want.

Have students try out for two or three roles by reading and acting from portions of the script. You may want to give yourself until the next day to make your decisions and announce the cast. Use the written tryouts to help you assign these roles.

## Learning the Stage Areas

**Goal:** To teach students the basic stage areas so that they can move to them as directed.

**Materials:** Stage-area diagram as given in chapter 3.

**Procedure:** Explain that different areas on the stage have names to help the director tell the actors where they should be positioned at a given time. Draw the stage area diagram on the board.

Explain that upstage comes from a time when stages sloped upward so that audiences seated on one level could see what was happening at the back of the stage. Downstage, is the opposite of upstage. Stage right and stage left are identified from the actors' point of view, and center is obviously the center of the stage.

To help students learn the areas, have students practice moving to the various areas in the front of the classroom or onstage. Teacher Demetrice Davis uses the Mother Goose verse, "Jack and Jill" to teach the stage areas.

To do this, choose two students to play Jack and Jill and tell them they will go to different stage areas on each line. Have them begin by standing downstage center. Tell them on "Jack and Jill went up the hill," to go upstage; on "To fetch a pail of water," say to go upstage left. Tell Jack on "Jack fell down and broke his crown," to go to center stage left. Tell Jill on "Jill came tumbling after," to go downstage center. The term *stage* might be eliminated when giving the directions, and you might just say, "Go up right" or "Move down left."

## Introducing Blocking Techniques

**Goal:** To teach the students movement techniques that will enable them to share the play effectively and dramatically with an audience.

**Procedure:** Explain that you'll give actors blocking or movement instructions during rehearsals so that they'll know where to go and when. Mention the three blocking techniques actors need to know to assure that the audience can see what's happening on the stage and enjoy the show.

1. Open up to the audience.

2. Don't get blocked.

3. Share the stage.

Demonstrate and practice the techniques, using the guidelines provided in chapter 3.

## Highlighting Chorus and Sound Crew

**Goal:** To prepare students to rehearse so that the chorus and sound crew will be ready to perform on cue.

**Materials:** Copies of the script and highlighting pens for the chorus and sound crew members only.

**Procedure:** Explain that only the chorus and the sound crew use scripts at rehearsals, and it is essential they highlight their parts so they will come in and perform on cue. Otherwise, the flow of the story will be disrupted.

Explain actors do not use scripts onstage so that they are able to move freely. Actors' lines are usually fed to them by the chorus, and if they forget a line, a chorus member will whisper it to them.

## Onstage Rehearsals

**Procedure:** Arrange for all of the staging of the play to be done on the stage or in the area where the play will be performed so that students become familiar and comfortable with it and know how much projection is required.

## Learning the Greek Dance (Optional)

**Goal:** To teach the opening and finale dance.

**Materials:** Dance instructions and taped music suggestions in chapter 5.

**Procedure:** Explain that the play begins and ends with a traditional Greek dance and that a sound crew member will play the music for the dance on the tape. Mention that all performers may dance if they desire. Choose as lead dancers one or two of the most talented dancers or enthusiastic students motivated to practice at home. Practice the steps and stances for the dance.

## Blocking the Play

**Goal:** To give students their stage movement.

**Materials:** Scripts for chorus and sound crew only. Rhythm instruments, props, and costume pieces for the scene you are rehearsing. (See Costumes Suggestions in the Production Notes of the script.)

**Procedure:** Set up the stage according to the stage layout with actors' chairs in a semi-circle and the sound crew's tables with instruments on them. Be sure to position the tables so they can see the stage action and be visible to the audience.

Blocking takes about six hours for each play. Chapter 3 describes in detail techniques of effective blocking. With this type of production, blocking can be loose and flexible. The only essentials are that actors be visible to everyone in the audience, that the focus is on the main action occurring on the stage at that time, and that the whole stage is used in scenes with lots of movements so it doesn't look cramped.

Begin introducing costume pieces and props that must be put on and taken off and manipulated from the first rehearsal so they'll get used to using them. Full costumes aren't needed until the dress rehearsal. Choose several responsible students to take charge of setting out and packing up the instruments and costume pieces. Tunics and full cosumes need not be worn until the dress rehearsal.

### Developing Acting, Speaking, and Sound-Effects Skills

**Goal:** To develop acting, narrating, and sound-effects techniques to communicate the play theatrically to the audience.

**Procedure:** Chapters 1, 2, and 3 describe how to train each member of the performance team to communicate their parts effectively and dramatically.

These skills should be emphasized and practiced during every rehearsal as these techniques and skills communicate the play. As mentioned, it is good to begin each rehearsal with a vocal warm-up to prepare students to use their stage-speaking voice.

# POLISHING THE PLAY— THREE DRESS REHEARSALS

It is good to have three dress rehearsals—two back-to-back dress rehearsals the day before the performance and a final warm-up dress rehearsal just before the performance.

The two back-to-back rehearsals should be nonstop run-throughs to help the performers get the flow of the show and to feel how it will be for the performance.

The final dress rehearsal is a rehearsal just before the play is performed. With beginners, it is beneficial to rehearse just before performance. This helps them warm up, gets them involved in the acting, and helps work out nervous jitters.

The central emphasis of all of these rehearsals is to build confidence. The following suggestions will help you conduct these rehearsals.

### First Dress Rehearsal

**Goal:** To polish major rough spots and to give students the feeling of the flow of the action.

**Materials:** All costumes and props (see Costume Suggestions for the script).

**Procedure:** Explain that there will be two dress rehearsals, one after the other. The first is to polish rough spots. Say that you will not verbally interrupt but will use four hand signals to communicate what needs to be done, and what's effective. Explain and demonstrate that cupping your hand to your ear means speak louder; pushing both hands from the chest slowly to the floor means slow down;

sweeping an arm across the body means don't crowd together, move aside and open up the action; and thumbs-up means everything is effective—keep it up.

At the end of this rehearsal, discuss what was good about the rehearsal and what they might do next time to enhance the production.

## Second Dress Rehearsal

**Goal:** To build students' confidence and enthusiasm and to teach them how to work as a team and "go on" if anything goes wrong.

**Procedure:** During this rehearsal, try to bring in a few sympathetic observers to give the performers the experience and excitement of an audience. Explain again that this is a nonstop rehearsal, and no matter what happens, students must cover it up and go on. Discuss with students what they might do if an actor forgets a line, drops a prop, or has difficulty with a costume piece. Mention that even in the professional theater there are mistakes. Ask why the audience usually never notices when something goes wrong.

After this rehearsal, heartily praise what was done well. Students need this reassurance to be excited and confident for the performance.

## Warm-Up Rehearsal Just Before the Play Is Performed

**Goal:** To warm students up, to focus their nervous jitters into effective performing, and to build confidence to perform their best.

**Procedure:** Explain that students will have the chance to warm up by running through the play once more before the audience arrives. Mention all the things that the performers have been doing well—to boost confidence. Ask them what they might do to create a good performance. Students' comments at this time are often most perceptive and helpful.

During this run-through, take note of who acts nervous or makes a lot of errors. Then you can be ready to help them with a few encouraging words in the "performance counseling" session just prior to the performance.

# THE PERFORMANCE

## Before-Performance Counseling

**Goal:** To build confidence and give students guidance and reassurance to help them enjoy the experience and do their best.

**Procedure:** Nervousness before a performance is normal even for professionals. Performing before an audience is exhilarating and a little nerve-wracking. Performers need the director's guidance and reassurance to gain a feeling of confidence. Ways to avoid the burden of perfectionism are suggested in chapter 3.

Psychologist Jack Sanford suggests going around and asking how each student is feeling just before the performance. This acknowledges the students' feelings and shows that you as a director care. If some say they're nervous, reassure them by explaining that jitters are normal and that all performers feel them.

Then reassure all students individually that they are doing a great job. It's helpful to point out one specific thing that each is doing well, such as speaking with a loud voice or moving with dignified grace. This helps students focus on what they do well, giving them confidence, and it helps them emphasize this strength during the performance.

To help the sound crew be ready and secure, check that all members have their first instruments ready in front of them, so they'll be ready to perform on cue.

### Training the Audience and Acknowledging Their Role

**Goal:** To acknowledge the audience's significant role and to train the audience to observe what performers do to create a good performance. Also, to give the performers final performance tips.

**Procedure:** This play and production style offers many opportunities for the audience to get involved. It also develops their imaginations and lets them experience directly how theater works because so many of the theatrics are out in the open for all to see.

Counsel the audience before the performance. Thank the audience for entering the auditorium and waiting for the performance respectfully. Point out the importance of an audience. Mention that their respectful, attentive manner will help the performers do their best job.

Explain they will see scenes from *The Odyssey*, a story about ancient Greek culture. Explain that *The Odyssey* along with its companion piece *The Iliad* is the oldest literary work. Give a brief synopsis of the scenes they'll see.

Ask the audience to observe how the actors use their imaginations and pretend they are the characters they are playing. Give examples such as watching how the actor playing Penelope uses her voice and movement to portray a royal majestic queen. Mention several other characters to observe and their character types—for example the bold, heroic Odysseus, the prowling lion, and the swirling whirlpool. Explain how these actors will use their voices and bodies to play their parts. This also gives the actors some last-minute reminders.

Tell the audience to watch the chorus and see what they do with their voices and bodies to make the story clear and exciting. Last, point out how the sound crew will play their sound effects crisply and on cue to make the action exciting and to help the actors act.

Explain that after the performance you will ask the audience to tell you and the performers what they noticed and liked about the production.

## Audience Follow-Up and Reflection

**Goal:** To reiterate the importance of the audience and to give the audience a chance to voice its reactions to the performance; to give the performers positive feedback; to train the audience by elaborating on their comments—pointing out the skills necessary to achieve what they liked.

**Procedure:** Thank the audience for being attentive. Be sure to express your appreciation and the performers' appreciation. Ask audience members to say loudly what they enjoyed so everyone can hear what they have to say. Respond to their reactions, pointing out the skills required to achieve what they liked. For example, if someone liked the portrayal of the monster Scylla, point out how the actors used their movements—leaping forward and crouching down to show aggression. If someone mentions the dance movements, reinforce how the dancers moved with dignity and how much control they had dancing together in a limited space.

Make sure that every performance element is included—actors, inanimate objects, chorus, and sound crew. Elicit comments on performers who are not mentioned. Ask the adults in the audience too.

## Audience Follow-Up: Writing, Art, and Reading

**Goal:** To give the audience a chance to reflect on the performance through art and writing; to use this performance to stimulate viewers to read myths and perhaps dramatize them; to give the performers written and artistic feedback.

**Procedure:** Tell the audience that you and the performers would greatly appreciate letters and pictures describing favorite parts of the performance. Mention that these will be read and displayed in the classroom and kept in a special book.

## Performers' Follow-Up and Reflection

**Goal:** To give the performers an opportunity to describe their reaction to the experience and reflect on its meaning to them.

**Procedure:** Performing is a heightened, meaningful experience. A follow-up reflection session helps students artistically evaluate the performance and articulate what it meant to them. Reflection also provides a calm transition back to the daily business of the classroom. Reflection is an ideal opportunity to take advantage of students' excitement and enthusiasm to discuss possible future drama project, including other full-scale plays, informal classroom dramatizations, as well as plays and dramatizations that they may want to write and stage on their own. (In chapter 12 we explore how students can write their own narrative mime scripts.) There are always several students who are highly excited by this experience and want to do more.

Some possible written reflection questions:

1. What did you enjoy most during this production?

2. What was most difficult?

3. What was your reaction to having an audience?

4. How did you feel during the performance?

5. What future drama projects would you like to do?

Students might make their own class album describing and drawing their favorite part of the performance. To expose them to more myths through drama, you might also copy the TV Interviews of other myths for students to perform informally in the classroom.

# PART II: DRAMATIZATIONS

# The Creation and Birth of the Olympian Gods

*There were many creation myths among the Greek and Romans. The poet Hesiod was the only one who gave a complete explanation of how the gods, the universe, and human beings came into being. This play is based on the version by Hesiod in his Theogony (account of the birth of the gods) from about 700 B.C.*

In the beginning of the universe, there was Chaos, a formless swirling mass. From Chaos, came Ge, Mother Earth. Ge created Uranus, the sky god to cover her Earth and to make a home for the gods. Ge also created the mountains and the sea.

Together Ge and Uranus created the hundred-handed Hecatonchires and the one-eyed Cyclopes. Uranus feared these powerful children would overcome him and banished them underground. Ge was furious and asked her other children, the Titans, to kill Uranus.

Cronus, her craftiest Titan son, agreed. In the darkest night, Cronus killed his father Uranus with a sickle and tossed his body into the sea. Cronus was now supreme leader and determined he would never be overcome by any of his children. So, when Cronus united with the goddess Rhea, he swallowed his first five children. Only Zeus, the sixth child, survived because Rhea hid him in a cave.

When Zeus became a young god, he wanted to overcome Cronus and retrieve his swallowed sisters and brothers. The goddess Metis gave Zeus a special drink that tasted like ambrosia, the drink of the gods, but it contained mustard and salt. Zeus gave his father Cronus the drink that made him spit out Zeus's five sisters and brothers. These were the six original Olympian gods and goddesses. Besides Zeus, they are Hestia, goddess of the hearth and home; Demeter, goddess of all growing things; Hera, the goddess queen and wife of Zeus; Poseidon, god of the sea; and Hades, god of the underworld. These original Olympians ascended to Mount Olympus, their home.

These first Olympians declared their brother Zeus, king of the gods, and with him they became rulers of the Greek universe. Later, these six Olympians were joined by Zeus's children—Hephaestus, god of the forge and fire; Athena, goddess of wisdom and arts and crafts; Apollo, god of intelligence, music, and light; Artemis, goddess of the hunt and the moon; Hermes, the messenger and trickster god; and Aphrodite, goddess of beauty and love. These twelve created the pantheon of the Olympian gods.

**Summary for the Teacher:** TV Interview with the Characters in *The Creation and the Birth of the Olympian Gods*

**Goal:** To introduce the characters and story of the myth through dramatization and as a possible casting method.

**Materials:** Copy of the TV Interview for all students, or students might share copies.

**Procedure:** Explain that they will perform a TV Interview playing the characters in the myth telling their story. Read the TV Announcer's introduction in a low monotone. Ask students what was wrong with the way you read and how you might make it more effective.

Cast the roles using the cast list. Choose students with animated, projected voices to play the TV Announcer, Ge, and Uranus. They will model the techniques desired and inspire the playing of the others. Before dramatizing, practice the pronunciation of the characters' names using the cast list.

Characters stand in front of the classroom with the TV Announcer sitting or standing to one side. Characters step forward when introduced and when speaking, and step back when finished. Students might wear signs with their character names to identify them. Use a wooden spoon or a wire whisk as a microphone. There are 15 roles in the interview, so perhaps dramatize it twice to give all students a chance to participate. To further increase roles, use a different student as announcer for each page. After dramatizing, review the characters and the story events.

# TV INTERVIEW

CAST OF CHARACTERS (16):
   TV Announcer
   Ge (**jee**)
   Uranus (you **ran** us)
   Hecatonchire #1 (hek a ton **keye** ree)
   Hecatonchire #2
   Cyclops #1 (**sigh** klopz; plural is Cyclopes, sigh **klow** peez)
   Cyclops #2
   Cronus (**crow** nus)
   Rhea (**ree** ah)
   Zeus (zoose)
   Metis (**mee** tis)
   Hestia (**hes** tee uh)
   Demeter (de **mee** ter)
   Hera (**hair** a)
   Poseidon (puh **sigh** dun)
   Hades (**hay** deez)

• • •

TV ANNOUNCER: Today we meet the characters who were there when the universe began. Characters, please step forward when introduced. First, meet **Ge,** the Earth goddess and her husband **Uranus,** the sky god. We'll hear from their children—the giant **Hecatonchires** with one-hundred hands and the **Cyclopes** with one huge eye. We'll see **Cronus,** the craftiest of their Titan children and his wife **Rhea.** We'll hear how **Zeus** was able to overcome Cronus with the help of **Metis.** Finally, we'll meet the six original Olympian goddesses and gods—**Hestia, Demeter, Hera, Poseidon, Hades,** and, Zeus, king of the gods. Now, let's listen to the dramatic story of how the ancient Greeks felt the universe began. Ge, you were here first. What was the world like when you came?

GE: There was nothing but whirling Chaos. I came forth from the Chaos. I was the first creator. I created the Earth, the mountains, and the sea. And, I wanted a sky so I created Uranus, the sky god.

TV ANNOUNCER: Uranus, sky god, what was your role?

URANUS: First, I made my sky cover Ge, the Earth. Later, we had children. First there were the Hecatonchires with one-hundred hands and the Cyclopes with one eye in the middle of their foreheads. They were very powerful.

TV ANNOUNCER: Hecatonchires, what made you powerful?

HECATONCHIRE #1: With our ONE-HUNDRED HANDS, a Hecatonchire could pummel a mountain or a village to bits.

TV ANNOUNCER: Cyclopes, were you as powerful as the Hecatonchires?

CYCLOPS #1: Yes. We Cyclopes have ONE HUGE EYE that can see through mountains and into the bottom of the sea. No one can escape our gaze.

URANUS: I feared one of those Hecatonchires or Cyclopes would overcome me. I wanted to get rid of them. So, I hid them under the earth.

HECATONCHIRE #2: It was miserable!

CYCLOPS #2: We could not see the light of day.

TV ANNOUNCER: Ge, how did you feel about Uranus putting your children underground?

GE: I was furious that Uranus would do such a cruel thing. I wanted revenge. So, when I gave birth to our other children the Titan gods, I asked them to kill Uranus. Cronus, my craftiest son, agreed.

TV ANNOUNCER: Cronus, why did you kill your father, Uranus?

CRONUS: I wanted to be supreme ruler of the universe. So, I waited until Uranus covered himself with his dark night sky. Then I sneaked up and lunged at him with a huge sharp sickle. I tossed his body into the sea. Then, I WAS the supreme leader of the universe.

**GE:** I warned Cronus not to get too high and mighty because someday he too would be overcome by one of his children.

**CRONUS:** I determined that would never happen.

**TV ANNOUNCER:** What did you do?

**CRONUS:** Each time my wife Queen Rhea had a child, I swallowed the baby whole. I swallowed five babies.

**TV ANNOUNCER:** *(Shocked.)* Rhea, how could you have allowed your husband Cronus to swallow your children?

**RHEA:** It was horrible. So when my sixth child, Zeus, was about to be born, on the advice of Ge, I hid baby Zeus in a cave.

**TV ANNOUNCER:** Was that successful?

**RHEA:** Yes. And to fool Cronus, I put a stone the size of a baby in a blanket and pretended it was the baby Zeus. I handed the stone covered in a blanket to Cronus.

**TV ANNOUNCER:** Didn't Cronus suspect it was a stone and not a baby in the blanket?

**RHEA:** Cronus was so eager to overcome his children that he swallowed the stone whole.

**TV ANNOUNCER:** Amazing!

**RHEA:** Then, when Zeus grew to be a strong young god, he was determined to overcome his evil father, Cronus, and to rescue his brothers and sisters.

**TV ANNOUNCER:** Zeus, how could you rescue your brothers and sisters when Cronus had already swallowed them?

**ZEUS:** I went to Metis, known for her trickery.

**METIS:** I gave Zeus a potion that tasted like nectar, the drink of the gods, but it was mixed with mustard and salt. I told him to give this drink to Cronus.

**ZEUS:** Cronus greedily swallowed it. The potion made him sick, and he spit out first a stone and then my five sisters and brothers.

**TV ANNOUNCER:** Were they still alive?

**ZEUS:** Yes, being Olympian gods and goddesses, they emerged whole.

**TV ANNOUNCER:** This whole story is astounding. Will those first Olympian goddesses and gods introduce themselves.

**HESTIA:** I am Hestia, goddess of the hearth and home.

**DEMETER:** I am Demeter, goddess of all growing things.

**HERA:** I am Hera, the goddess queen.

POSEIDON: I am Poseidon, god of the sea.

HADES: I am Hades, god of the underworld.

ZEUS: And I am Zeus, king of the gods.

TV ANNOUNCER: Did you Olympians then rule the universe?

ZEUS: Not yet. First we had to defeat Cronus and his brothers, the other Titan gods, including Atlas, who was very powerful and our worst enemy of all.

TV ANNOUNCER: How did you do it?

ZEUS: I set free the Hecatonchires and the Cyclopes, from their dark underworld. They were grateful and helped me. The Cyclopes gave me a huge thunderbolt to throw. The hundred-handed Hecatonchires hurled hundreds of boulders at the Titans who thought the mountains were falling and retreated. Even Atlas, the most powerful Titan, retreated. They were so scared they went into the underworld to escape.

TV ANNOUNCER: That was quite a victory.

ZEUS: It was. Then we Olympians climbed to the top of Mt. Olympus, our home. Then I created the muses of song, music, art, poetry, and dance to lead us in a joyful celebration. We Olympians, later joined by my six children, have been up there reigning ever since.

TV ANNOUNCER: Well, viewers, now we know how the universe evolved in the ancient Greek world and how the Olympian gods and goddesses that we study today became the rulers of the Greek universe. I've got to admit this is THE most astounding story I've heard in all of my broadcast career.

# ACTING EXERCISES

Use the following exercises to involve all students in dramatizing and to develop the stage-speech and acting skills.

## *Practicing Effective Stage Speech*

**Goal:** To practice the stage-speaking skills using introductory verse from the script.

**Procedure:** First, discuss and practice the four stage-speaking skills. (See chapter 1, "The Four Stage-Speaking Principles.") Then, recite each line of the following introduction modeling the good speaking skills using gestures. Have the students echo you. (This is a good vocal warm-up to use before any rehearsal or use the rhymed couplet speeches in the following exercise.)

*(Waving and very energetically.)* Welcome audience, and "yas sas" or to your health too.

*(Pointing on "you.")* Today we'll act a myth for you.

*(Arms down on "old," up on "new.")* From ancient Greece, it's old yet new.

*(Opening arms up.)* We'll make it come alive for you. This myth tells of the world's creation, and the birth of the gods.

*(Raising arms.)* It's quite a sensation.

## *Warming up the Voice Using the Rhymed Couplet Verses of the Olympian Gods and Goddesses*

**Goal:** To develop expressive stage speech in a vocal warm-up.

**Procedure:** Tell students that they will warm up their voices reciting rhymed couplet verses of the Olympian gods and goddesses. Mention that the goal is to use the stage-speaking skills of projection, articulation, colorization, while speaking slowly and distinctly. First, you recite each line of the following verse or verses, and then the students recite the line with you. (Perhaps do two or three of these before each rehearsal.)

I am HESTIA, goddess of hearth and home
From this place I never roam.
I love to tend a friendly fire
And never let the flames expire.

I am DEMETER goddess of the growing grain.
I make things grow with sun and rain.
So when you eat your daily bread,
I'm the one who keeps you fed.

I am HERA, the goddess queen.
My husband Zeus is the god supreme.
I enjoy my place as queen of the skies
Over all of society I supervise.

I am POSEIDON, god of the sea.
I am lively. I am free.
I make waves tumble. I make waves toss.
Over all the world's oceans, I am the boss.

I am HADES, god of the world below
Where everyone eventually goes.
I felt gloomy in my world down there.
And captured Persephone so bright and so fair.

I am ZEUS king of the gods.
I rule the sky with thunder rods.
The lightning bolt's my other tool.
Who interferes would be a fool.

## Developing Majestic Bearing

**Goal:** To stand, sit and move with dignity, nobility, and majesty.
**Acting Principles:** Belief, Movement.
**Materials:** Drum (optional).
**Procedure:** Tell students that the characters in this play have a majestic stance. Explain that they sit and stand erectly with excellent posture. Model poor posture. First, slouch, then lean on one foot, shift from one foot to another, put your hands in pocket. As you do each of these, ask what was I doing wrong to convey royal stance? Finally, stand with a royal bearing. Then, have them do the following majestic bearing activity.

- Sit with head up, shoulders back, feet together and firmly on the ground.

- Place your hands on each side of the chair to help lift you. Then keeping head up, press hands on chair to help lift you and slowly rise.

- Walk slowly with head up, shoulders back and hands by sides perhaps to the accompaniment of a steady majestic drum beat.

- Finally, stand with feet planted firmly on the floor, hands by sides, shoulders back and head looking slightly up to the back wall of the auditorium. Lift arms up and out in a gesture showing you are ready to lead your people.

*Using Movement to Become*
*the Characters and Inanimate Objects*

**Goal:** To develop expressive movement skills with control.
**Acting Principles:** Belief, Control, Movement.
**Materials:** Use a bell to start and end each scenario.
**Procedure:** Explain that students will become the characters and inanimate objects from the myth. Provide enough space between students for movement. Ring a bell to start and stop each action and end each action in a "freeze." Perhaps, divide the class in half, with each half doing every other one of the actions. Girls perform females, and boys, male roles. All play inanimate objects, giants, and monsters.

- Become whirling Chaos. Use your arms and shoulders and whole body. Use all levels—move up, down and all around. Freeze.

- Become the sea. First, move your arms and body as gentle rippling waves. Next create big sweeping breakers. Finally, create a high stormy roller. Freeze.

- Girls: Become the Earth goddess Ge. On a slow count of five, stoop and rise slowly from Chaos. Open your arms out majestically creating your great expanse of Earth. Gesture to make mountains push up. Gesture to form a rippling sea. Freeze.

- Boys: Become the sky god Uranus. On a slow count of five, stoop and emerge from deep within the Earth. Thrust your arms up powerfully, and open them out to create your huge expanse of sky. Freeze.

- Become a tall, mighty mountain, or with others form a mountain range. Freeze.

- Become a powerful hundred-handed Hecatonchire. Stand ferociously, feet apart, display your huge hands. Pick up a big boulder and hurl it mightily. Now, use your powerful hands to pummel everything to bits. Freeze aggressively.

- Become a giant Cyclops. Make your huge eye pierce through a massive rock searching for enemies. Peer with your powerful eye into the depths of the sea tracking down enemies. Glare forward to assert your dominance. Freeze.

- Boys: Become power-greedy Cronus. Smile menacingly. Reach out, grab baby Hestia bundled in a blanket, swallow the baby whole, and then abruptly toss the empty blanket aside. Sneer and freeze.

- Girls: Become a protective Nymph. Reach out and take precious baby Zeus. Cradle and rock the baby gently to sleep. Freeze.

- Boys: Become Cronus. Reach eagerly for the drink Zeus hands you thinking it will make you more powerful, gulp it greedily, cough violently, and spit out a stone. Freeze.

- Girls: Become a graceful muse. Spin and bow to Zeus ready to celebrate the joyful victory of the Olympian gods. Freeze.

- Boys and Girls: Become the Olympian god or goddess of your choice. Stand majestically, chin up, shoulders back, ready to command the world. Freeze.

*Developing Character Stance and Convincing Character Speech*

**Goal:** To develop character stance and speech, and to experience the characters in key action moments in the play.

**Acting Principles:** Belief, Control, Voice and Movement, Creative Flexibility.

**Materials:** Use a bell to start each scenario.

**Procedure:** Tell the students they will become characters in the play and say their dialogue. Explain the goal is dramatic expression with control. Read each scenario first so they are familiar with it and then read it again coaching them through it. Ring a bell to start and stop action. End each action in a "freeze." Boys perform male roles, and girls, female roles.

- Girls: Become Ge. Assert your power, say, "I am Ge, goddess of the Earth."
- Boys: Become Uranus. Assert your dominance. Declaim powerfully, "I am Uranus, god of the sky."
- Boys: Become Cronus. Toss Uranus's body into the sea. Say triumphantly, "I am the supreme ruler of the universe."
- Girls: Become Rhea. See Cronus swallow your baby Hestia, say with horror, "What have you done!"
- Boys: Become Zeus say confidently, "I will overcome my evil father Cronus."
- Girls: Become crafty Metis. Helpfully advise Zeus, "Give this drink to Cronus."
- Girls and Boys: Become your favorite Olympian goddesses or god (other than Zeus). Tell Zeus, "Lead us brother Zeus."

# THE CREATION AND BIRTH
# OF THE OLYMPIAN GODS
Adapted from a version by Hesiod

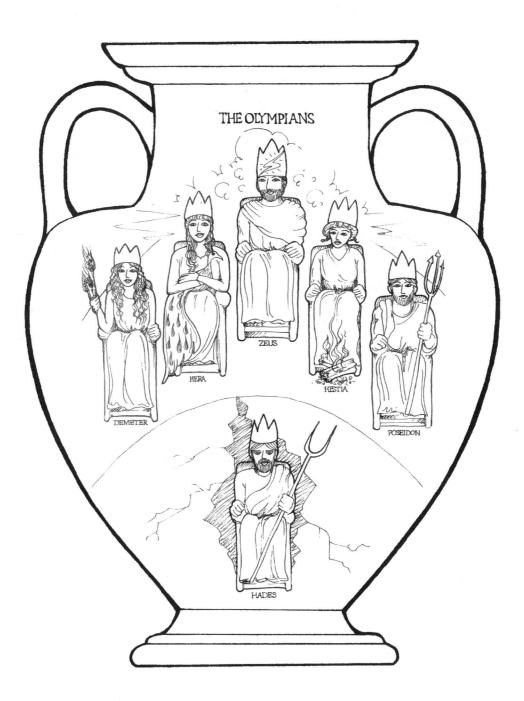

CAST OF CHARACTERS: (In order of appearance.)

    CHORUS 1 Leader, very responsible, strong voice

    CHORUS 2, 3, 4 Strong voices; ability to follow and pick up cues

    WHIRLING CHAOS (3 or more)

    GE (**jee**) Leading role; strong voice; commanding presence; requires line memorization

    URANUS (you **rah** us) Powerful voice and presence

    SEA (2)

    MOUNTAINS (4)

    HECATONCHIRE # 1 (hek a ton **keye** ree) Powerful, aggressive

    HECATONCHIRE # 2

    CYCLOPS # 1 (**sigh** klopz)—plural is Cyclopes pronounced (sigh **klow** peez) Powerful, aggressive

    CYCLOPS # 2 Powerful, aggressive

    CYCLOPS # 3 Powerful, aggressive

    TITANS (5 ) (**tie** tanz)

    PROP PERSON

    CRONUS (**crow** nus)

    RHEA (**ree** ah) Strong role; strong voice; stage presence and dramatic flair

    NYMPHS (3 or 4) Protective

    ZEUS (**zoose**) Leading role; strong voice; powerful stance; requires line memorization

    METIS (**mee** tis)

    HESTIA (**hes** tee uh) Majestic; strong voice; requires minimal line memorization

    DEMETER (de **mee** ter) Majestic; strong voice; requires minimal line memorization

    HERA (**hair** a) Majestic; strong voice; requires minimal line memorization

    POSEIDON (puh **sigh** dun) Majestic; strong voice; requires minimal line memorization

    HADES (**hay** deez) Powerful

    MUSES (**mew** zes) (4) Graceful dancers

*Sound Crew*

    SOUND CREW 1 triangle

    SOUND CREW 2 jingle bells, drum, rattle

    SOUND CREW 3 jingle bells, wood block, rattle

    SOUND CREW 4 tambourine, rattle

    SOUND CREW 5 handbell, rattles, gong

    SOUND CREW 6 tone bells, jingle bells, guiro, handbell

## Basic Stage Setup

The actors sit in chairs arranged in a semicircle in view of the audience. Two Chorus members stand on each side of the stage. Costumes and props are stored under the actors' chairs. The Chorus and actors who wear tunics throughout the play are in their tunics.

The Sound Crew sit at one or two tables to the right or left of the stage area with their instruments on in view of the audience. Tables are set so that the crew can see the stage action.

## Stage Setup

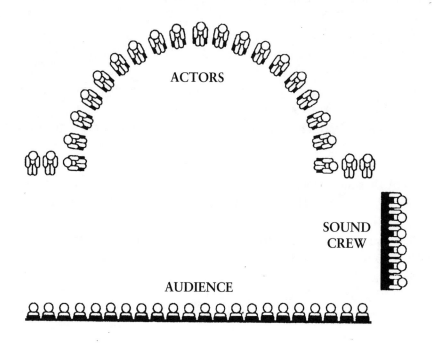

ACTORS

SOUND
CREW

AUDIENCE

*The play might begin with a Greek dance. (See chapter 5 for dance instructions and music suggestions.)*

# PROLOGUE

*(SOUND CREW 1 strikes triangle three times slowly to signal the play will begin.)*

**CHORUS 1:** *(Very energetically.)* Welcome audience, and "yas sas" or to your health too.

*("Yas sas" is Greek for "to your health" and is used for both hello and good-bye.)*

**CHORUS 2:** *(Pointing on "you.")* Today we'll act a myth for you.

**CHORUS 3:** *(Arms down on "old," up on "new.")* From ancient Greece, it's old yet new.

**CHORUS 4:** *(Opening arms up colorfully.)* We'll make it come alive for you.

**CHORUS 1:** *(Gesturing to audience.)* This myth tells of the world's creation

**CHORUS 2:** And the birth of the gods.

**CHORUS 3:** *(Raising arms.)* It's quite a sensation.

*(SOUND CREW 1 strikes triangle. SOUND CREW 2 might play tape of opening movement of Beethoven's Fifth Symphony to set the powerful tone of this myth.)*

# SCENE ONE
## *The Beginning*

Characters: Chorus, Chaos, Ge, Uranus, Mountains

**CHORUS 4:** Scene One: The Beginning

*(SOUND CREW 1 strikes triangle.)*

**CHORUS 1:** In the beginning there was nothing—only whirling Chaos.

*(SOUND CREW 2 strikes drum rapidly and SOUND CREW 4 shakes tambourine vigorously as CHAOS ACTORS take different stage areas and swirl atmosphere sticks or fabric up, down, and all around for a slow count of eight. Then, SOUND CREW 2 strikes drum once emphatically and SOUND CREW 4 slaps tambourine in the center, as CHAOS freeze for a count of three in "chaotic," jagged positions.)*

**CHORUS 2:** From Chaos, sprang Ge, the Earth.

*(SOUND CREW 4 shakes tambourine as CHAOS shimmer atmosphere sticks above GE, who kneeling center stage rises slowly. SOUND CREW 4 slaps tambourine in the center as GE opens arms out and freezes. SOUND CREW 4 shakes tambourine as CHAOS actors return to their chairs.)*

**GE:** *(Powerfully.)* I am Ge, goddess of the Earth.

> *(SOUND CREW 2 strikes drum once emphatically.)*

**CHORUS 3:** Ge commanded Uranus, the sky god, to come forth.

**GE:** *(Powerfully.)* Come forth Uranus and create a sky to cover my Earth.

> *(SOUND CREW 4 shakes tambourine as URANUS steps next to GE.)*

**URANUS:** *(Powerfully, thrusting arms up.)* I am Uranus, the sky god. I will create my sky to cover your Earth.

> *(SOUND CREW 2 strikes drum three times as URANUS gestures to sky and opens arms out showing heaven.)*

**CHORUS 4:** Then, Ge beckoned the sea to come forth.

**GE:** *(Beckoning with arm and powerfully.)* Come forth, sea.

> *(SOUND CREW 1 strikes triangle slowly eight times and SOUND CREW 3 and 6 shake jingle bells as SEA actors form the sea downstage and ripple SEA fabric. SEA actors sit.)*

**CHORUS 1:** And GE beckoned the mountains to come forth.

**GE:** *(Thrusting fist up.)* Come forth, mountains.

> *(SOUND CREW 3 strikes wood block five times as MOUNTAINS stoop, and on a slow count of five stand, thrusting peaks up. SOUND CREW 2 then strikes wood block three times as MOUNTAINS freeze and then sit.)*

# SCENE TWO
## The Hecatonchires and the Cyclopes
Characters: Chorus, Hecatonchires, Cyclopes, Uranus, Ge


**CHORUS 2:** Scene Two: The Hecatonchires and the Cyclopes

> *(SOUND CREW 1 strikes triangle.)*

**CHORUS 3:** Ge and Uranus became the parents of the HUNDRED-HANDED Hecatonchires.

**URANUS:** *(Gesturing to Hecatonchires.)* Our first children were the POWERFUL Hecatonchires.

> *(SOUND CREW 2 strikes drum as HECATONCHIRES step forward, legs apart standing firmly.)*

**GE:** Each Hecatonchire had one hundred hands.

> *(SOUND CREW 2 strikes drum once as HECATONCHIRES thrust hands forward assertively and freeze for a count of five with hands extended.)*

**CHORUS 4:** With their hundred hands, each HECATONCHIRE could hurl one hundred rocks at enemies.

**HECATONCHIRE #1:** *(Glaring and aggressively.)* With MY hundred hands, I can HURL one hundred rocks at my enemies.

*(SOUND CREW 2 strikes drum five times as HECATONCHIRE #1 mimes hurling five rocks, and freezes for a count of three on the last hurl.)*

**HECATONCHIRE # 2:** *(Glaring and aggressively.)* With MY hundred hands, I can PUMMEL ANYTHING to bits.

*(SOUND CREW 2 strikes drum rapidly five times as HECATONCHIRE #2 punches five times and freezes on last punch for a count of three.)*

**CHORUS 1:** The Hecatonchires were powerful!

**HECATONCHIRE #1:** *(Raising fist.)* We are POWERFUL.

*(SOUND CREW 2 strikes drum once firmly as HECATONCHIRE #1 raises fist.)*

**HECATONCHIRE #2:** *(Raising fist.)* We are VERY POWERFUL.

*(SOUND CREW 2 strikes drum twice firmly as HECATONCHIRE #2 raises two fists.)*

**HECATONCHIRE #1 and #2:** *(Raising both fists.)* We are VERY, VERY POWERFUL.

*(SOUND CREW 2 strikes drum 3 times as both HECATONCHIRES raise both fists and freeze for a count of three.)*

**CHORUS 2:** Ge and Uranus also became parents of three GIANT Cyclopes.

**URANUS:** *(Gesturing toward Cyclopes.)* Our second children were the giant Cyclopes.

*(SOUND CREW 2 strikes drum as CYCLOPES step forward, chins up, feet apart. HECATONCHIRES step back but remain standing.)*

**GE:** Each Cyclops had one HUGE EYE in the middle of his forehead.

*(SOUND CREW 3 strikes wood block firmly as the CYCLOPES point aggressively at their single eyes.)*

**CHORUS 3:** With this huge eye, each Cyclops could see thousands of miles.

**CYCLOPS #1:** *(Pointing at eye and aggressively.)* I can spot an enemy wherever he goes.

*(SOUND CREW 3 strikes wood block firmly.)*

**CYCLOPS #2:** *(Peering over heads of audience.)* I can see through mountains.

*(SOUND CREW 3 strikes wood block firmly.)*

**CYCLOPS #3:** *(Peering down.)* I can see into the bottom of the ocean.

*(SOUND CREW 3 strikes wood block firmly.)*

**CYCLOPS #1:** *(Raising fist and loudly.)* We are POWERFUL.

*(SOUND CREW 2 strikes drum once firmly.)*

**CYCLOPS #2:** *(Raising fist and more loudly.)* We are VERY POWERFUL.

*(SOUND CREW 2 strikes drum twice firmly.)*

**CYCLOPS #3:** *(Raising both fists and most loudly.)* WE are VERY, VERY POWERFUL.

*(SOUND CREW 2 strikes drum three times firmly as all CYCLOPES raise fists and freeze.)*

**CHORUS 4:** Uranus HATED these powerful children, the Hecatonchires and the Cyclopes. He feared someday they would overcome him.

**URANUS:** *(Plotting, to audience:)* I HATE these powerful children. Someday they might overcome me. I will put them UNDERGROUND and NEVER let them see the light of day.

**CHORUS 1:** His wife, Ge, begged Uranus not to put their children underground.

**GE:** *(On knees.)* Uranus, do NOT put our children, the Hecatonchires and the Cyclopes, underground. It is CRUEL to make them live in DARKNESS.

**CHORUS 2:** But Uranus took pleasure in the banishment.

**URANUS:** *(Pointing.)* Ha! Ha! Ha! I BANISH YOU children beneath the earth. May you live in DARKNESS and NEVER see the light of day.

*(SOUND CREW 2 strikes drum slowly and rhythmically as the HECATONCHIRES and CYCLOPES scowling and with bowed heads, return to their chairs, kneeling with backs to audience and putting their heads on their chair seats to symbolize going underground.)*

**CHORUS 3:** The Hecatonchires and the Cyclopes hated their father, Uranus, for putting them underground.

**HECATONCHIRE #1:** *(Rising.)* I hate our father Uranus.

**HECATONCHIRE #2:** *(Rising.)* He banished us here to the dark underground.

**CYCLOPS #1:** *(Rising.)* We Cyclopes also hate our father.

**CYCLOPS #2:** *(Rising.)* Now we can NEVER see the light of day!

**CYCLOPS #3:** *(Rising.)* Someday we will get our revenge.

*(SOUND CREW 2 strikes drum once firmly.)*

**ALL CYCLOPES and ALL HECATONCHIRES:** *(Very assertively and raising fists.)* WE WILL GET OUR REVENGE!

*(SOUND CREW 2 strikes drum twice firmly. HECATONCHIRES and CYCLOPES freeze with raised fists for count of five and then sit.)*

# SCENE THREE
## The Titans and the Ascent of Cronus

Characters: Chorus, Uranus, Ge, Titans, Cronus

**CHORUS 4:** Scene Three: The Titans and the Ascent of Cronus

*(SOUND CREW 1 strikes triangle.)*

**CHORUS 1:** Ge and Uranus gave birth to more children. These children were THE TITANS, THE FIRST GODS.

*(SOUND CREW 2, 3, 4, and 5 shake rattles vigorously as TITANS stand by chairs stage left and thrust arms up majestically.)*

**CHORUS 2:** Uranus did not fear the Titans for they were not as powerful as the Hecatonchires or the Cyclopes. So he let them live in the world above.

**URANUS:** *(Gesturing to TITANS.)* I will let you Titans live above.

**TITANS:** *(Bowing heads.)* Thank you, father Uranus.

*(SOUND CREW 5 strikes gong as TITANS bow to URANUS and then return to their chairs.)*

**CHORUS 3:** Ge loved her Titan children. But Ge despised Uranus for putting their first children, the Hecatonchires and the Cyclopes, underground. Ge wanted revenge.

**GE:** *(Angrily pacing.)* Uranus should NOT have put our first children underground. *(Raising fist.)* I WANT REVENGE.

*(SOUND CREW 5 strikes gong.)*

**CHORUS 4:** So, Ge went to her Titan children and asked them to kill Uranus.

*(TITANS stand and SOUND CREW 3 strikes wood block to accompany GE'S walking to TITANS standing in semicircle with CRONUS in the center.)*

**GE:** *(To TITANS.)* One of you Titan children must kill Uranus. Then you will rule the universe.

**CHORUS 1:** Her craftiest son Cronus agreed. He wanted to rule the universe.

**CRONUS:** *(Stepping forward enthusiastically.)* I agree with you mother. I will kill Uranus. THEN I WILL RULE THE UNIVERSE.

*(SOUND CREW 5 strikes gong.)*

**CHORUS 2:** Ge gave Cronus a huge, black sickle.

*(SOUND CREW 1 strikes triangle as PROP PERSON hands sickle to GE. CRONUS kneels.)*

**GE:** *(Holding sickle reverentially as instrument of power.)* Cronus, my son, take this sickle. Kill your evil father Uranus and toss his body into the sea.

**CRONUS:** *(Bowing head and craftily.)* I gladly obey, Mother.

**CHORUS 3:** Crafty Cronus waited until his father the sky pulled his black night cloak over him. *(SOUND CREW 4 shakes tambourine as URANUS goes center and kneels covering himself with night cloak. )*

**CHORUS 4:** Then, in the blackest dark when no one could see, Cronus circled Uranus stealthily.

*(SOUND CREW 6 strikes guiro slowly to accompany CRONUS slowly circling URANUS.)*

**CHORUS 1:** Quickly, he lunged with the sickle and killed Uranus in one blow.

**URANUS:** *(Falling slowly, holding wound and loudly.)* AOOOOW!

*(SOUND CREW 5 strikes gong. CRONUS freezes arms raised triumphantly.)*

**CHORUS 2:** Ge beckoned the sea to come forth and carry Uranus's body away.

**GE:** *(Powerfully gesturing to SEA.)* Come forth sea and carry away the body of EVIL URANUS. May he NEVER be seen again.

*(SOUND CREW 4 shakes tambourine and SOUND CREW 2, 3, and 6 shake jingle bells as GE beckons SEA ACTORS who ripple sea fabric covering URANUS who stooping disappears as SEA and URANUS return to their chairs.)*

**CHORUS 3:** Now, Cronus was the supreme ruler of the universe, and he gloried in his absolute power.

**CRONUS:** I am SUPREME RULER of the universe. I GLORY in my ABSOLUTE POWER.

*(SOUND CREW 5 strikes gong.)*

**CHORUS 4:** But his mother Ge mother warned Cronus not to glory too much in his power, for someday he too would be overthrown by one of HIS children.

**GE:** Cronus, don't glory too much in your power. Some day YOU TOO will be overcome by one of your children.

**CHORUS 1:** Cronus determined that NONE of his children would EVER OVERCOME HIM. He made plans to get rid of all of his children.

**CRONUS:** *(Craftily.)* None of my children will EVER overcome ME! *(Rubbing hands.)* I have plans to get rid of ALL OF MY CHILDREN. I will ALWAYS be the SUPREME RULER.

*(SOUND CREW 2 strikes drum firmly and then SOUND CREW 5 strikes gong.)*

# SCENE FOUR
## *The Children of Cronus*

Characters: Chorus, Rhea, Cronus, Prop Person

**CHORUS 2:** Scene Four: The Children of Cronus

*(SOUND CREW 1 strikes triangle.)*

**CHORUS 3:** Later Cronus united with the goddess Rhea, and they had children. These children were the Olympian gods.

*(SOUND CREW 1 strikes triangle six times as CRONUS and RHEA stand side by side.)*

**CHORUS 4:** The first child of Cronus and Rhea was the Olympian goddess Hestia. Rhea was delighted with the baby girl Hestia and handed the first born to the father, Cronus.

*(PROP PERSON hands RHEA a blanket wrapped around a towel, as if a baby were in the blanket.)*

**RHEA:** *(Happily handing baby to Cronus.)* Cronus, here is our first child, the goddess Hestia. Come and embrace her.

**CHORUS 1:** BUT, instead of EMBRACING Hestia, Cronus grabbed the baby and SWALLOWED HER WHOLE!

*(SOUND CREW 4 shakes tambourine as CRONUS takes blanket and mimes eating the baby. Then, CRONUS turns back to audience and abruptly drops baby on floor as SOUND CREW 4 slaps tambourine in the center. PROP PERSON removes blanket. This sequence should be done in a stylized way with the exact sequence repeated for each of the following "baby swallowing" sequences.)*

**RHEA:** *(Pulling hair and hysterically.)* What have you done!

*(SOUND CREW 4 slaps tambourine in the center. RHEA, bowing head and putting hands to face in agony, turns back to CRONUS.)*

**CHORUS 2:** Rhea gave birth to four more baby Olympian gods—two daughters, Demeter and Hera, and two sons, Poseidon and Hades. Each time Cronus did the SAME despicable thing—reaching out as if to embrace the babies and then swallowing them whole.

*(SOUND CREW 1 strikes triangle on the name of each god and goddess. PROP PERSON hands different colored blankets, again wrapped around towels to look like a baby, to RHEA who in turn hands blankets to CRONUS who mimes eating each baby and tossing the blankets abruptly in a choreographed, stylized way on the floor as was done previously. SOUND CREW 4 shakes the tambourine each time for eating and slaps it in the center for tossing. RHEA reacts in horror each time. This sequence should be done quickly like a choreographed dance.)*

# SCENE FIVE
## The Birth of Zeus and the Defeat of Cronus

Cast: Chorus, Rhea, Nymphs, Metis, Cronus

**CHORUS 3:** Scene Five. The birth of Zeus and the defeat of Cronus. Rhea was now TERRIFIED of Cronus.

**RHEA:** Cronus terrifies me. He has SWALLOWED four of our children!

**CHORUS 4:** When Rhea learned that her last baby Zeus was to be born, she went to her mother Ge for advice.

**RHEA:** Oh great mother goddess Ge, what can I do to keep Cronus from SWALLOWING our last child Zeus?

**GE:** Hide baby Zeus in a cave and have the Nymphs guard him.

**CHORUS 1:** So, Rhea put her new born babe Zeus in a cave and asked the Nymphs to care for him.

*(SOUND CREW 1 strikes triangle as PROP PERSON hands RHEA blue, blanket-towel bundled to represent baby Zeus. NYMPHS step forward to cave center stage.)*

**RHEA:** *(Handing baby to Nymphs.)* Nymphs, please care for my baby Zeus. Let no one find him. Protect him and treat him as a god.

**NYMPHS:** *(Bowing heads.)* We will.

*(SOUND CREW 1 strikes triangle as the NYMPHS go into imaginary cave and kneel cradling the baby.)*

**CHORUS 2:** The Nymphs guarded Zeus. To distract attention from baby Zeus's cries, some of the Nymphs marched around the cave banging spears against shields to drown out baby Zeus's cries.

*(ONE or TWO NYMPHS march around CAVE striking pot-lid shields with metal spoons for a count of ten.)*

**CHORUS 3:** Then, Rhea placed a STONE the size of a baby in a blanket and handed it to her husband, Cronus, PRETENDING it was the baby Zeus.

*(RHEA displays stone to audience. PROP PERSON hands RHEA blanket and RHEA mimes placing stone in blanket. Then, RHEA turns back to audience and hands stone back to PROPS so it appears CRONUS is eating stone in the blanket.)*

**RHEA:** *(Handing blanket to CRONUS.)* Cronus, here is our last-born child, Zeus. Come and embrace him.

**CHORUS 3:** Cronos again greedily grabbed for the baby, but this time he swallowed a STONE WHOLE.

*(SOUND CREW 4 shakes tambourine as CRONUS mimes eating and slaps it in the center as he tosses blanket on the floor in similar fashion to the other "baby swallowing" sequences.)*

**CHORUS 4:** Later, baby Zeus grew to be a strong god.

*(SOUND CREW 6 sweeps tone bells low to high three times as the young god ZEUS steps majestically center with head high and shoulders back.)*

**CHORUS 1:** He vowed to overcome his father Cronus and get back his sisters and brothers whom Cronus had SWALLOWED.

**ZEUS:** *(Assertively.)* I WILL overcome my evil father Cronus. Cronus SWALLOWED my sisters and brothers. I must find a way to set my brothers and sisters free.

**CHORUS 2:** Zeus went to Metis, known for her trickery.

**ZEUS:** Metis, my father Cronus has swallowed my sisters and brothers. How can I overcome Cronus and set my brothers and sisters free?

**CHORUS 3:** Metis knew just how to trick Cronus.

**METIS:** *(Craftily.)* I know just how to trick Cronus. *(Handing imaginary drink.)* Give this drink to Cronus. It tastes like nectar, the drink of the gods, but I added mustard and salt.

# SCENE SIX
## *The Rebirth of the Olympian Gods and Goddesses*

Cast: Chorus, Zeus, Hestia, Demeter, Hera, Poseidon, Hades, Muses

**CHORUS 4:** Scene Six. The rebirth of the Olympian gods and goddesses

*(SOUND CREW 1 strikes triangle.)*

**CHORUS 1:** Zeus went to Cronus and gave him the drink.

**ZEUS:** Father Cronus, drink this nectar. It is the drink of the gods and will make you even more powerful.

**CRONUS:** *(Greedily grasping.)* Give me that drink.

**CHORUS 2:** Cronus greedily swallowed the drink. The mustard and salt made him cough violently.

*(SOUND CREW 4 shakes tambourine and SOUND CREW 3, 4, 5, and 6 shake rattles as CRONUS facing the audience swallows and coughs violently. Then turning back to audience CRONUS takes out stone concealed in his clothing.)*

**CHORUS 3:** Then, out popped FIRST a STONE.

*(SOUND CREW 3 strikes wood block firmly as CRONUS places stone near his mouth and then turning to audience tosses it on the floor.)*

**CHORUS 4:** Then out popped the five, undigested children—the Olympian gods and goddesses and each proclaimed his or her name and special power.

*(SOUND CREW 5 strikes gong as all the OLYMPIAN GODS and GODDESSES rise quickly from their chairs and raise arms up as if popping out. When announced by CHORUS, each GODDESS or GOD steps forward center, speaks his or her dialogue in a grand style, and steps back, remains standing as the next GODDESS or GOD takes center stage.)*

**CHORUS 1:** *(Majestically declaiming.)* HESTIA!

*(SOUND CREW 1 strikes triangle.)*

**HESTIA:** *(Holding up flame.)*

I am HESTIA, goddess of hearth and home.

From this place I never roam.

I love to tend a friendly fire

And never let the flames 'expire.

*(SOUND CREW 6 strums tone bells low to high three times as HESTIA freezes with flame raised and then steps back remaining standing.)*

**CHORUS 2:** *(Majestically declaiming.)* DEMETER!

*(SOUND CREW 1 strikes triangle.)*

**DEMETER:** *(Holding up sheaves of wheat.)*

I am DEMETER goddess of the growing grain.

I make things grow with sun and rain.

So when you eat your daily bread,

I'm the one who keeps you fed.

*(SOUND CREW 6 strums tone bells low to high three times as DEMETER freezes with grain raised and then steps back remaining standing.)*

**CHORUS 3:** *(Majestically declaiming.)* HERA!

*(SOUND CREW 1 strikes triangle.)*

**HERA:** *(Holding up peacock feather.)*

I am HERA, the goddess queen.

My husband Zeus is the god supreme.

I enjoy my place as queen of the skies,

Over all of society I supervise.

*(SOUND CREW 6 strums tone bells low to high three times as HERA freezes with peacock feather raised and then steps back remaining standing.)*

**CHORUS 4:** *(Majestically declaiming.)* POSEIDON!

*(SOUND CREW 1 strikes triangle.)*

**POSEIDON:** *(Holding up trident.)*

I am POSEIDON, god of the sea.

I am lively. I am free.

I make waves tumble. I make waves toss.

Over all the world's oceans, I am the boss.

*(SOUND CREW 6 strums tone bells low to high three times as POSEIDON freezes with trident raised and then steps back remaining standing.)*

**CHORUS 1:** *(Majestically declaiming.)* HADES!

*(SOUND CREW 1 strikes triangle.)*

**HADES:** *(Holding up pitchfork.)*

I am HADES, god of the world below

Where everyone will eventually go.

I felt lonely in my world down there.

And captured Persephone so bright and so fair.

*(SOUND CREW 6 strums tone bells low to high three times as HADES freezes with pitchfork raised and then steps back remaining standing.)*

**CHORUS 2:** *(Majestically declaiming.)* ZEUS!

**ZEUS:** *(Holding up thunderbolt and lightning rod and mightily.)*

I am Zeus, king of the gods.

*(Holding up thunderbolt in one hand.)* I rule the sky with thunder rods.

*(Holding up lightning bolt in other hand.)* The lightning bolt's my other tool.

*(Powerfully.)* Who interferes would be a fool.

*(SOUND CREW 6 strums tone bells low to high three times as ZEUS raises thunder and lightning bolts and remains center.)*

**CHORUS 3:** The grateful Olympian gods and goddesses bowed to their brother Zeus and thanked him for saving them.

**ALL GODDESSES and GODS:** *(Bowing heads.)* Thank you, brother Zeus.

**CHORUS 4:** They made Zeus their leader.

**ALL GODDESSES and GODS:** *(Enthusiastically.)* Lead us, Brother Zeus.

**CHORUS 1:** Then Zeus led the Olympian gods and goddesses, his brothers and sisters, to the top of Mount Olympus, their home.

**ZEUS:** Come brothers and sisters to Mount Olympus, our home.

*(SOUND CREW 1 strikes triangle as ZEUS leads all GODS and GODDESSES who stand on their chairs with ZEUS in the center chair to represent Mt. Olympus.)*

**CHORUS 2:** And Zeus called forth the Muses of song, music, art, and dance to help them celebrate their victory.

**ZEUS:** Come forth, Muses.

*(SOUND CREW 6 strums tone bells low to high three times as MUSES spin gracefully around ZEUS.)*

**ZEUS:** Now, Muses, make our hearts lively and make our feet prance.

And lead everyone here in a bright circle dance.

**CHORUS 3:** And the Muses happily complied.

**MUSES:** *(Bowing to Zeus.)* Happily we comply.

**MUSE OF DANCE:** Now watch our arms lift. Watch our feet prance as we lead this whole group in a bright circle dance.

*(MUSES spin and then take position. MUSES do a variation of the Greek dance—first circling with backs to audience, then circling facing the audience, then going in and out of the circle three times and finally spinning and returning to their chairs. See chapter 5 for dance and music suggestions.)*

**CHORUS 4:** And then led by Zeus everyone joined in the dance.

*(SOUND CREW 6 plays taped music as ALL ACTORS including the OLYMPIANS do the beginning dance with this time ZEUS in the center of the front line. Then, SOUND CREW SIX fades the music, and ALL ACTORS sit ready for the Finale.)*

# FINALE

**CHORUS 1:** And that is the story of "The Creation and Birth of Olympian Gods." It's quite a sensation!

*(ALL CHORUS members go center stage for the finale. They should memorize this part.)*

**CHORUS 1:** "Efharisto," (Ef ha **ree** stoh) friends and thank you too.

*(Efharisto, pronounced Ef ha **ree** stoh, is Greek for "thank you" and literally means good graces and joy.)*

**CHORUS 3:** For watching so kindly our myth for you.

**CHORUS 4:** From ancient Greece, it's old yet new.

**CHORUS 1:** We hope it came alive for you.

**CHORUS 2:** *(Pointing to audience.)* And here's a last tip from the Chorus, your friends.

**CHORUS 3:** *(Holding up book.)* Read a book of these myths from beginning to end.

**CHORUS 4:** And study ancient Greece with its great majesty.

**CHORUS 1:** *(Making big circular gesture.)* For the more that you know, the more you'll be free.

*(CHORUS return to their respective sides of stage to introduce the cast and crew.)*

*(To end the performance, CHORUS 1–4 introduce the performers, having them stand and say their names loudly and clearly. When all are standing, CHORUS 1–4 thank the audience and then turn toward ACTORS and raise their arms. Everyone follows, raising their arms and bringing them down together for a group bow. Performers then sit for the audience performance discussion.)*

**CHORUS 1:** The Actors are . . .

*(SOUND CREW 6 strikes one high tone bell after each cast member stands, and introduces her- or himself. CAST and CREW remain standing after they are introduced.)*

**CHORUS 2:** The Sound Crew is . . .

**CHORUS 3:** The Chorus members are . . .

# PRODUCTION NOTES

## *Costume Suggestions*

For narrative mime presentations students wear all black clothing—black shirts and black pants—with individual, character costumes worn as additional pieces to the all-black attire. If actors play characters wearing tunics throughout the play, they need not wear black clothes as long as their clothes don't show under the tunic.

**Chorus:** Use pattern for simple, knee-length tunic. Make the tunic from a wrinkle-free fabric. Use purple, dark blue, burgundy, dark green, off-white, or any dignified, but not overpowering, color. Might use similar or different colors for each chorus member. Tie with black cord. Wear gold, store-bought, laurel-leaf headpieces or make headpieces with foliage from floral-supply store. (See chapter 4, *Creating Costumes, Props, and Scenery* for making tunic and headpieces.)

**Whirling Chaos:** Atmosphere sticks with black steamers and scarves of vivid colors such as red, deep blue, and purple tied to it. Two sticks for each Chaos actor. (See chapter 4, *Creating Costumes, Props, and Scenery* for making atmosphere sticks.)

**Ge:** Brown tunic of cotton or other lightweight fabric and green cloak of sheer fabric; gold belt; headdress with branches, green and autumn leaves, and perhaps berries.

**Uranus:** Dark blue tunic, possibly with one sun or several small suns on it. Small narrow blue crown with spikes that are not too tall, so his night sky cloak can be tossed over him. Silver or gold belt. For black night cloak, use black cloak or lightweight, black fabric.

**Sea:** Transparent, lightweight, blue fabric extending the length of the stage and about two or three feet wide.

**Mountains:** No costume other than black clothing is necessary. Actors use their bodies to form mountain peaks.

**Hecatonchires:** Draw hands with a black, felt-tip pen on the front, back, and sleeves of a white, long-sleeved, man's shirt; headbands with two tagboard, hand shapes attached.

**Cyclopes:** Cut in half a white Styrofoam ball and draw a black pupil and red iris with felt-tip pens; attach ball to a headband that resembles hair. Or use small, white paper cups and color the bottom of the cup black, leaving a large slit like that of a cat's eye in the center and color it red.

**Titans:** No costume other than black clothing is necessary.

**Cronus:** Black tunic; tall black crown with costume jewelry attached; silver belt.

**Rhea:** Pink tunic; multicolored headband; dark pink belt.

**Nymphs:** Pretty, matching headbands and belts.

**Zeus:** Sky-blue tunic; tall headpiece of dark blue poster board with white or silver lightning bolts; silver belt.

**Metis:** Silver tunic and contrasting belt; silver crown with junk jewelry attached.

**Hestia:** Yellow or orange-yellow tunic; gold crown decorated with orange flames representing the hearth; gold or orange belt.

**Demeter:** Golden yellow tunic; golden yellow crown or tall headpiece decorated with cutout sheaths of wheat or autumn leaves; gold belt.

**Hera:** Purple tunic; silver crown with lots of junk jewelry attached, or attach a peacock feather to a hat; silver or other contrasting belt.

**Poseidon:** Green tunic; green and blue crown or headpiece with wave pattern on top; black cord belt.

**Hades:** Red cape (no tunic is necessary as red cloak contrasts with the all-black clothes); black headpiece of black poster board with points shaped like flames and accented with red glitter.

**Muses:** Short, white tunics; gold elasticized headbands with artificial flowers attached; gold sashes or cord for belts.

## Prop Suggestions

**Sickle:** Black dowel with foam core shaped like a sickle and covered with tagboard attached and painted all black.

**Baby Blankets:** Small bath towels with colors similar to the costumes of each of the god and goddesses whom the blankets represent—e.g., bright blue for Zeus; green for Poseidon; red, Hades; gold, Demeter; orange, Hestia; and purple, Hera.

**Nymphs' Brass Shields:** Pot lids struck with metal spoons.

**Stone:** Two, heavy, gray socks tied to resemble stones—one for Rhea to display and another for Cronus to conceal in his clothes.

**Hestia's Flame:** Paper towel roll covered with gold foil and with flames of red, orange, and yellow construction paper coming from the top.

**Demeter's Wheat:** Sheaves of wheat from floral-supply store.

**Hera's Peacock Feather:** Tall, peacock feather.

**Poseidon's Trident:** Dowel with a three-pronged head of poster board covered with aluminum foil.

**Hades' Pitchfork:** Paint-stirring stick with two-pronged head of Flexi-foam attached and painted black.

**Zeus's Lightning and Thunderbolt:** Stiff cardboard about 18 inches long, cut like streaks of lightning in a jagged fashion. Make two—a thunder rod (covered in silver foil) and a lightning bolt (covered in blue foil).

# STORY QUESTIONS, WRITING, ART, AND CLASSICAL CONNECTIONS (DEVELOPING LANGUAGE)

The following questions are listed scene by scene. Interpretive questions are indicated by an asterisk (*). A separate list of general and personal response questions are at the end of this section as well as a Classical Connections language section with questions on words from the myths that have entered our English vocabulary.

SCENE ONE: *The Beginning*

1. According to this myth, what did the universe consist of originally?

2. Who was the first creator and what did she create first?

3. Why did the first creator make the sky?

4. What else did the first creator create besides the sky?

5. *Who do you think was the more powerful—Earth goddess Ge or sky god Uranus? Explain your answer.

SCENE TWO: *The Hecatonchires and the Cyclopes*

1. What was unusual about the Hecatonchires, and what made them powerful?

2. What was unusual about the Cyclopes, and what made them powerful?

3. What cruel action did Uranus take against the Hecatonchires and the Cyclopes? Why did he do it?

4. *What was Ge's reaction to what Uranus did to their first children? Why did she feel that way?

5. How did the Hecatonchires and the Cyclopes feel about what Uranus had done to them? What did they say they would do?

SCENE THREE: *The Titans and the Ascent of Cronus*

1. Who were the Titans? Why didn't Uranus treat the Titans in the same way he had his other children, the Hecatonchires and the Cyclopes?

2. What did Ge ask the Titans to do and why?

3. Who is Cronus and why did he help Ge with her plan?

The Creation and Birth of the Olympian Gods  85

4. *Why do you think Cronus—but none of his brothers and sisters—agreed to help Ge execute her plan?

5. What did Cronus do to Uranus, and how did he do it?

6. How did Cronus feel after he executed his plan? What did he say?


SCENE FOUR: *The Children of Cronus*

1. *How do you know Rhea trusted Cronus when they first had children?

2. What did Cronus do to try to guarantee none of his children would ever overcome him?

3. How did Rhea react to what Cronus did to her children?

4. What did Rhea do to save baby Zeus?


SCENE FIVE: *The Birth of Zeus and the Defeat of Cronus*

1. Who gave Rhea advice on what to do to prevent Cronus from devouring baby Zeus? What did she tell Rhea to do?

2. How did Rhea fool Cronus into thinking she was giving him baby Zeus to hold?

3. Who helped Zeus overcome Cronus, and what did she do to help him?

4. What was effective about the help Zeus received?

5. *Zeus deceived Cronus. Do you think he was justified in deceiving him? Explain.


SCENE SIX: *The Rebirth of the Olympian Gods and Goddesses*

1. In what unusual way did five of the six Olympian gods become "reborn"?

2. Name the six original Olympian gods and tell their specialties.

3. Who did Zeus create to help the Olympians celebrate their ascendance to Mt. Olympus as the Olympian gods? What did they do to celebrate?

## General Interpretive and Personal Response Questions

1. Which character in this myth do you think is most powerful? Why?

2. The Greek word *hubris* means "reckless behavior." Which characters in this myth demonstrate hubris? What do they do?

3. Which character in the myth do you admire the most? Why?

4. In what way might it correctly be said of Cronus "like father, like son."

5. Which characters in this myth try to win power by using brute force? What are the consequences of their actions?

## Research

1. Research the names of Zeus's children who later became the six other Olympian gods and goddesses.

2. Find names of three minor gods and goddesses who don't live on Mount Olympus and tell their responsibilities.

## Writing

Choose one of the twelve Olympian god or goddesses that you most admire and write a fan letter to him or her telling what you admire. Perhaps draw a picture of him or her.

## Classical Connections: Developing Language

The following are questions on words in the myth that have entered the English language. Use the Glossary to answer these questions.

1. What is the original meaning of *chaos*? What does *chaos* mean now?

2. Which character in this play is connected to the word *uranium?* What is uranium?

3. What Greek figures inspired the name of the ship, the *Titanic?* Why was the ship named the *Titanic?* What happened to the *Titanic* that showed it was not invincible?

4. Name the fields of study that come from the name of Ge, the Earth goddess.

5. The word *chronology* comes from the name of what Greek figure in this play? What is a chronology?

6. What words in use today come from the muses?


### Art

• Draw your interpretation of a Cyclops or a Hecatonchire.

• Draw one, or all six, of the original Olympians.

• Draw the sea and mountains that Ge created.

8

# The Myth of Demeter and Persephone
## or *The Origin of the Seasons*

*This myth is the ancient Greek explanation for the seasons of the year. It is one of the oldest stories in the world. The play is based on the version by the poet Homer from the 8th century B.C.*

Persephone was picking flowers and reached out to pick a beautiful white narcissus. The Earth opened and Hades, the king and god of the underworld, sprang up in his gold chariot with the black horses. He snatched Persephone who screamed, and he carried her to the underworld.

Demeter, Persephone's mother and goddess of the harvest, was performing her magic rites to make the crops grow and heard her daughter scream. Demeter searched for her daughter. Hecate, the moon goddess, advised going to Helios, the sun god, who sees everything. Helios said that Hades seized Persephone and carried her to his underworld home. He said Zeus, king of the gods, gave Persephone to Hades as a present.

Demeter was furious with Zeus. She disguised herself as an old woman, so no one would recognize her and went to the city of Eleusis. There, she sat by the well, where the daughters of King Celeus came to draw water and asked who she was.

Demeter asked them to find her work caring for a baby. The girls took Demeter home. The girls' mother, Queen Metaneira, saw Demeter's nobility and gave Demeter her son to care for. Then one night, Metaneira shrieked when she saw Demeter place her baby in the fire. Demeter snatched the boy from the flames and said she was putting him there so he might live forever like the gods, but now because of Metaneira's interference, the boy would grow old like all humans and die.

Demeter changed back into a goddess and commanded the people of Eleusis to build her a temple. The people obeyed, but Demeter remained depressed and commanded the land to die.

Zeus, the king of the gods, saw the crops dying and sent Iris the rainbow goddess to offer presents to Demeter to make the crops sprout. Demeter refused and said the crops would not grow until she saw her daughter. So, Zeus sent Hermes to the underworld to demand that Hades return Persephone to her mother. Hades agreed but slyly gave Persephone a pomegranate.

Demeter and Persephone happily reunited, but then Persephone revealed she had eaten four seeds of a pomegranate in the land of the dead. Zeus decreed that since

Persephone had eaten the four seeds she must always live four months or one-third of the year with her husband, Hades, in the land of the dead. The other eight months, she could be in the world above with her mother. Demeter was satisfied and let the land bloom again.

**Summary for the Teacher:** TV Interview with the Characters in *The Myth of Demeter and Persephone* or *the Origin of the Seasons*

**Goal:** To introduce the characters and story of the myth through dramatization and as a possible casting method.

**Materials:** Copy of the TV Interview for all students or students might share copies.

**Procedure:** Explain that they will perform a TV Interview playing the characters in the myth telling their story. Read the TV Announcer's introduction in a low monotone. Ask students what was wrong with the way you read and how you might make it more effective.

Cast the roles using the cast list. Choose students with animated projected voices to play the TV Announcer, Persephone, and Demeter. They will model the desired techniques and inspire the other students to improve their playing. Before dramatizing, practice the pronunciation of the characters' names using the cast list.

Characters stand in front of the classroom with the TV Announcer sitting or standing to one side. Characters step forward when introduced and when speaking, and they step back when finished. Students might wear signs with their character names to identify them. Use a wooden spoon or a wire whisk as a microphone. There are 13 roles in the Interview, so perhaps dramatize it twice to give all students a chance to participate. To further increase roles, use a different student as Announcer for each page. After dramatizing, review the characters and the events of the story.

# TV INTERVIEW

CAST OF CHARACTERS (13)
> TV Announcer
> Persephone (purr **sef** oh nee)
> Demeter (deh **mee** ter)
> Hecate (**hek** a tee)
> Helios (**hee** lee ohs)
> Daughters of King Celeus (**See** lee us):
>> Daughter #1, Daughter #2, Daughter #3
> Queen Metaneira (met a **nee** ra)
> Zeus (**zoose**)
> Iris (**eye** ris)
> Hermes (**her** meez)
> Hades (**hay** deez)

TV ANNOUNCER: *(Energetically.)* Today we meet the characters in the ancient Greek story that explains the seasons of the year. Characters, please step forward when introduced. The Greek gods and goddesses who will appear are **Demeter,** goddess of the growing grain; **Hades,** king and god of the underworld; **Persephone,** daughter of Demeter and wife of Hades; **Hecate,** the moon goddess; **Helios,** the sun god; **Zeus,** king of the gods; **Iris,** the rainbow goddess; and **Hermes,** the messenger god. The mortals are the eldest **daughters of King Celeus** and their mother, **Metaneira.** This myth is one of the oldest myths in the world.

    Now we'll hear from the characters in the myth. We begin with Persephone since the story revolves around her.

PERSEPHONE: *(Excitedly.)* I was picking flowers in a meadow. Suddenly, I saw this beautiful narcissus, and I reached out to pluck it. The Earth opened and Hades, the king and god of the underworld, sprang up and charged at me with his black horses. He snatched me into his gold chariot and carried me screaming to the world below.

TV ANNOUNCER: Demeter, Persephone's mother, what were YOU doing at the time?

DEMETER: *(Urgently.)* I was performing my magic rites to make the crops grow. Suddenly, I heard the mountains and ocean echo with my daughter's scream. I grabbed my heart and rushed like a bird looking for Persephone. For nine days, I wandered calling for her. On the tenth, I met Hecate, the moon goddess.

TV ANNOUNCER: Hecate were you able to help Demeter?

HECATE: *(Helpfully.)* I told Demeter that I had heard Persephone scream, but I did not see what happened. I suggested we go to Helios, the sun god. He sees everything.

DEMETER: *(Urgently.)* We went together. I begged Helios to tell what had happened to my daughter.

TV ANNOUNCER: Helios, what did you see?

HELIOS: *(Strongly.)* I told Demeter that I saw Hades seize Persephone in his chariot and carry her to the underworld. I said it was ZEUS, king of the gods, who gave Persephone to Hades as a present.

    Demeter was terribly upset. But I told her to accept her fate. I said that Persephone had a noble husband who is king of the underworld, and that Persephone was now a queen.

DEMETER: *(Angrily.)* But I was furious with Zeus. I disguised myself as an old woman and went among humans. I didn't want anyone to know I was goddess of the harvest. I went to the city of Eleusis and sat by the well where people come for water. The daughters of King Celeus came with bronze pitchers to draw water from the well.

The Myth of Demeter and Persephone or The Origin of the Seasons 91

**TV ANNOUNCER:** King Celeus's eldest daughters, what did you think?

**DAUGHTER #1:** *(Kindly.)* The woman looked so lonely, and we asked who she was. She said that she'd been kidnapped by pirates and taken here by ship from Crete. We know now that was a lie, but we didn't then.

**DAUGHTER #2:** She begged my sisters and me to help her find work taking care of a baby. So we took her home.

**DAUGHTER #3:** When she stood in the doorway, the room filled with a sparkling light. Our mother, Metaneira, could see there was something noble about her, and she gave Demeter her son to care for.

**TV ANNOUNCER:** Demeter, were you happy to have a baby to care for?

**DEMETER:** *(Happily.)* The baby made me feel somewhat better. And I wanted to make the boy immortal, so he could live forever like the gods. So I fed him ambrosia, the food of the gods. At night I lay him in the fire to burn away his mortality.

**TV ANNOUNCER:** Metaneira, did you know what Demeter was doing to your baby?

**METANEIRA:** *(Urgently.)* From what I saw, she was gentle and loving to the baby. But then one night, I saw her place my baby in the fire, and I shrieked in horror.

**DEMETER:** *(Angrily.)* I snatched the boy from the flames and told her that she, like all mortals, was stupid and ignorant. I said that I was putting the boy in the flames to make him live forever like the gods. Then I removed my disguise so she could see that I was goddess of the harvest.

**METANEIRA:** *(Sincerely.)* She told me because I had interfered, the boy would now grow old like all humans and die. She said, though, that because he had slept in a GODDESS'S arms, he would always be filled with honor.

    Then, she commanded all the people of Eleusis to build a temple in her honor. She transformed into a goddess, and the house was filled with sparkling light. I knelt and begged Demeter's forgiveness.

**TV ANNOUNCER:** Demeter, did the people build you a temple?

**DEMETER:** *(Angrily.)* Yes, but I was so depressed without my daughter. I wouldn't perform my magic rites as goddess of the harvest to make the food crops grow. I commanded all of the land to wither and die. I would have destroyed the human race except that Zeus, the king of the gods, noticed.

**TV ANNOUNCER:** Zeus, what did YOU do?

**ZEUS:** *(Powerfully.)* I was horrendously upset. I knew that if all the food crops died, people would die too. Soon, there wouldn't be anyone to give presents to the gods. This could not go on. So, I sent Iris, the rainbow goddess, down from Mt. Olympus to bargain with Demeter to make the food grow.

**TV ANNOUNCER:** Iris, what was the bargain?

**IRIS:** *(Brightly.)* Zeus had me offer Demeter gifts from all of the gods and any honor she desired. But Demeter refused. She said she'd never allow food to sprout from the earth until she saw her daughter.

**ZEUS:** *(Authoritatively.)* So then I sent Hermes, the messenger god, down to Hades in the underworld to tell him he had to let Persephone go back to her mother.

**TV ANNOUNCER:** What happened Hermes?

**HERMES:** *(Urgently.)* When I arrived in the underworld, Hades was sitting on a couch with Persephone, his wife. I told Hades that Demeter planned to destroy all humans by refusing to let the earth sprout if she did not see her daughter. I said he MUST let Persephone go to her mother.

**TV ANNOUNCER:** Hades, did you agree ?

**HADES:** *( Slyly.)* I pretended to. But I didn't want Persephone to leave me. She's my wife even if I did capture her against her will. She's beautiful and sweet, and I truly love her. But I knew better than to disobey Zeus, the king of the gods. So, I told Hermes I would obey. But craftily, I gave Persephone a delicious pomegranate to eat—plotting that she wouldn't spend all her days with her mother. Then, I gave Hermes my gold chariot with the immortal horses to take Persephone to her mother

**HERMES:** *(Enthusiastically.)* Those immortal horses were so powerful that they cut through the deep Earth into the air above. We arrived immediately at the temple where Demeter waited.

**TV ANNOUNCER:** Demeter and Persephone, how did you feel when you saw each other?

**DEMETER:** *(Joyfully.)* At the sight of Persephone, I rushed out from my temple like a winged-spirit.

**PERSEPHONE:** *(Excitedly.)* I leaped from the chariot and ran throwing my arms about my mother's neck.

**DEMETER:** *(Knowingly.)* But while Persephone was in my arms, my heart sensed treachery, and I asked Persephone if she had eaten any food in the underworld.

**PERSEPHONE:** *(Anxiously.)* I said I'd eaten FOUR SEEDS of a POMEGRANATE that Hades gave me. My mother said that was a big mistake.

**TV ANNOUNCER:** Zeus, was Persephone's eating of the pomegranate a big mistake? If so, what were the consequences?

**ZEUS:** *(Powerfully.)* Only dead people who go down and will remain in the world of the dead should eat the food of the dead. Otherwise, you have to stay down there. But since Persephone ate only the four seeds of the pomegranate, I determined that she must live four months or one-third of the year below with

Hades, her husband. The other two-thirds she could live above with her mother.

**TV ANNOUNCER:** And everyone agreed.

**ZEUS:** *(Powerfully.)* It was the best I could do. And at least they each got Persephone to be with them for part of the year. And, of course, Demeter got to be with her the most.

**TV ANNOUNCER:** And did all the crops begin growing again?

**ZEUS:** After my decree, I asked Demeter to quickly make the life-bringing crops grow for humans.

**DEMETER:** *(Joyfully.)* And I commanded everything to grow in abundance.

**ZEUS:** *(Enthusiastically.)* It was a great sight to see. Everything sprang forth, and the whole wide land was laden with crops and flowers. I couldn't help smiling and nodding in approval. Demeter and Persephone seemed happy too. In fact, I saw mother and daughter take hands, step forward, and open out their arms welcoming spring.

**TV ANNOUNCER:** *(Slowly and dramatically.)* And THAT is the ancient Greek explanation for the seasons of the year. So, remember when it's cold and the land dies and winter comes, Persephone is below with her husband, Hades. And when the birds begin singing and crops burst forth, and it's spring, she comes up to the world of the living to be with her mother, Demeter.

# ACTING EXERCISES

Use the following exercises to involve all students in dramatizing and to develop stage speech and acting skills.

## Practicing Good Speaking Skills Using the Script

**Goal:** To practice the stage-speaking skills using introductory verse from the script.
**Procedure:** First, discuss and practice the Four Stage Speaking Skills. (See chapter 1, "Developing the Four Stage-Speaking Principles.") Next, recite each line of the following introduction modeling the good speaking skills using gestures and then have all of the students recite it with you. (This is a good vocal warm-up to use before any rehearsal or recite opening dialogue from the scene you are rehearsing.)

*(Very energetically.)* Welcome audience, and "yas sas" or to your health too.

*(Pointing on "you.")* Today we'll act a myth for you.

*(Arms down on "old," up on "new.")* From ancient Greece, it's old yet new.

*(Opening arms up colorfully.)* We'll make it come alive for you.

*(Gesturing to audience.)* So please attend. Please watch and hear.

*(Opening arms out.)* Of Demeter and Persephone and the seasons of the year.

## Developing Majestic Bearing

**Goal:** To stand, sit and move with dignity, nobility and majesty.
**Acting Principles:** Belief, Movement.
**Materials:** Drum (optional).
**Procedure:** Tell students that the characters in this play have a majestic stance. Explain that they sit and stand erectly with excellent posture. Model poor posture. First, slouch, then lean on one foot, shift from one foot to another, put your hands in your pockets. As you do each of these, ask what was I doing wrong to convey royal stance? Finally, stand with a royal bearing.

Then, have them do the following majestic-bearing activity.

* Sit with head up, shoulders back, feet together and firmly on the ground.

* Place your hands on each side of the chair to help lift you. Then keeping head up, press hands on chair to help lift you and slowly rise.

* Walk slowly with head up, shoulders back and hands by sides perhaps to the accompaniment of steady majestic drumbeat.

* Finally, stand with feet planted firmly on the floor, hands by sides, shoulders back and head looking slightly up to the back wall of the auditorium. Lift arms up and out in a gesture showing you are ready to lead your people.

## Becoming the Characters and Integrating Sound Effects

**Goal:** To experience the characters' actions and to practice coordinating acting with sound effects.

**Acting Principles:** Belief, Control, Voice, and Movement.

**Materials:** Bell. A copy of this exercise for the Sound Crew only and the instruments they will use in the play.

**Procedure:** Tell students they will do characters' actions from the play and speak their dialogue expressively. Tell the Sound Crew they will play sound effects to help the actors act. All students (except the Sound Crew) act the following scenarios. Read each scenario through once to familiarize students with it. Then, ring a bell and coach them through it. All traveling actions are done "in place." Girls act female roles, and boys, male roles. Both act animals and inanimate objects. (Perhaps dramatize ten or so of these, and do the rest another day.)

- Become Persephone. See a beautiful narcissus. *(Sound Crew 5 and 6 ring handbells.)* Pluck it. Freeze: Say enthusiastically, "How beautiful!"

- Become Hades. Spring from the underworld. *(Sound Crew 2 strikes drum emphatically.)* Reach to snatch Persephone. Freeze. Say assertively, "Come with me to the underworld."

- Become Demeter. Gesture over the Earth to make the crops grow. *(Sound Crew 2, 3, and 4 shake jingle bells.)* Freeze. Chant magically, "Grow, grow grow."

- Become one of Hades' horses eager to prance back to the underworld. *(Sound Crew 3 strikes wood block.)* Freeze. Whinny energetically.

- Become Demeter. Hear your daughter scream. *(Sound Crew 4 shakes tambourine.)* Freeze. Call frantically, "Persephone, Persephone, Persephone."

- Become Helios. Strongly advise Demeter to let Persephone remain with Hades. *(Sound Crew 5 strikes gong.)* Freeze. Declaim, "Accept your fate!"

- Become Metaneira. See Demeter place your baby in the flames. *(Sound Crew 3, 4, and 5 shake rattles.)* Freeze. Terrified say, "What ARE you doing?"

- Become Demeter. Snatch the baby from flames. *(Sound Crew 4 shakes tambourine and slaps it in the center.)* Freeze. Say furiously, "Mortals are stupid and ignorant."

- Become Demeter. Gesture over the Earth to force the plants to die. *(Sound Crew 6 scrapes guiro three times.)* Freeze. Say powerfully, "Die, die, die!" *(Sound Crew 3 strikes wood block three times.)*

- Become Zeus. Open your eyes in shock at seeing all of the dead plants. *(Sound Crew 5 strikes gong.)* Freeze. Say assertively, "This will NOT do!"

- Become Hermes. Fly in place to Hades to the underworld. *(Sound Crew 2, 3, and 4 shake jingle bells.)* Freeze. Say assertively, "Let Persephone go."

- Become Hades. Hand Persephone the pomegranate. *(Sound Crew 1 strikes triangle three times.)* Freeze. Say slyly, "Eat this delicious pomegranate."

- Become Persephone. See your mother after your long separation. *(Sound Crew 2, 3, and 4 shake jingle bells.)* Freeze. Say joyfully, "Mother, I've been thinking of you every day."

- Become Zeus. Examine the new spring growth. Freeze. *(Sound Crew 6 strikes tone bells from low to high.)* Say enthusiastically, "Thank you Demeter for your life-giving power."

- Become Persephone or Demeter. Open out your arms welcoming the new spring growth. Freeze. Say joyfully, "Welcome." *(Sound Crew 2, 3, and 4 shakes jingle bells and Sound Crew 5 and 6 shake handbells.)*


## Creative Movement

**Goal:** To develop expressive movement skills.
**Acting Principles:** Belief, control, movement.
**Materials:** Bell.
**Procedure:** Tell students they will use their face and bodies to become the inanimate objects in the play. Half of the class acts every other one of the following activities. The other half observes, commenting on controlled expressive movement. Ring a bell to start and stop each action.

Become:

- A growing plant. Begin as seeds tucked into the ground. On slow count of five, grow into tall healthy plants with outstretched branches reaching out to luxuriate in the sun. Freeze.

- A dying plant. Begin with outstretched branches. On a slow count of five, feel Demeter's power sap all of your energy and make your branches wither, die, and droop to the ground.

- Yawning earth. Fold body in, becoming an inert piece of earth. Feel the push of Hades' horses and chariot and open up, split apart, and freeze.

- Divine light surrounding Demeter. With arms and hands become a shimmering light to illuminate Demeter's divinity. Freeze.

- Fireplace flames. With arms, head, and hands become flickering flames in a fireplace. Freeze.

- Winter vegetation. Express with whole face and body how vegetation feels in darkest cold winter. Freeze.

- Spring vegetation. Express feeling of vegetation when spring comes and vegetation is full of life. Freeze.

# THE MYTH OF DEMETER AND PERSEPHONE
## or THE ORIGIN OF THE SEASONS

Adapted from the version by Homer

CAST OF CHARACTERS (In order of appearance.)

CHORUS 1 Leader; very responsible, strong voice
CHORUS 2, 3, 4 Strong voices; ability to follow and pick up cues
PERSEPHONE (per **sef** oh nee) Innocent, graceful
DAUGHTERS OF OCEANUS (oh **see** a nus) (3 or as many as desired) Graceful
FLOWERS (3 or more)
NARCISSUS (nar **sis** us)
EARTH (2 or 3)
HADES (**hay** deez) Assertive, single-minded
HORSES (2)
DEMETER (deh **mee** ter) Strong, majestic, motherly
HECATE (**hek** a tee) Sisterly, helpful
HELIOS (**hee** lee ohs) Assertive
PROP PERSON 1
PROP PERSON 2
DAUGHTERS OF KING CELEUS (**See** lee us) (2 or more) Kind, gracious
QUEEN METANEIRA (met a **nee** ra) Regal
SHIMMERING LIGHT (1 or 2)
FIRE (2)
TEMPLE BUILDERS (3 or 4)
PLANTS (3 or 4)
SEEDS (3 or 4)
ZEUS (**zoose**) Powerful, takes charge
IRIS (**eye** ris) Lively, colorful, graceful
HERMES (**her** meez) Fleet, agile
WINTER BRANCHES (1 or 2)

*Sound Crew*
    SOUND CREW 1  triangle
    SOUND CREW 2  jingle bells, drum, rattle
    SOUND CREW 3  jingle bells, wood block, rattle
    SOUND CREW 4  tambourine, jingle bells, rattle
    SOUND CREW 5  handbell, rattle, gong, wind chimes
    SOUND CREW 6  guiro, tone bells, handbell

# BASIC STAGE SETUP

The actors sit in chairs arranged in a semicircle in view of the audience. Two Chorus members stand on each side of the stage. Costumes and props are stored under the actors' chairs. The Chorus, and characters wearing tunics throughout the play, wear their tunics.

The Sound Crew sits with instruments on a table (or two) to the right or left of the stage area and in view of the audience. Tables are set so that the Crew can see the stage.

*Stage Setup*

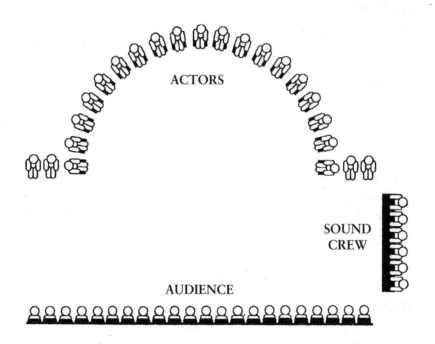

*The play might begin with a Greek dance. (See chapter 5 for dance instructions and music suggestions.)*

# PROLOGUE

*(SOUND CREW 1 strikes triangle slowly three times to signal the play will begin.)*

**CHORUS 1:** *(Very energetically.)* Welcome audience, and "yas sas" or to your health too.

> *("Yas sas" is Greek for "to your health" and is used for both hello and goodbye.)*

**CHORUS 2:** *(Pointing on "you.")* Today we perform a myth for you.

**CHORUS 3:** *(Arms down on "old," up on "new.")* From ancient Greece, it's old yet new.

**CHORUS 4:** *(Opening arms up colorfully.)* We'll make it come alive for you.

**CHORUS 1:** *(Gesturing to audience.)* So please attend. Please watch and hear.

**CHORUS 2:** Of Demeter and Persephone and the seasons of the year.

**CHORUS 3:** *(Clearly and emphatically.) The Myth of Demeter and Persephone*

> *(SOUND CREW 1 strikes triangle)*

**CHORUS 4:** or *The Origin of the Seasons*

> *(SOUND CREW 1 strikes triangle.)*

**CHORUS 1:** An ancient Greek myth based on a version by Homer from the 8th century B.C.

> *(SOUND CREW 1 strikes triangle.)*

# SCENE ONE
## *The Abduction of Persephone by Hades*

Characters: Chorus, Persephone, Daughters of Oceanus, Flowers, Narcissus, Hades, Horses

**CHORUS 2:** Persephone was with the daughters of Oceanus skipping and dancing in a circle.

> *(SOUND CREW 2, 3, and 4 shake jingle bells as DAUGHTERS swinging arms and, with knees high, skipping around in a circle. They then go in and out of the center three times raising arms as they go in.)*

**CHORUS 3:** The daughters waved to Persephone and skipped away.

*(SOUND CREW 2, 3, and 4 shake jingle bells as DAUGHTERS skip once more around circle and then skip to their chairs.)*

**CHORUS 4:** Persephone saw a soft meadow with roses, crocuses, and violets.

*(SOUND CREW 5 and 6 shake handbells as each FLOWER bunch forms along front of stage.)* **CHORUS 1:** Persephone skipped there and plucked some from each bunch.

*(SOUND CREW 5 and 6 shake handbells as PERSEPHONE plucks each bunch. FLOWERS return to their chairs.)*

**CHORUS 2:** *(Dramatically.)* Suddenly, the earth magically produced a beautiful white narcissus with a hundred blossoms and a smell so sweet.

*(SOUND CREW 6 sweeps tone bells from low to high as NARCISSUS stoops center stage right and thrusts flower dramatically up.)*

**CHORUS 1:** Persphone threw up her hands in delight and exclaimed.

**PERSEPHONE:** *(Excitedly.)* How beautiful!

*(SOUND CREW 1 strikes triangle three times.)*

**CHORUS 2:** She stretched out both hands to pluck it.

*(SOUND CREW 1 strikes triangle as PERSEPHONE plucks NARCISSUS. NARCISSUS ACTOR returns to chair.)*

**CHORUS 3:** *(Dramatically.)* Suddenly, a mound of Earth yawned.

*(SOUND CREW 3 strikes drum rapidly creating threatening rumble as EARTH actors stand facing and concealing HADES and HORSES in their chairs. Then, EARTH kneel and slowly rise lifting arms up and out creating yawning Earth.)*

**CHORUS 4:** Instantly, the Earth split apart.

*(SOUND CREW 2 strikes drum once firmly as EARTH actors jump aside. EARTH return to their chairs.)*

**CHORUS 1:** And Hades, king and god of the underworld, charged up in his chariot with the prancing horses.

*(SOUND CREW 3 strikes wood block for hoofbeats as HORSES lead HADES who urges HORSES in a circle around the stage and then arrives by PERSEPHONE. PROP PERSON 1 takes flowers from PERSEPHONE.)*

**CHORUS 2:** Hades froze and reached out his arms to Persephone.

*(SOUND CREW 2 strikes drum once firmly as HADES freezes reaching out.)*

**HADES:** *(Still "freezing" says urgently.)* PERSEPHONE!

*(SOUND CREW 6 sweeps tone bells from low to high.)*

**CHORUS 1:** Persephone stepped back and froze in terror.

*(SOUND CREW 2 strikes drum once firmly.)*

**CHORUS 2:** Hades leaped from his chariot and grabbed her arm. Persephone pulled back.

*(SOUND CREW 3, 4, and 5 shake rattles on "grabbed her arm." SOUND CREW 3 strikes wood block on "pulled back.")*

**CHORUS 3:** Hades demanded that Persephone come with him to the underworld.

**HADES:** *(Urgently.)* You MUST come with me and be my queen in the underworld.

**CHORUS 4:** Persephone begged Hades to let her remain on Earth.

**PERSEPHONE:** *(Kneeling.)* *Please* let me stay here on the Earth with the sun and flowers and my mother.

**CHORUS 1:** But Hades said NO.

**HADES:** *(Firmly.)* NO, Zeus gave you to me as a present. You will come with ME and be my WIFE and QUEEN.

**CHORUS 2:** Persephone called to Zeus to help her.

**PERSEPHONE:** *(Prayerfully facing audience.)* Zeus, king of the gods, help me.

> *(SOUND CREW 3 and 5 shakes rattles. SOUND CREW 4 shakes tambourine.)*

**CHORUS 3:** But Zeus did not answer.

**CHORUS 4:** Hades pulled Persephone into his chariot while Persephone shouted NOOO!

**PERSEPHONE:** NOOOO!

> *(SOUND CREW 2, 3, 4, and 5 shake rattles as PERSEPHONE leans away resisting HADES.)*

**CHORUS 1:** The Earth swallowed them up. They disappeared into the underworld.

> *(SOUND CREW 2 rumbles drum on "swallowed them up" and strikes drum once firmly on "disappeared." EARTH ACTORS act as a shield covering and guiding HORSES, HADES, and PERSEPHONE to their chairs. EARTH returns to their chairs.)*

# SCENE TWO
## *Demeter Searches for Persephone*
### Characters: Chorus, Demeter, Crops, Hecate, Helios, Mountains, Sea

**CHORUS 2:** Meanwhile, Demeter, Persephone's mother and goddess of the harvest, was performing her magic rites making the crops grow.

> *(CROPS form a line downstage on both sides of DEMETER. They kneel, tucking heads down becoming seeds.)*

**DEMETER:** *(Dramatically gesturing over the seeds.)* Grow little seeds into food for the people.

> *(SOUND CREW 3 strikes wood block slowly five times as PLANTS slowly stand on count of five with outstretched arms. DEMETER raises her arms as PLANTS grow.)*

**CHORUS 3:** In the midst of her magic, Demeter heard the peaks of the mountains and the depths of the sea echo with Persephone's scream, NOOO!

**PERSEPHONE:** NOOOO!

> *(PLANTS return to their chairs. After PERSEPHONE'S "NOOOO!," all seated ACTORS become MOUNTAINS or SEA, divided into three groups. Each group of five or so loudly echoes each other saying "NOOOO!" MOUNTAINS sit on stage left and right in the semicircle and SEA, center.)*

**MOUNTAINS STAGE LEFT:** *(Standing creating peaks with arms.)* NOOOO!

> *(SOUND CREW 4 shakes tambourine.)*

**SEA:** *(Sitting making wave motions.)* NOOOO!

> *(SOUND CREW 4 shakes tambourine.)*

**MOUNTAINS STAGE RIGHT:** *(Standing creating peaks.)* NOOOO!

> *(SOUND CREW 4 shakes tambourine.)*

**CHORUS 4:** Demeter grabbed her heart and peered in all directions.

> *(SOUND CREW strikes triangle three times as DEMETER peers into audience left, center, and right.)*

**CHORUS 1:** She searched nine days frantically calling and calling for her daughter.

**DEMETER:** *(Becoming increasingly frantic.)* Persephone, Persephone, Persephone.

> *(SOUND CREW 1 strikes triangle 3 times.)*

**CHORUS 2:** On the tenth, she met Hecate, the moon goddess, and asked if she'd seen Persephone.

**DEMETER:** *(Anxiously.)* Sister moon goddess, have you seen my beautiful daughter?

**HECATE:** *(Concerned.)* I HEARD Persephone scream, but I did NOT see what happened.

**CHORUS 3:** Hecate suggested they go to Helios, the sun god.

**HECATE:** *(Eagerly.)* Let's go to HELIOS the sun god. He sees EVERYTHING.

**CHORUS 4:** Arm in arm, Hecate and Demeter hastened to Helios looking down from his realm in the sky.

> *(SOUND CREW 3 strikes wood block as HECATE and DEMETER hasten. PROP PERSON TWO places chair center for HELIOS who walks regally to it and stands on it.)*

**CHORUS 1:** Demeter beseeched Helios to tell what he had seen of her daughter.

**DEMETER:** *(Urgently.)* Helios, have you seen my daughter?

**CHORUS 2:** Helios raised an arm.

> *(SOUND CREW 5 strikes gong.)*

**HELIOS:** *(Slowly pronouncing.)* I saw Hades take your daughter in his chariot and carry her *(Pointing down dramatically.)* to the underworld. *(Pointing up.)* It was ZEUS, king of the gods, who gave Persephone to Hades as a present.

**CHORUS 3:** Demeter wrung her hands and clasped her face in despair.

(*SOUND CREW 6 scrapes guiro for wringing hands.*)

**CHORUS 4:** But Helios advised Demeter to accept her fate.

**HELIOS:** (*Assertively, arms across chest.*) ACCEPT your fate! Persephone has a noble husband. Hades is KING of the underworld, and Persephone is now a QUEEN.

(*SOUND CREW 5 strikes gong after "ACCEPT your fate."*)

**CHORUS 1:** But Demeter was FURIOUS with Zeus.

**CHORUS 2:** She turned away in anger and grief.

(*SOUND CREW 3 strikes wood block as DEMETER stamps foot. HECATE and HELIOS sit. PROP PERSON 2 removes chair.*)

# SCENE THREE

## *Demeter Disguises Herself as an Old Woman*

Characters: Chorus, Demeter, Daughters of King Celeus

**CHORUS 3:** In her anger and sorrow, Demeter removed her goddess attire.

**CHORUS 4:** She wanted no one to recognize that she was goddess of the harvest.

(*DEMETER removes goddess attire, handing it to PROP PERSON 1. PROP PERSON 2 hands cape to DEMETER in such a way that she can easily put it on.*)

**CHORUS 1:** Demeter disguised herself as an old woman so she might go among humans.

**DEMETER:** (*To audience.*) I will disguise myself as an old woman. I will go among people, and no one will recognize that I am goddess of the harvest.

(*DEMETER puts on cape covering her head.*)

**CHORUS 2:** Demeter traveled among the cities and fields of humans.

(*SOUND CREW 3 strikes wood block as DEMETER bent like an old woman travels around the stage and arrives stage right.*)

**CHORUS 3:** She arrived at the city of Eleusis.

(*SOUND CREW 1 strikes triangle. SOUND CREW 6 sweeps tone bells high to low.*)

**CHORUS 4:** Bent over in despair, she sat by the well where people come for water.

(*PROP PERSON 2 places chair center stage left.*)

**CHORUS 1:** The daughters of King Celeus came skipping along with bronze pitchers to draw water from the well.

(*SOUND CREW 4 shakes tambourine for skipping.*)

**CHORUS 2:** The daughters saw Demeter's sadness and asked who she was.

**DAUGHTER ONE:** *(Concerned.)* Who are you, old woman?

**DAUGHTER TWO:** *(Concerned.)* Where are you from?

**CHORUS 3:** To keep her disguise, Demeter lied saying she was kidnapped by pirates.

**DEMETER:** *(Deviously.)* I was kidnapped by pirates and taken here from Crete.

**CHORUS 4:** She begged the girls to find her work taking care of a newborn child.

**DEMETER:** Please help me find work taking care of a baby.

**CHORUS 1:** The girls' mother had a newborn.

**DAUGHTER ONE:** Our mother has a newborn baby.

**DAUGHTER TWO:** Come with us and meet our mother.

**CHORUS 2:** The gracious girls took Demeter home.

> *(SOUND CREW 3 strikes wood block for walking. PROP PERSON 2 removes chair.)*

# SCENE FOUR
## *Demeter Becomes a Child's Nursemaid*

> Characters: Chorus, Demeter, Daughters of King Celeus, Queen Metaneira, Shimmering Light, Temple Builders

**CHORUS 3:** Their mother, Queen Metaneira, was inside holding her baby.

> *(QUEEN stands center holding baby. DAUGHTERS kneel on either side of QUEEN.)*

**CHORUS 4:** When Demeter stood in the doorway, the room filled with a shimmering light.

> *(SOUND CREW 6 sweeps tone bells low to high three times as LIGHT actors shimmer light over DEMETER'S head.)*

**CHORUS 1:** Queen Metaneira felt Demeter's nobility and handed the baby to her.

**METANEIRA:** *(Enthusiastically.)* Please care for my baby.

> *(SOUND CREW strikes triangle three times as QUEEN METANEIRA hands baby to DEMETER.)*

**CHORUS 2:** Demeter smiled.

**CHORUS 3:** She planned to give the child godly powers.

**CHORUS 4:** She fed the boy ambrosia, the food of the gods, to make him as strong and powerful as the gods.

> *(SOUND CREW 1 strikes triangle. DAUGHTERS and QUEEN sit.)*

**DEMETER:** *(To baby.)* Eat this ambrosia, dear child. It is the food of the gods and will give you the strength and power of the gods.

> *(SOUND CREW 6 sweeps tone bells from low to high.)*

**CHORUS 1:** Each night, Demeter lay the boy in the fire to burn away his mortality and to make him live forever.

*(SOUND CREW 2, 3, and 4 shake jingle bells as FIRE actors kneel and create flickering fire in fireplace.)*

**DEMETER:** *(Reverently.)* I place you in the fire my little one to make you live forever like the gods.

*(SOUND CREW 6 rings handbell and SOUND CREW 5 shakes wind chimes as DEMETER places baby among flames.)*

**CHORUS 2:** But one night Queen Metaneira came into the room and saw Demeter place her baby in the fire. She froze, threw up her hands, and shrieked, NOO!

*(SOUND CREW 2, 3, and 5 shake rattles vigorously emphasizing NOO!)*

**METANEIRA:** NOOO!

*(SOUND CREW 4 shakes tambourine and slaps it in the center.)*

**CHORUS 3:** Demeter snatched the boy from the flames.

*(SOUND CREW 4 shakes tambourine and slaps it in the center. FIRE sits.)*

**CHORUS 4:** Demeter scorned the ignorance and stupidity of mortals.

**DEMETER:** *(Scornfully.)* Mortals are ignorant and stupid. I was putting the boy in the fire to make him immortal, so he would live forever like the gods. Now that you have interfered, your son will grow old and die like all humans, but since he has slept in my arms, he will always be filled with nobility.

**CHORUS 1:** Then Demeter transformed back into a goddess.

*(PROP PERSON 1 hands DEMETER goddess attire and takes "old woman" cape. SOUND CREW 1 strikes triangle three times as DEMETER transforms.)*

**CHORUS 2:** And the room filled with shimmering light.

*(SOUND CREW 6 sweeps tone bells from low to high, as LIGHT actors shimmer light for a slow count of three and then return to their chairs.)*

**CHORUS 3:** Queen Metaneira kneeled and begged forgiveness.

**METANEIRA:** Please forgive my ignorance, great goddess of the harvest.

**CHORUS 4:** Then, Demeter held up a hand and commanded all the people of Eleusis to build a temple to honor her.

**DEMETER:** *(Gesturing stage left.)* Build a temple here to honor me.

*(SOUND CREW 6 sweeps tone bells from low to high.)*

**CHORUS 1:** The people built Demeter a splendid temple.

*(SOUND CREW 3 strikes wood block in pounding rhythm as TEMPLE BUILDERS stoop and slowly stand miming hammering and building a temple from bottom up.)*

**CHORUS 2:** But Demeter remained sitting there depressed.

*(PROP PERSON 2 brings chair for sitting.)*

**CHORUS:** She was wasted with longing for her beautiful daughter.

# SCENE FIVE

## *Demeter Causes a Great Drought*

### Characters: Chorus, Demeter, Plants, Seeds, Zeus, Iris

**CHORUS 3:** And she decided to neglect her goddess-of-the-harvest duties of making the crops grow.

*(PLANTS form a line on both sides of DEMETER.)*

**CHORUS 4:** She gestured over the Earth commanding all living plants to wither and die.

**DEMETER:** *(Gesturing.)* Wither and die. Wither and die. Do not survive, but wither and die.

*(SOUND CREW 3 strikes wood block five times as PLANTS wither and fall to ground.)*

**CHORUS 1:** She thrust her arm toward the ground and commanded the seeds to never sprout but to die, die, die.

*(SEEDS kneel on other side of DEMETER and crouch covering their heads to die).*

**DEMETER:** *(Gesturing at the Earth.)* Die, seeds, die, die, DIE.

**CHORUS 2:** Zeus, king of the gods, gazed down from the sky and his eyes blazed in shock.

*(ZEUS stands on his chair placed in center of semicircle. SOUND CREW 5 strikes gong firmly on "eyes blazed in shock.")*

**CHORUS 3:** He folded his arms across his chest in worry and alarm.

**CHORUS 4:** He realized that all humans would soon die of hunger, and there would be no one to give the gods presents and sacrifices.

**ZEUS:** *(Powerfully concerned.)* This will NOT DO. We gods need humans to offer us gifts and sacrifices. With NO PEOPLE there is NO ONE to worship us gods.

*(PLANTS return to chairs.)*

**CHORUS 1:** He ordered Iris, the rainbow goddess, to fly down and bargain with Demeter to make the Earth sprout again.

**ZEUS:** Iris, offer Demeter golden jewelry or any gift she wants if she will let the Earth sprout again.

**CHORUS 2:** Iris flew quickly to Demeter.

*(SOUND CREW 2 and 3 ring jingle bells as IRIS on tip toes runs lightly flapping arms.)*

**IRIS:** *(Imploring.)* Zeus will give you golden jewelry and any gift or honor you want to make the Earth sprout again.

**CHORUS 3:** But Demeter refused.

The Myth of Demeter and Persephone or The Origin of the Seasons 109

**DEMETER:** I will NEVER let the Earth sprout until Zeus returns to me my beautiful daughter.

**CHORUS 4:** Iris flew back to Zeus and shook her head no with Demeter's message.

*(SOUND CREW 2 and 3 shake jingle bells for flying.)*

**IRIS:** Demeter will NEVER let the Earth sprout again until she sees her daughter.

*(IRIS flies to her chair and sits.)*

# SCENE SIX
## *Hermes Commands Hades to Let Persephone Go*
Characters: Chorus, Zeus, Hermes, Hades, Persephone, Horses

**CHORUS 1:** So, Zeus summoned Hermes, the messenger god, to go down to Hades and make Hades return Persephone to her mother.

**ZEUS:** *(Assertively pointing down.)* Hermes, fly to the underworld.

*(SOUND CREW 6 shakes handbell and SOUND CREW 5 shakes wind chimes as HERMES swoops with wings pulled back using a different flight style than IRIS.)*

**CHORUS 2:** Hades was sitting on a couch with Persephone his wife.

*(HADES and PERSEPHONE bring their chairs center side by side creating a couch and sit.)*

**CHORUS 3:** Hermes announced that Demeter planned to destroy all human beings if she did not see her daughter.

**HERMES:** Demeter will NEVER let the earth sprout to make food for humans if she doesn't see her daughter. Zeus says you MUST let Persephone go back to her mother.

**CHORUS 4:** Hades did NOT want Persephone to leave him and spend all her days with her mother. But he knew better than to disobey the great god, Zeus.

**HADES:** *(To Hermes.)* Persephone is MY WIFE, but I know better than to disobey, Zeus, king of all gods. So, *(Bowing head.)* I will obey.

**CHORUS 1:** Hades told Persephone to go to her mother.

**HADES:** Persephone, go now with Hermes to your mother.

**CHORUS 2:** Persephone smiled with pleasure.

*(SOUND CREW 5 shakes wind chimes for smiling.)*

**CHORUS 3:** But then Hades offered Persephone a delicious pomegranate to eat in hopes that she would NOT spend all her days with her mother.

**HADES:** *(Slyly.)* Eat this DELICIOUS pomegranate.

**CHORUS 4:** Persephone ate FOUR SEEDS from the pomegranate.

*(SOUND CREW 1 strikes triangle slowly four times as PERSEPHONE slowly eats each seed.)*

**CHORUS 1:** Then, Hades gave Hermes his chariot with the prancing horses.

> *(HORSES prance downstage.)*

**HADES:** Take my chariot to bring Persephone to her mother.

**CHORUS 2:** Persephone and Hermes stepped inside. The horses tossed their heads.

> *(SOUND CREW 3 and 4 shake rattles for "tossing.")*

**CHORUS 3:** The chariot cut through the Earth.

> *(EARTH ACTORS form the two sides of a cave. HORSES, HERMES, and HADES go between the sides arriving at DEMETER'S temple. SOUND CREW 2 strikes drum rapidly like thunder as chariot cuts through the Earth. SOUND CREW 2 strikes drum once firmly as EARTH mime coming together to close cave and return to their chairs.)*

# SCENE SEVEN
## *Demeter and Persephone Reunite and The Origin of the Seasons*

> Characters: Chorus, Hermes, Horses, Demeter, Persephone, Zeus, Plants, Flowers, Hades Persephone, Winter Branch

**CHORUS 4:** The chariot arrived at the temple. Demeter rushed out and exclaimed in joy. . .

> *(SOUND CREW 2, 3, and 4 shake jingle bells and SOUND CREW 5 and 6 shake handbells as PERSEPHONE steps out of chariot and freezes gracefully with arms outstretched toward DEMETER. HERMES and HORSES return to their chairs.)*

**DEMETER:** *(Very enthusiastically.)* My daughter, at last you have come home to me.

**CHORUS 1:** Persephone threw her arms about her mother's neck.

**PERSEPHONE:** *(Joyfully.)* Mother, I've been thinking of you every day.

**CHORUS 2:** But while Demeter embraced Persephone, she sensed something was wrong.

**CHORUS 3:** Demeter asked Persephone if she had eaten any food in the underworld.

**DEMETER:** Did you EAT anything in the underworld?

**PERSEPHONE:** I ate FOUR seeds from a pomegranate that Hades gave me.

> *(SOUND CREW 1 strikes triangle four times.)*

**CHORUS 4:** Demeter frowned saying that eating food from the underworld was a mistake.

**DEMETER:** Persephone, you SHOULDN'T have eaten FOOD from the underworld. Only those who will remain forever in the underworld should eat the food there.

**CHORUS 1:** Then, Zeus came down from the skies and raised an arm with this pronouncement.

*(SOUND CREW 6 sweeps tone bells from high to low as ZEUS steps down from his chair.)*

**ZEUS:** *(Slowly.)* Since Peresphone ate FOUR seeds of the pomegranate, she must live ONE-THIRD of the year or FOUR months with her husband below. The other TWO-THIRDS of the YEAR she will live above with her mother.

*(SOUND CREW 1 strikes triangle four times for each seed eaten.)*

**CHORUS 2:** Demeter and Persephone took hands.

**CHORUS 3:** Then, Zeus asked Demeter to quickly make all the crops grow.

**ZEUS:** Demeter, please make all the crops grow for humans.

**CHORUS 4:** Demeter gladly agreed.

**DEMETER:** Gladly, I will.

**CHORUS 1:** Demeter opened out her arms gesturing over the earth.

**DEMETER:** *(Gesturing.)* Grow little seeds. Grow into food for the people.

*(SOUND CREW 3 strikes wood block five times slowly as PLANTS form line down stage becoming seeds and grow into healthy food plants. SOUND CREW 6 sweeps tone bells up and down three times for abundant growing.)*

**CHORUS 2:** Zeus nodded in approval as the earth filled with green spring growth.

*(SOUND CREW 6 strikes tone bells from low to high three times for spring growth.)*

**CHORUS 3:** Zeus thanked Demeter for performing her magic.

**ZEUS:** Thank you, Demeter, for your magic, life-saving help.

*(SOUND CREW 6 sweeps tone bells from low to high.)*

**CHORUS 4:** Then, Demeter and Persephone looked at each other and smiled.

*(SOUND CREW 5 shakes handbell for smiling.)*

**CHORUS 1:** Persephone took her mother's hand, and the two women opened out their arms welcoming spring.

*(SOUND CREW 6 sweeps tone bells low to high three times welcoming spring.)*

**CHORUS 2:** So, remember when it is cold and the land dies and winter comes, Persephone is below with her husband, Hades.

*(PLANTS return to their chairs. SOUND CREW 2 strikes drum rapidly creating underground rumble as HADES and Persephone stand stage right in a tableau with WINTER BRANCHES holding branches above their heads. Then, HADES sits. WINTER BRANCHES remain stage right.)*

**CHORUS 3:** And when the birds sing and crops burst forth, and it's spring, she comes up to the world of the living to be with her mother, Demeter.

*(DEMETER AND PERSEPHONE create a tableau center left with FLOWERS and PLANTS in front of and on either side of them. SOUND CREW*

*6 sweeps tone bells three times slowly creating joyous springtime effect as all freeze.)*

CHORUS 4: *(Gesturing over stage.)* And THIS is the ancient Greek explanation for the seasons of the year.

*(ALL CHORUS members go center stage. They should memorize this next part.)*

CHORUS 2: "Efharisto" *(Ef ha **ree** stoh)* friends and thank you too.

*("Efharisto," pronounced Ef ha **ree** stoh, is the Greek word for thank you. It means good graces and joy.)*

CHORUS 2: For watching so kindly our myth for you.

CHORUS 3: From ancient Greece, it's old yet new.

CHORUS 4: We hope it came alive for you.

CHORUS 1: *(Pointing to audience.)* And here's a last tip from the chorus, your friends.

CHORUS 2: *(Holding up book.)* Read a BOOK of these myths from beginning to end.

CHORUS 3: And study ancient Greece with its great majesty.

CHORUS 4: *(Making big circular gesture.)* For the more that you know the more you'll be free.

*(CHORUS return to their respective sides of stage to introduce the cast and crew.)*

*(To end the performance, CHORUS 1–4 introduce the performers, having them stand and say their names loudly and clearly. When all are standing, CHORUS 1–4 thank the audience and then turn toward ACTORS and raise their arms. Everyone follows, raising their arms and bringing them down together for a group bow. Performers then sit for the audience-performance discussion.)*

CHORUS 1: The Actors are. . .

*(SOUND CREW 6 strikes one high tone bell after each cast member stands and introduces her- or himself. CAST and CREW remains standing after they are introduced.)*

CHORUS 2: The Sound Crew is. . .

CHORUS 3: The Chorus are. . .

# PRODUCTION NOTES

## *Costume Suggestions*

For narrative mime presentations students wear all black clothing—black shirts and black pants—with individual character costumes worn as additional pieces to the all-black attire. If actors wear tunics throughout the play, they need not wear black clothes as long as the clothes underneath don't show under the tunic.

**Chorus:** Use pattern for simple knee-length tunic. Make tunic from a wrinkle-free fabric. This might be purple, dark blue, burgundy, dark green, off-white, or any dignified but not overpowering color. Might be similar or different colors for each chorus member. Tie the tunic with a black cord. Wear gold, store-bought, laurel-leaf headpieces or make headpieces with foliage from a floral-supply store. (See chapter 4, "Creating Costumes, Props and Scenery," for making tunics and headpieces.)

**Persephone:** Pink tunic; headband with pink and white, artificial flowers attached; pink or white belt.

**Daughters of Oceanus:** Headbands with artificial flowers attached.

**Flowers:** Plastic flowers of different, bright colors from floral-supply store.

**Narcissus:** Large, white, plastic flower.

**Hades:** Red cloak; headpiece of black poster board with points shaped like flames and enhanced with red glitter.

**Horses:** Black baseball caps with ears attached and with long streamers of ribbons for manes.

**Demeter:** Gold tunic; tall headdress with sheaves of wheat or autumn leaves attached; gold belt. For old-lady disguise, black, hooded sweatshirt cut down the center to wear as a cloak.

**Plants:** Plastic branches and greenery from floral-supply store.

**Hecate:** Lavender tunic; three-inch wide, black, tagboard headband with a crescent moon of tagboard covered with aluminum foil attached; silver belt.

**Helios:** Yellow tunic tied with gold cord; headpiece of gold or yellow poster board with points resembling a sunburst. (See chapter 4, "Creating Costumes, Props and Scenery" for making headpiece.)

**Daughters of King Celeus:** Small, store-bought, gold tiaras or make tiaras from yellow poster board; gold belts.

**Queen Metaneira:** Light blue tunic; gold crown (taller than the daughters' tiaras); gold belt.

**Shimmering Light:** Dowels with gold-foil strips attached.

**Fire:** Orange, filmy fabric manipulated so it resembles flickering flames.

**Zeus:** Bright blue tunic; headpiece of dark blue poster board with white or silver thunderbolts placed diagonally; silver belt.

**Iris:** Elasticized headband with ribbons of different colors tied on it; wand with multicolored ribbons; colorful belt.

**Hermes:** Tunic of lamé, or similar metallic fabric; three-inch wide, black, tagboard headband with poster board or tagboard wings covered with aluminum foil attached; silver belt.

**Winter Branches:** Branches with a few dead leaves or bare branches.

## Prop Suggestions

**Queen Metaneira's Baby:** Small, light blue, bath towel bundled like a blanket with a baby in it.

# STORY QUESTIONS, WRITING, ART, AND CLASSICAL CONNECTIONS (DEVELOPING LANGUAGE)

The following questions are listed scene by scene. Interpretive questions are indicated by an asterisk (*). A separate list of general and personal response questions is at the end of the section as well as a Classical Connections section with questions on words from the myths that have entered our vocabulary.

SCENE ONE: *The Abduction of Persephone by Hades*

1. What is the season of the year in the beginning of the play? What is Persephone doing?

2. How does Hades kidnap Persephone and why?

3. Why doesn't Persephone want to go with Hades? What is her feeling toward him?

4. Why do you think anyone might find Persephone's experience with Hades frightening?

5. Why do you think that Hades used these tactics to get Persephone to go with him?

6. Who does Persephone beg to help her? Why doesn't he help her?

SCENE TWO: *Demeter Searches for Persephone*

1. What is Demeter doing in the beginning of this scene that shows she is the goddess of growing things?

2. How does Demeter know Persephone is in trouble?

3. What does Demeter do to find out what happened to Persephone?

4. What did Hecate suggest Demeter and she do to get help?

5. How is Helios, the sun god, able to help Demeter?

6. What advice does Helios give Demeter? Why isn't Demeter enthusiastic about his advice?

7. *Do you think the advice Helios gives Demeter is wise or good? Explain.

8. Why is Demeter "furious with Zeus"?

SCENE THREE: *Demeter Disguises Herself as an Old Woman*

1. How did Demeter disguise herself? Why?

2. To what city did Demeter go?

3. *Why do you think she sat by the well?

4. Who were hospitable to Demeter? In what way were they hospitable?

5. What did they suggest she do?

6. *Why do you think Demeter wanted a job taking care of a baby after Hades seized her daughter?

SCENE FOUR: *Demeter Becomes a Child's Nursemaid*

1. What happened when Demeter stood in the doorway of Queen Metaneira's house?

2. Why did Queen Metaneira so readily give Demeter her child to care for?

3. What extraordinary things did Demeter do as she cared for the baby?

4. What caused Queen Metaneira to be frightened for the life of her baby?

5. What was Demeter's reaction when Queen Metaneira got upset at her treatment of the baby?

6. How did Demeter prove she was not an old woman?

7. How did Queen Metaneira react when she saw who Demeter really was?

8. *Why do you think Demeter commanded the people of Eleusis to build her a temple?

9. Why didn't the building of the temple make Demeter happy?

SCENE FIVE: *Demeter Causes a Great Drought*

1. Why did Demeter cause a great drought?

2. Who became most alarmed when he saw the crops dying? Why was he so alarmed?

3. Who does Zeus first send to Demeter to convince her to make the crops grow? What is Demeter offered? What is Demeter's reaction to the offer and why?

4. *Do you think Demeter has a good reason for refusing to let the crops grow even though humans will die as a result? Explain.

SCENE SIX: *Hermes Orders Hades to Let Persephone Go*

1. What message does Hermes give Hades? What is Hades' reaction to the message?

2. Why does Hades give Persephone a pomegranate to eat while she's in the underworld?

3. What does Persphone do when she gets the pomegranate?

4. How do Persephone and Hermes get out of the underworld?


SCENE SEVEN: *Demeter and Persephone Reunite and The Origin of the Seasons*

1. How do Demeter and Persephone react when they see each other after their separation?

2. What did Demeter ask Persephone if she'd done when she sensed something was wrong?

3. What does Zeus say that Persephone must do because she ate four seeds of the pomegranate?

4. *How does Persephone's eating the pomegranate change her life? What might have happened if she hadn't eaten any of the pomegranate? What do you think would have happened if she ate twelve seeds or more?

5. What does Demeter do at the end of the story that makes Zeus joyous?

6. How does this myth explain the birth of the seasons?

7. What season is it now, and according to the myth, where is Persephone?


*General Interpretive and Personal Response Questions*

1. Experts say Greek myths are great stories because they plunge the listener immediately into a very dramatic situation. What dramatic situation happens at the beginning of this myth?

2. Many writers, painters, and choreographers have created their own versions of the myth of Demeter and Persephone. In some versions, Persephone initially resists going with Hades, but then she willingly goes back to the underworld yearly. Do you think Persephone will ever enjoy being with Hades in the underworld? Explain.

3. Which character in this myth do you think is the most powerful? Explain.

4. In what way did Zeus make a mistake when he gave Persephone to Hades as a present? What were the consequences of his mistake?

5. In a play or story, each character is motivated to want one thing more than any other. For example, Persephone wants to stay on the earth with her mother. What does Hades want? Demeter? Zeus?

6. In Greek society, hospitality or being kind, gracious, and helpful to all people is considered important behavior for all citizens. Which characters in this myth are hospitable? What do they do that show their hospitality?

7. Demeter is called "The Mother of Wealth." What power does she have that makes her a "Mother of Wealth"?

## Writing

1. Write a three or four sentence description of each of the four major characters—Persephone, Hades, Demeter, and Zeus. Refer to the script and use something the characters say or do to support your answer.

2. Become Hades and write a letter to Demeter telling her why you captured Persephone and why she should be allowed to stay with you. Or become Demeter and write to Hades and tell him why he must return Persephone to you.

## Research

1. Research myths of other cultures describing the origin of the seasons.

2. Research different versions of the myth of Demeter and Persephone. Find a version of the story that mentions a different number of pomegranate seeds that Persephone eats. In that version of the story, does the number of pomegranate seeds Persephone eats affect the number of months she must stay with Hades?

## Classical Connections: Developing Language

The following are questions on words in the myth that have entered the English language. Use the Glossary to answer these questions.

1. Demeter had a temple built for her in the city of Eleusis. Where is Eleusis, and how was the temple used by Greek citizens?

2. What words are derived from the name of the god Helios?

3. What words are derived from name of the goddess Iris?

4. Demeter fed ambrosia to the baby of Queen Metaneira. What does it mean today if someone said a dessert tasted like ambrosia?

5. Demeter gave the baby nectar to drink? What common food today comes from the word nectar?

6. Why was Hermes the appropriate god for Zeus to send to the underworld?

## Eleusinian Mysteries

When Demeter loses her daughter, she goes to Eleusis and commands the people to build her a temple there. People still visit Eleusis. In the days of the ancient Greeks, people went to participate in an elaborate rite developed to honor Demeter and her daughter.

Participants walked fourteen miles from Athens to Eleusis. There they participated in a ceremony that re-enacted the story of the myth. The ritual included nine days of fasting (to represent the nine days Demeter searched for her daughter), sitting by the well where Demeter came to find work as a nurse maid, and possibly a symbolic trip to the underworld. During the ceremony sacred objects, such as grain, were shown. The ceremony culminated in an ultimate revelation that only initiates knew. Initiates were sworn to absolute silence and not allowed to tell anyone what occurred. This religious rite, called the Eleusinian Mysteries, lasted 2,000 years until Christianity conquered the Mediterranean.

## Art

- Demeter is called "the goddess of ripe grain" and Persephone is called "the goddess of the budding tender shoots." Draw a picture showing the two goddesses representing these characteristics—either by their surroundings or by their carrying of certain objects.

- Advertising agencies often use Greek gods, goddesses, and heroes as symbols to sell their products. For example, Demeter is goddess of the grain. Her Roman name is Ceres from which the word *cereal* is derived. Draw a picture of Demeter or a symbol of her to advertise a breakfast cereal.

9

# The Labors of Hercules

*Hercules is the most famous god-hero of all times. He was revered in the 5th century B.C. and is admired today. His labors are depicted more than any other Greek myth in story, film, comic strips, painting, and on pottery. Hercules was brave, hard-working, and strong. He overcame the passions of anger and the use of brute force, and he chose right action rather than a life of ease. The themes of Hercules adventures are the slaying and capturing of wild animals, fighting fabulous creatures, and heroic deeds.*

Hercules' mother was a mortal, and his father was Zeus, king of the gods. When Hercules was a boy, he was strong enough to strangle two snakes with his bare hands. As a young man, Hercules consulted the oracle at Delphi to find out how he might best live his life. The oracle told him to go to cruel Eurystheus and do whatever labors he gave him for twelve years. Hercules hesitated, but he obeyed the divine decree.

Eurystheus gave Hercules many difficult, dangerous labors. Among them were destroying the vicious, six-headed Hydra, capturing a golden-horned deer, getting rid of evil brass-feathered birds, cleaning the filthy Augean stables, obtaining the precious, jeweled belt of the Amazon queen, getting golden apples from a tree guarded by a dragon, and bringing the ferocious, guard dog Cerberus from the underworld to the land of the living. Hercules patiently and courageously fulfilled all of his labors and later was made a god for his bravery and service.

**Summary for the Teacher:** TV Interview with the Characters in *The Labors of Hercules*

**Goal:** To introduce the characters and story of the myth through dramatization. This may also serve as a possible casting method.

**Materials:** Copy of the TV Interview for all students, or pairs might share a script.

**Procedure:** Explain that they will perform a TV Interview playing the characters in the myth telling their story. Read the TV Announcer's introduction in a low monotone. Ask students what was wrong with the way you read this and how you might make it more effective.

Cast the roles using the cast list. Choose students with animated projected voices to play the TV Announcer, Hercules, and Eurystheus to model the techniques desired and to inspire the playing of other students. Before dramatizing, practice the pronunciation of the characters' names using the cast list.

Characters stand in front of the classroom with the TV Announcer sitting or standing to one side. Characters step forward when introduced and when speaking, and they step back when finished. Students might wear signs with their character names to identify them. Use a wooden spoon or a wire whisk as a microphone. There are 14 roles in the interview, so perhaps dramatize it twice to give all students a chance to participate. To further increase roles, use a different student as interviewer for each page. After dramatizing, review the characters and the events of the story.

# TV INTERVIEW

CAST OF CHARACTERS (14)

TV Announcer

Hercules (**her** cue leez)

Mother of Hercules

Priestess

Eurystheus (you **riss** thee us)

Hydra (**high** dra)

Artemis (**are** tuh miss)

Deer of Cerynea (se ri **nee** a)

King Augeas (aw **jee** us)

Hippolyta (hip **pol** i ta)

Atlas

Athena (a **thee** na)

Hermes (**her** meez)

Hades (**hay** deez)

Cerberus (**sir** ber us)

TV ANNOUNCER: Today we meet the characters in the Greek myth, *The Labors of Hercules*. Characters, please step forward when introduced. First, meet our hero, **Hercules**, and his **mother**. When Hercules was young, he consulted the **Priestess** at Delphi. The Priestess sent him to the cruel **Eurystheus** who gave him many hard labors. First, Hercules was to destroy the five-headed **Hydra**. Next, he had to capture the golden-horned **Deer of Cerynea** that the goddess **Artemis** also wanted. The goddess **Athena** helped Hercules in his labor to drive away the wicked birds of Stymphalia. He also had to clean the stables of the neglectful **King Augeas**, and he had to obtain the jeweled belt of **Hippolyta**, the Amazon queen. He got help from **Atlas** in his labor to obtain golden apples from a tree guarded by a dragon. Finally, **Hermes**, the messenger god, and **Athena**, goddess of wisdom, led him into the underworld. There he had to convince **King Hades** to let him bring the guard dog **Cerberus** to the land of the living.

TV ANNOUNCER: Hercules' mother, when did you notice Hercules had special strength?

MOTHER: When Hercules was a boy, two snakes slithered into his room. Hercules strangled them.

TV ANNOUNCER: Amazing! Hercules, when you grew up, why were you made to do difficult and dangerous labors?

HERCULES: When I was eighteen, I went to the oracle at Delphi and asked the Priestess what I should do to help people.

TV ANNOUNCER: Priestess, what was the advice?

PRIESTESS: I told Hercules to go to King Eurystheus and do whatever labors he gave him to do for twelve years.

TV ANNOUNCER: Hercules, what was your reaction to this?

HERCULES: Eurystheus is cruel, and I didn't want to serve him. But the oracle had spoken, and so I obeyed.

TV ANNOUNCER: Eurystheus, what was your reaction when Hercules came willing to do any labors you gave him?

EURYSTEHUS: I was delighted. I dislike Hercules. Everyone admires him because he is good and strong. I wanted to give him the most difficult and dangerous labors I could think of. First, I sent him to get rid of the horrible hydra.

TV ANNOUNCER: Hydra what makes you horrible?

HYDRA: I have six, vicious heads, and I like to destroy humans. If you chop off one of my heads, another grows in its place.

TV ANNOUNCER: Hercules, how did you get rid of the Hydra?

HERCULES: I took a burning branch and burnt off each head so it couldn't grow back again.

TV ANNOUNCER: How resourceful!

EURYSTHEUS: Next, I sent Hercules to capture the Deer of Cerynea.

TV ANNOUNCER: Goddess Artemis, you own four of these golden-horned deer, why did you want the fifth deer?

ARTEMIS: I am the goddess of wild animals. I wanted all of these deer. But I couldn't catch the fifth one.

TV ANNOUNCER: Hercules how did you catch it?

HERCULES: I chased it for a year and couldn't catch it. Finally it lay down in some flowers, and I put a beautiful halter on it.

TV ANNOUNCER: Deer of Cerynea, how did you feel about Hercules capturing you?

DEER OF CERYNEA: Hercules was kind and gentle to me. I was not afraid of him.

ARTEMIS: After Hercules fulfilled the labor, he gave the deer to me.

TV ANNOUNCER: How gallant of Hercules!

EURYSTHEUS: (Cruelly.) Then, I sent Hercules to the island of the Birds of Stymphalia and thought they would shoot him with their brass feathers.

TV ANNOUNCER: Goddess Athena, I heard you helped Hercules with this labor.

ATHENA: Yes. The birds hate the sound of a gong. I gave Hercules a gong and told him to strike it three times. The birds flew off and were never seen again.

TV ANNOUNCER: Hercules, did you get any rest between your labors?

EURYSTHEUS: (Angrily.) Why should I let him rest? I wanted to get as many labors as I could from him. Next I gave him the horrendous labor of cleaning the stables of King Augeas in one day. They hadn't been cleaned for thirty years.

TV ANNOUNCER: King Augeas, why didn't you clean your stables?

KING AUGEAS: I have a herd of 3,000 and have been too busy to clean my stables.

TV ANNOUNCER: Hercules, how did you manage to clean those stables in one day?

HERCULES: I used my club and knocked huge holes through the back and front walls of the stables. Then, I diverted the flow of a mighty river through the stables and washed them clean.

TV ANNOUNCER: Wow!

EURYSTHEUS: Hercules still had more labors to go. Next I sent him to bring back the precious, jeweled belt of Hippolyta, the Amazon Queen.

TV ANNOUNCER: Queen Hippolyta, why was this belt so precious to you?

**HIPPOLYTA:** My jeweled belt was given to me by my father.

**TV ANNOUNCER:** Hercules, why was this difficult? Hippolyta and the other Amazons are all women.

**HERCULES:** These Amazons have more stamina and are in better condition than men. I watched Queen Hippolyta run for hours and never tire. I saw her shoot arrows and never miss the mark. She even forced a bull to its knees.

**TV ANNOUNCER:** Hippolyta, how did Hercules manage to get your belt?

**HIPPOLYTA:** Hercules told me he'd traveled miles to see me and admired my athletic skills. We spent days running and riding horseback together. Hercules admired the belt, and I gave it to him as a present. It was a mistake.

**EURYSTHEUS:** Then, I sent Hercules to bring me golden apples from a tree guarded by a fire-breathing dragon who never sleeps.

**TV ANNOUNCER:** Hercules, how did you get the apples?

**HERCULES:** The only one able to soothe the dragon was Atlas. So I convinced Atlas to help me.

**TV ANNOUNCER:** Atlas, how did Hercules convince you?

**ATLAS:** I have the job of holding up the sky. That sky is mighty heavy and it's a boring, tiring job. Hercules said he'd hold up the sky for a while if I calmed the dragon and got him some apples. I agreed and got two apples for him.

**EURYSTHEUS:** I still had time for one more labor. I tried to think of the most dangerous and frightening labor I could. So I sent Hercules to the land of the dead to bring back the vicious, three-headed, guard dog, Cerberus.

**TV ANNOUNCER:** Hermes and Athena, how did you help Hercules in this labor?

**HERMES:** I am the messenger god who brings souls into the underworld.

**ATHENA:** I wanted to help Hercules complete his final labor. So Hermes and I guided Hercules to King Hades in the underworld.

**TV ANNOUNCER:** King Hades, did you agree to let Hercules bring the three-headed, guard dog to the land of the living?

**HADES:** Hercules is a valiant hero. I admire him. I said he could bring Cerberus to the land of the living if he could master him without using weapons. Then I called Cerberus to go with Hercules.

**TV ANNOUNCER:** Cerberus, did you go willingly with Hercules?

**CERBERUS:** At first I snarled and showed my vicious claws. But Hercules grasped me firmly by the shoulders and kept staring into my eyes. He said he wouldn't stop until I yielded to him. I knew he meant it, and so I let him tame me and become my master.

**TV ANNOUNCER:** Hercules had performed twelve years of service. He accomplished every labor you gave to him, Eurystheus. How did you feel now?

**EURYSTHEUS:** I disliked Hercules more than ever. And do you know what he did? He brought that vicious guard dog Cerberus up close to me. That savage brute of a dog nearly ripped me apart. I ran off screeching and have never been heard from again.

**TV ANNOUNCER:** Hmmmmm, I see! Well, Hercules how did you feel after all those years of labors?

**HERCULES:** I was pleased that I had fulfilled my obligations and glad that I'd been able to help people.

**TV ANNOUNCER:** And for your bravery and service, you, Hercules were made into a god and brought to the top of Mt. Olympus. There you joined the other Olympian gods and goddesses. I'm sure all of our viewers today agree with me when I say this is a remarkable story of a remarkable hero.

# ACTING EXERCISES

Use the following exercises to involve all students in dramatizing and to let everyone experience being all of the characters. The exercises also develop stage-speech and acting skills.

## Practicing Effective Stage Speech Using the Script

**Goal:** To practice the stage-speaking skills using introductory verse from the script.
**Procedure:** First, discuss and practice the Four Stage-Speaking Skills (see chapter 1, "Developing the Four Stage-Speaking Principles"). Next, recite each line of the following introduction modeling the good, speaking skills using gestures, and then have all of the students recite it with you. (This is a good vocal warm-up to use before any rehearsal or recite opening dialogue from the scene you are rehearsing.)

*(Waving.)* Good morning students, adults too,

*(Pointing on "you.")* Today we'll act a myth for you.

*(Hands down on "old" and up on "new.")* From Greece and Rome, it's old yet new.

*(Opening arms up colorfully.)* We'll make it come alive for you.

*(Gesturing to audience.)* So watch our myth of Hercules.

*(Opening arms out and freezing.)* Whose noble deeds will you please.

## Developing Majestic Bearing

**Goal:** To stand, sit, and move with dignity, nobility, and majesty.
**Acting Principles:** Belief, Movement.
**Materials:** Drum (optional).
**Procedure:** Tell students that Hercules, the Priestess of Delphi, Artemis, Athena, Hippolyta, Hermes, Hades, and the Chorus have a royal stance. Explain that they sit and stand erectly with excellent posture. Model posture flaws. First slouch, then lean on one foot, shift from one foot to another, put your hands in your pockets. As you do each of these, ask what was you were doing wrong to convey a royal stance? Then, stand with a royal bearing. Have students do the following majestic bearing activity.

- Sit with head up, shoulders back, feet together and firmly on the ground.

- Place your hands on each side of the chair to help lift you. Then keeping head up, press hands on chair to help lift you and slowly rise.

• Walk slowly with head up, shoulders back and hands by sides (perhaps to the accompaniment of a steady, majestic drumbeat).

## Creating Tableaux of the Myth

**Goal:** To convey the heightened drama of the characters and their situations in frozen pictures.

**Acting Principles:** Belief, Control, Movement.

**Materials:** Make a copy of the tableaux list below. Cut it apart and give each pair or group of students the title of one tableaux.

**Procedure:** Tell students they will form pairs or groups of three or four to create dramatic pictures of scenes from the play. Explain that they will pose without moving, exaggerating the expression and the action to communicate to the audience what is happening. After practicing in groups for about ten minutes, groups reassemble and show their tableaux in sequence to the class. Groups begin with one member announcing the title of their tableau.

Tableau One: Young Hercules holds strangled snakes as his astonished mother looks on.
Characters (2): Hercules, his Mother

Tableau Two: Hercules kneels to the priestess who pronounces the oracle.
Characters (2): Hercules, Priestess

Tableau Three: Bully Eurystheus sneers at the dignified hero Hercules.
Characters (2): Eurystheus, Hercules

Tableau Four: Hercules graciously gives the deer to Artemis who pets it.
Characters (3): Hercules, Deer of Cerynea, Artemis

Tableau Five: The Frightened Birds of Stymphalia fly off as Hercules strikes a gong.
Characters (4): Hercules, Birds (3)

Tableau Six: Dishonest King Augeas refuses to give honest Hercules his reward for cleaning the Augean Stables.
Characters (2): Hercules, King Augeas

Tableau Seven: The vicious dragon guards the beautiful golden apple tree.
Characters (2): Dragon, Tree with Golden Apples

Tableau Eight: Atlas strains to hold up the sky and Hercules reaches out to take it.
Characters (2): Atlas, Hercules

Tableau Nine: Hades beckons the ferocious Cerberus to go to Hercules.
Characters (3): Hades, Cerberus, Hercules

Tableau Ten: Hercules tames Cerberus by holding him and staring into his eyes.
Characters (2): Hercules, Cerberus

Tableau Eleven: Hercules brings snarling Cerberus to Eurystheus who freezes in terror.
Characters (3): Hercules, Cerberus, Eurystheus

Tableau Twelve: Athena crowns Hercules who poses as an Olympian god.
Characters (2): Athena, Hercules

## Developing Character Stance and Believable Character Speech

**Goal:** To experience effective character stance and convincing character speech.
**Principles:** Belief, Voice and Movement, Control.
**Materials:** Bell.
**Procedure:** First read each of the following scenarios to familiarize student with them. Then coach them through emphasizing dramatic, character speech. Girls play female roles, and boys, male roles. Both play animals and monster. Ring the bell to start and stop each action.

### SCENE ONE: *Young Hercules and the Prediction of His Greatness*

- Become Hercules' mother wishing her son a peaceful sleep, say, "Pleasant dreams Hercules, my son."

### SCENE TWO: *Hercules Consults the Oracle at Delphi*

- Become a vicious snake trying to attack Hercules, "Hiss!"

### SCENE THREE: *King Eurystheus and the Labor of the Hydra of Lerna*

- Become Eurystheus trying to dominate Hercules, say, "Ha, Ha, Ha, Hercules!"

- Become Hercules refusing to let Eurystheus bully him, say, "I'll do as requested."

- Become the Hydra, roaring to terrorize people. Say, "RRRRRRR!"

- Become the people grateful that Hercules saved you from the Hydra, say enthusiastically, "Thank you, Hercules."

### SCENE FOUR: *The Labor of the Deer of Cerynea*

- Become Artemis, proclaim your title proudly, "I am Artemis, goddess of the hunt."

- Become the shy, graceful deer say, "I am the magic deer of Cerynea."

- Become Hercules eager to reassure the deer, say, "Do not be afraid, magical deer.

- Become assertive Artemis say, "Give me the deer of Cerynea."

SCENE FIVE: *The Labor of the Birds of Stymphalia*

- Become one of the birds of Stymphalia trying to destroy people. Say, "Caw, Caw, Caw, Caw, Caw."

- Become Athena proclaiming your title proudly, say, "I am Athena, goddess of wisdom."

- Become Athena wanting to help Hercules, say, "I want to help you, Hercules."

- Become Eurystheus, wanting to hurt Hercules' feelings, by saying, "Who cares!"

SCENE SIX: *The Labor of the Augean Stables*

- Become King Augeas trying to impress the world with your wealth, say, "I own a huge herd."

- Become Hercules proclaiming his accomplishment, say, "I cleaned your stables."

- Become Augeas trying to cheat Hercules say, "No, the river cleaned my stables, not you."

SCENE SEVEN: *The Labor of the Belt of Hippolyta*

- Become proud Hippolyta. Say, "I am Hippolyta the Amazon Queen."

- Become Hippolyta, confident of her power. Say, "Watch this bull fall."

- Become impressed Hercules say, "This woman is strong."

- Become Hippolyta, wanting to befriend Hercules, say, "Take my precious belt."

SCENE EIGHT: *The Labor of the Golden Apples of the Hesperides*

- Become the fire-breathing dragon, roaring to protect your golden tree, "RRRRRRR!"

- Become Atlas, eager to put down the heavy sky. Say, "I hate this job holding up this heavy sky."

- Become Hercules straining to hold up the sky. Say, "This sky IS heavy!"

- Become Atlas hypnotizing the dragon, and say, "Sleep great dragon. Sleep, sleep, sleep."

- Become greedy Eurystheus. Say, "Give me those apples."


SCENE NINE: *The Labor of the Guard Dog Cerberus*

- Become Athena or Hermes, helping Hercules to the underworld, and say, "Follow us."

- Become powerful King Hades wanting to help Hercules and say, "Hercules I admire you."

- Become authoritative King Hades, say, "Come Cerberus."

- Become ferocious Cerberus, and growl to frighten Hercules, "GRRRRRRR!"

- Become Cerberus wanting Hercules to stop staring at you and say, "I yield. I yield."

- Become Eurystheus terrorized by Cerberus. Say, "Get that dog out of here."

- Become modest Hercules elevated to the rank of god. Say, "Thank you for the honor."

# THE LABORS OF HERCULES

Adapted from versions by the Roman poets, Theocritus and Apollodorus

CAST OF CHARACTERS (In order of appearance.)

Each of the nine scenes in this play is complete in itself. A director might choose to produce only some scenes. Each scene has a cast list.

CHORUS 1 Leader, very responsible, strong voice
CHORUS 2, 3, 4 Strong voices; ability to follow and pick up cues
Hercules (**her** cue leez) Leading role; strong voice; bright confident manner; robust
Mother of Hercules Loving, enthusiastic, and proud of her son
Snakes (2)
Mist (3)
Priestess of Delphi (del **feye**) Mysterious, dramatic
Prop Person 1
Prop Person 2
Eurystheus (you **riss** thee us) Aggressive, mean-spirited
Trees (3 or more)
Hydra of Lerna (**high** dra) (**ler** na) (3) Three use hands and heads to create nine-headed monster, or use as many as desired by changing the number of monster heads.
Artemis (**are** tuh miss) Goddess of the hunt, assertive
Deer of Cerynea (se ri **nee** ah) Graceful, shy
Flowers (4 or more)
Stymphalian Birds (stim **faa** li an) Evil, malicious
Athena (a **thee** na) Assertive, helpful
King Augeas (aw jee us) Pompous, dishonest
River (2)
Amazons (3 or more) Strong, graceful, athletic
Hippolyta (hip **pol** i ta) Very strong, graceful and athletic
Bull Big, lumbering
Tree with Golden Apples
Dragon Watchful, vicious
Atlas Strong, weary
Hermes (**her** meez) Messenger god, helpful
Hades (**hay** deez) Majestic, powerful
Cerberus (**sir** ber us) Ferocious
Pot (3 or 4)

*Sound Crew*
  SOUND CREW 1 triangle
  SOUND CREW 2 jingle bells, drum, rattle
  SOUND CREW 3 jingle bells, wood block
  SOUND CREW 4 tambourine, jingle bells, rattle, handbell
  SOUND CREW 5 handbell, rattles, gong
  SOUND CREW 6 tone bells, wind chimes, rattle, guiro, handbell

*Basic Stage Setup*

The actors sit in chairs arranged in a semicircle in view of the audience. Two Chorus members stand on each side of the stage. Costumes and props are stored under the actors' chairs. The Chorus and characters wearing tunics throughout the play are dressed in their tunics.

The Sound Crew sits at a table, or two, to the right or left of the stage area with their instruments on a table and in view of the audience. Tables are set so that the crew can see the stage action.

*Stage Setup*

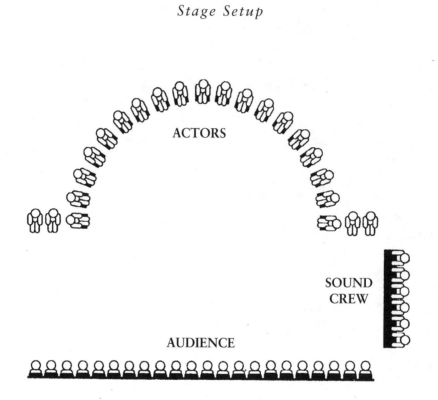

ACTORS

SOUND
CREW

AUDIENCE

The play might begin with a Greek dance. (See chapter 5 for dance instructions and music suggestions.)

# PROLOGUE

*(SOUND CREW 1 strikes triangle three times slowly to signal the play will begin.)*

**CHORUS 1:** *(Very energetically.)* Welcome audience, and "yas sas" or to your health too.

*("Yas sas" is Greek for "to your health" and is used for both hello and good-bye.)*

**CHORUS 2:** *(Pointing on "you.")* Today we'll act a myth for you.

**CHORUS:** *(Hands down on "old" and up on "new.")* From Greece and Rome, it's old yet new.

**CHORUS 3:** *(Opening arms up colorfully.)* We'll make it come alive for you.

**CHORUS 4:** So watch our myth of Hercules whose noble deeds will you please.

**CHORUS 1:** *(Clearly and emphatically.)* The Labors of Hercules

*(SOUND CREW 1 strikes triangle.)*

**CHORUS 2:** A Greek Myth based on versions by the Roman writers Theocritus and Apollodorus.

*(SOUND CREW 1 strikes triangle.)*

# SCENE ONE
## *Young Hercules and the Prediction of His Greatness*

Characters (3): Chorus, Mother, Hercules, Snakes

**CHORUS 3:** Scene One: Young Hercules and the Prediction of His Greatness

*(SOUND CREW 1 strikes triangle.)*

**CHORUS 4:** Hercules and his mother lived in a fine house in Greece.

*(SOUND CREW 1 strikes triangle continually to accompany HERCULES and his MOTHER walking majestically center.)*

**CHORUS 1:** One night when Hercules was young, his mother sent him to bed and wished him pleasant dreams.

**MOTHER:** *(Cheerfully.)* Pleasant dreams, Hercules, my son.

*(SOUND CREW 1 strikes triangle continually as MOTHER returns to her chair.)*

**CHORUS 2:** Hercules lay down.

*(SOUND CREW 6 strums tone bells low to high three times as HERCULES lies down with his legs curled up and lying on side, facing audience.)*

**CHORUS 3:** Two vicious snakes hissed and slithered into his room.

**SNAKES:** *(Loudly and viciously.)* HISSSSSSSSS!

*(SOUND CREW 2, 5, and 6 shake rattles vigorously as SNAKES slither and hiss, one going on each side of HERCULES.)*

**CHORUS 4:** Hercules grasped each snake.

*(SOUND CREW 3 strikes wood block twice—once for each snake HERCULES grasps.)*

**CHORUS 1:** The snakes whipped back and forth and expired.

*(SOUND CREW 4 shakes tambourine vigorously as SNAKES whip back and forth. SOUND CREW 4 slaps the tambourine in the center as SNAKES drop dramatically and expire.)*

**CHORUS 2:** Hercules' mother entered the room rapidly and saw the dead snakes.

*(SOUND CREW 3 strikes wood block rapidly as MOTHER enters wide-eyed and freezes.)*

**MOTHER:** *(Astonished and proud.)* What an amazing child you are, Hercules! You are young, but YOU are strong and brave.

**HERCULES:** *(Rising and bowing modestly.)* Thank you, mother. It really was not difficult at all.

**MOTHER:** *(Enthusiastically.)* I predict someday Hercules my son, YOU will be a GREAT HERO.

*(SOUND CREW 1 strikes triangle three times as MOTHER and HERCULES freeze, gazing thoughtfully out as they consider HERCULES' future. MOTHER returns to chair. HERCULES remains center stage.)*

## SCENE TWO
### Hercules Consults the Oracle at Delphi

Characters (4 or more): Chorus, Hercules, Mist (1 or 2), Priestess

**CHORUS 3:** Scene Two: Hercules Consults the Oracle at Delphi

*(SOUND CREW 1 strikes triangle.)*

**CHORUS 4:** When Hercules was eighteen, he wanted to help people.

**HERCULES:** *(Determined, to audience.)* I want to help people.

*(SOUND CREW 1 strikes triangle.)*

**CHORUS 1:** So, Hercules journeyed to the cave at Delphi to seek advice from the oracle.

*(SOUND CREW 3 strikes wood block crisply as HERCULES with chin up and swinging arms strides confidently circling the stage clockwise, symbolizing going a distance. HERCULES stops down right and kneels with side to audience. NOTE: HERCULES circles the stage on each labor alternating the direction, clockwise and counterclockwise for each labor.)*

**HERCULES:** *(On knees, prayerfully.)* Oh, great oracle, what can I do to help people?

**CHORUS 2:** Mists swirled . . .

*(SOUND CREW 6 shakes wind chimes for a count of five as MIST swirls gracefully and lightly up, down and all around and freezes for the next sequence.)*

**CHORUS 3:** The Priestess who delivers oracles came forth from the mist.

*(SOUND CREW 6 shakes wind chimes as PRIESTESS slowly regally opening arms out steps from the MIST.)*

**PRIESTESS:** *(Raising a hand and slowly and prophetically.)* Hercules, go to King Eurystheus and do whatever labors he gives you for twelve years.

*(SOUND CREW 5 strikes gong.)*

**CHORUS 4:** King Eurystheus was cruel and cowardly. Hercules did NOT want to serve a cruel coward.

**HERCULES:** Priestess, must I serve the cruel coward Eurystheus?

**PRIESTESS:** *(Raising both arms, prophetically and slowly.)* Hercules, the oracle has spoken! Do whatever labors Eurystheus gives you for twelve years.

*(SOUND CREW 5 strikes gong.)*

**CHORUS 1:** Mists swirled again, and the priestess disappeared.

*(SOUND CREW 6 shakes wind chimes as MIST swirls around PRIESTESS for count of five. MIST and PRIESTESS, moving backwards regally and mysteriously, return to their chairs.)*

**HERCULES:** *(Bowing head and to audience.)* The oracle has spoken, and so I will obey.

**CHORUS 2:** The gods gave Hercules special gifts to help him. He received a golden belt, a helmet, a bow, a sword, horses, and a shield of gold with jewels from his father Zeus, king of the gods.

*(SOUND CREW 1 strikes triangle as each gift is mentioned.)*

**CHORUS 3:** But Hercules' most distinctive weapon was a club that he made himself.

*(SOUND CREW 5 strikes gong as PROP PERSON hands club to HERCULES who holds it high.)*

**HERCULES:** *(Raising club and brightly.)* I am off to King Eurystheus to do whatever labors he gives me for twelve years.

*(SOUND CREW 5 strikes gong. HERCULES places club over shoulder.)*

# SCENE THREE
## *King Eurystheus and The Labor of the Hydra of Lerna*

Characters (4 or more): Chorus, Eurystheus, Prop Persons 1 and 2, Trees (2 or 3), Hydra (3)

**CHORUS 4:** Scene Three: King Eurystheus and The Labor of the Hydra of Lerna

*(SOUND CREW 1 strikes triangle.)*

**CHORUS 1:** Hercules traveled to King Eurystheus.

*(SOUND CREW 3 strikes wood block crisply as HERCULES, club over shoulder, circles the stage, arriving center. EURYSTHEUS arms across chest strides arrogantly center.)*

**CHORUS 2:** Eurystheus greeted Hercules with a cruel laugh.

**EURYSTHEUS:** *(Hands on hips and maliciously.)* Ha! Ha! Ha! Hercules. The oracle has spoken. You must do whatever labors I give you for twelve years.

**HERCULES:** *(With dignity.)* I'll do as requested.

**CHORUS 3:** Eurystheus ordered Hercules to slay the horrible Hydra of Lerna.

**EURYSTHEUS:** *(Scowling and pointing.)* Go and slay the horrible Hydra of Lerna. He'll BITE you to BITS with his nine heads.

**HERCULES:** *(Chin up, hands on hips, to audience and brightly.)* I am off to slay the horrible Hydra of Lerna.

*(SOUND CREW 5 strikes gong. EURYSTHEUS swaggers to his chair.)*

**CHORUS 4:** Hercules traveled to Lerna.

*(SOUND CREW 3 strikes wood block as HERCULES confidently strides circling the stage, stopping upstage left.)*

**CHORUS 1:** The Hydra had nine horrible heads that bit people. The heads couldn't be chopped off because they grew back again.

**CHORUS 2:** Hercules waited for the Hydra by a grove of trees.

*(SOUND CREW 2, 4, and 5 shake rattles vigorously as TREES form.)*

**CHORUS 3:** The Hydra roared, encircling the trees and tearing them with its tough teeth.

*(SOUND CREW 6 strikes guiro as HYDRAS linking arms to create one monster circle and tear. TREES drop arms [as branches] and upper body as if torn.)*

**HYDRA:** *(Snarling.)* RRRRRRRRRRRR!

**CHORUS 4:** The Hydra roared toward people.

*(ACTORS IN CHAIRS become PEOPLE cringing as HYDRA moves around thrusting heads aggressively at them.)*

**HYDRA:** *(Reaching toward people and viciously.)* RRRRRRRRRRRR!

**CHORUS 1:** Hercules knocked each Hydra head off, but they grew back again.

*(SOUND CREW 3 strikes wood block as HERCULES using club mimes knocking each HYDRA head that bows down and SOUND CREW 3 strikes wood block again as each head pops up again. PROP PERSON 1 takes club from HERCULES.)*

**CHORUS 2:** Then Hercules got a burning branch. He set fire to each Hydra head that burned to ashes.

*(SOUND CREW 1 strikes triangle as PROP PERSON 2 hands branch to HERCULES. SOUND CREW 4 shakes tambourine as HERCULES touches each head with branch. Each individual HYDRA moans as each head is burned, and then HYDRA [as one monster] moans when last head is burned. SOUND CREW 4 shakes tambourine and slaps it in the center as the HYDRAS then collapse with a dramatic thud on the floor.)*

**HYDRA:** *(Moaning and collapsing on the floor.)* OHHHHHHHHHHHHHHH!

*(HYDRA actors return to chairs.)*

**CHORUS 3:** The people thanked Hercules.

**ACTORS IN CHAIRS:** *(Enthusiastically.)* Thank you Hercules.

**HERCULES:** *(Bowing head modestly to ACTORS.)* I was glad to serve.

*(SOUND CREW 1 strikes triangle.)*

**CHORUS 4:** Hercules returned to Eurystheus.

*(SOUND CREW 3 strikes wood block crisply as HERCULES circles stage returning to EURYSTHEUS who strides center.)*

**HERCULES:** *(Proudly.)* I slew the horrible Hydra of Lerna.

**EURYSTHEUS:** *(Sneering.)* So WHAT! You have MANY labors left.

**CHORUS 1:** Eurystheus ordered Hercules to capture the Deer of Cerynea.

**EURYSTHEUS:** *(Loudly snarling.)* Go and capture the Deer of Cerynea. *(Leering.)* No one, not even the goddess Artemis, can catch that deer.

*(EURYSTHEUS swaggers to his chair.)*

**HERCULES:** *(Chin up, hands on hips and brightly.)* I'm off to capture the Deer of Cerynea!

*(SOUND CREW 5 strikes gong.)*

# SCENE FOUR
## *The Labor of the Deer of Cerynea*

Characters(4 or more): Chorus, Artemis, Hercules, Deer of Cerynea, Flowers (2 or 3), Eurystheus

**CHORUS 2:** Scene Four: The Labor of the Deer of Cerynea

*(SOUND CREW 1 strikes triangle.)*

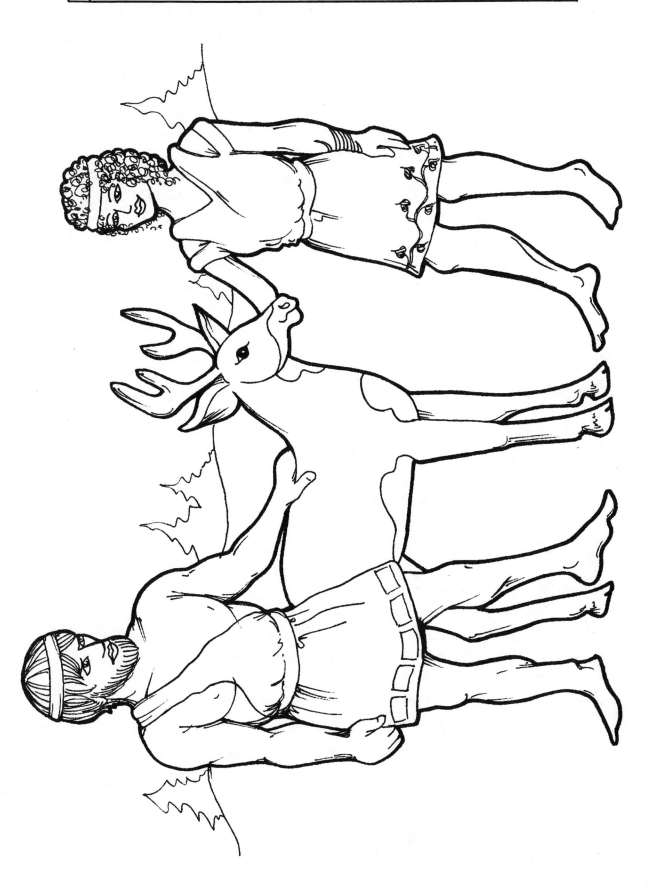

**CHORUS 3:** Hercules traveled to Cerynea.

*(SOUND CREW 3 strikes wood block as HERCULES circles stage stopping up right.)*

**CHORUS 4:** The Deer of Cerynea was one of five magical deer with golden horns. The Goddess Artemis caught four of these beautiful deer, but one escaped to the hills of Cerynea. Artemis wanted the fifth deer. Artemis appeared.

*(SOUND CREW 5 shakes wind chimes as ARTEMIS walks regally center.)*

**ARTEMIS:** *(Raising index finger high.)* I am Artemis, goddess of the hunt. I caught four of the golden-horned deer. I want the fifth deer, but I CANNOT catch it.

*(SOUND CREW 5 shakes wind chimes as ARTEMIS regally returns to her chair.)*

**CHORUS 1:** Hercules hunted the deer for a year.

*(SOUND CREW 6 strikes lowest note on tone bells continually as HERCULES searching leans over, shades his eyes, and walks in a serpentine pattern around the stage.)*

**HERCULES:** *(To audience shaking head.)* This deer IS difficult to catch. I've been chasing it for more than a year.

**CHORUS 2:** Hercules waited near a field of flowers.

*(SOUND CREW 5 and 6 shake handbells as FLOWERS form along front of stage.)*

**CHORUS 3:** Suddenly, Hercules saw the deer in the field of flowers.

*(SOUND CREW 2, 3, and 4 shake jingle bells as DEER trots gracefully among FLOWERS.)*

**DEER:** *(To audience.)* I am the magic Deer of Cerynea. I am so tired from this long chase with Hercules. I will sleep for a minute.

**CHORUS 4:** The deer lay down among the flowers.

*(SOUND CREW 2, 3, and 4 shake jingle bells as DEER lays down.)*

**CHORUS 1:** Hercules sneaked up to the sleeping deer.

*(SOUND CREW 4 and 6 shake rattles lightly as HERCULES sneaks.)*

**CHORUS 2:** Gently, Hercules put a harness around the deer.

*(SOUND CREW 2, 3, and 4 shake jingle bells as HERCULES mimes putting harness on DEER who stands.)*

**HERCULES:** Do not be afraid, magic deer. I will not harm you.

**CHORUS 3:** The goddess Artemis appeared and put up a hand

*(SOUND CREW 5 shakes wind chimes as ARTEMIS walks regally center.)*

**ARTEMIS:** *(Assertively and pointing to herself.)* Hercules, give ME the Deer of Cerynea.

**HERCULES:** Oh goddess Artemis, I MUST show this deer to Eurystheus to fulfill one of my labors. Then, I will give the deer to you.

**ARTEMIS:** Hercules, I trust you. *(Petting deer.)* Beautiful deer, I will wait for you.

*(SOUND CREW 4, 5, and 6 ring handbells as ARTEMIS sits.)*

**CHORUS 4:** Hercules returned to Eurystheus with the deer.

*(SOUND CREW 3 strikes wood block as HERCULES travels around stage and DEER trots behind him. EURYSTHEUS strides center. FLOWERS return to chairs.)*

**HERCULES:** *(Proudly.)* I have captured the Deer of Cerynea.

**EURYSTHEUS:** *(Angrily.)* Who needs a wild deer!

**HERCULES:** *(To Deer.)* Magic Deer, go now to the goddess Artemis.

**DEER:** *(Nodding head.)* Happily I obey.

*(SOUND CREW 2, 3, and 4 shake jingle bells as ARTEMIS beckons DEER who trots to her. ARTEMIS reaches out and pets DEER. ARTEMIS and DEER return to their chairs.)*

**EURYSTHEUS:** *(Aggressively.)* Don't rest. Go and get rid of the brass-winged Stymphalian birds They'll shoot you with their brass feathers.

*(EURYSTHEUS swaggers to his chair.)*

**HERCULES:** *(Hands on hips, chin up and brightly.)* I am off to get rid of the Stymphalian birds.

*(SOUND CREW 5 strikes gong.)*

# SCENE FIVE
## *The Labor of the Birds of Stymphalia*

Characters: Birds (3 or more), Hercules, Athena, Eurystheus


**CHORUS 1:** Scene Five: The Labor of the Birds of Stymphalia

*(SOUND CREW 1 strikes triangle.)*

**CHORUS 2:** Hercules traveled to Stymphalia.

*(SOUND CREW 3 strikes wood block crisply as HERCULES circles stage, arriving stage right.)*

**CHORUS 3:** The brass-winged Stymphalian birds cawed and flew all around viciously flapping their evil wings.

*(SOUND CREW 4 shakes tambourine for a count of ten as BIRDS cawing loudly fly all over stage flapping wildly and freeze after ten "CAWS.")*

**BIRDS:** *(Raucously.)* CAW! CAW! CAW! CAW! CAW! CAW! CAW! CAW! CAW!

**CHORUS 4:** The birds shot their brass feathers like arrows to hurt humans.

*(SOUND CREW 4 shakes tambourine vigorously and slaps it in the center as BIRDS thrust arms out as if shooting arrows at ACTORS IN CHAIRS who put hands up to dodge feathers.)*

**CHORUS 1:** Hercules shot at the birds with his bow and arrow. But the arrows would not penetrate their tough feathers.

*(SOUND CREW 3 strikes wood block each time HERCULES shoots an arrow at each BIRD. BIRDS freeze but with wings outspread unharmed and stare menacingly.)*

**HERCULES:** *(Shaking head.)* My arrows won't penetrate them. *(Pacing.)* What can I do?

**CHORUS 2:** Athena, the goddess of wisdom, appeared from behind an olive tree. She carried a gong.

*(SOUND CREW 5 and 6 shake hand bells as ATHENA holding gong up high walks regally center.)*

**ATHENA:** *(Regally.)* Hercules, I am Athena, goddess of wisdom. I want to help you. *(Handing Hercules gong.)* Strike this gong firmly three times.

**CHORUS 3:** Hercules struck the gong firmly three times.

*(HERCULES facing audience strikes gong to right, center, and left.)*

**CHORUS 4:** The frightened birds flew off frantically cawing and flapping their wings.

**BIRDS:** *(Raucously.)* CAW! CAW! CAW! CAW! CAW!

*(SOUND CREW 4 shakes tambourine vigorously as frightened BIRDS caw and fly rapidly to their chairs and sit.)*

**CHORUS 1:** Hercules thanked Athena.

**HERCULES:** *(Bowing head and handing Athena the gong.)* Thank you goddess Athena for your wise help.

**ATHENA:** I was happy to help you Hercules. Those belligerent birds hate the sound of a gong. Now, they will never be seen again!

*(SOUND CREW 5 and 6 shake handbells as ATHENA returns to her chair.)*

**CHORUS 2:** Hercules returned to Eurystheus.

*(SOUND CREW 3 strikes wood block as HERCULES travels around stage and EURYSTHEUS strides center.)*

**HERCULES:** *(Proudly.)* I got rid of the Stymphalian Birds.

**EURYSTHEUS:** *(Sneering.)* Who cares! Your next labor is HORRIBLE. Go and clean the Augean stables in one day. Ha! Ha! Ha! They haven't been cleaned in thirty years.

*(EURYSTHEUS swaggers to his chair.)*

**HERCULES:** *(Hands on hips, chin up.)* I am off to clean the Augean Stables in one day.

*(SOUND CREW 5 strikes gong.)*

# SCENE SIX
## *The Labor of the Augean Stables*

Characters: Chorus, Hercules, King Augeas, River (2), Eurystheus

**CHORUS 3:** Scene Six: The Labor of the Augean Stables

*(SOUND CREW 1 strikes triangle.)*

**CHORUS 4:** Hercules arrived at the kingdom of King Augeas.

*(SOUND CREW 3 strikes wood block as HERCULES circles stage, stopping up left.)*

**CHORUS 1:** King Augeas owned the largest herd of cattle in Greece.

*(SOUND CREW 2 strikes drum as KING AUGEAS arms across chest and nose in air walks arrogantly center.)*

**AUGEAS:** *(Pompously points at himself.)* I am King Augeas. *(Gesturing over audience.)* I own a HUGE HERD. *(Arms across chest.)* I have been too busy to clean my stables.

**CHORUS 2:** Hercules knew it would be an ENORMOUS task to clean the Augean Stables in one day. He wanted a REWARD to do this hard labor.

**HERCULES:** *(To Augeas.)* I will clean your stables in one day, but you must give me one-tenth of your herd to do so.

**AUGEAS:** *(Brashly and loudly.)* NO ONE can clean my stables in one day. So, yes I will give you one-tenth of my herd if you can do this IMPOSSIBLE labor.

*(SOUND CREW 2 strikes drum as AUGEAS swaggers to chair and sits.)*

**CHORUS 3:** With his club, Hercules smashed a huge hole in the front and back walls of the stables.

*(PROP PERSON 1 hands HERCULES a club. SOUND CREW 2 strikes drum very emphatically as HERCULES mimes smashing two holes in stable walls— one on stage left and one on stage right.)*

**CHORUS 4:** Then, Hercules diverted the flow of a mighty river through the stables.

*(SOUND CREW 4 shakes tambourine. SOUND CREW 2 and 3 shake jingle bells and SOUND CREW 5 and 6 shake handbells vigorously as RIVER moves fabric up and down, going alternately upstage to downstage two times and freezes.)*

**CHORUS 1:** The river washed the stables clean.

*(SOUND CREW 4 shakes tambourine. SOUND CREW 2 and 3 shake jingle bells and SOUND CREW 5 and 6 shake hand bells vigorously as RIVER moves fabric up and down from upstage to downstage once more and returns to chairs.)*

**CHORUS 2:** Hercules went to Augeas to claim his reward.

*(SOUND CREW 3 strikes wood block as HERCULES goes to KING AUGEAS who swaggers center.)*

**HERCULES:** King Augeas, I cleaned your stables in one day. Now, please give me my reward of one-tenth of your herd.

**CHORUS 3:** The greedy king did not want to give up any of his herd.

**AUGEAS:** *(Arms across chest, loudly and belligerently.)* NO! The RIVER cleaned my stables, NOT YOU.

**HERCULES:** *(Looking directly at Augeas.)* As you know sir, *(Pointing to himself.)* I diverted the river to clean your stables.

**CHORUS 4:** But dishonest Augeas scowled and shook his head no. Hercules, head held high returned to Eurystheus.

*(SOUND CREW 2 strikes drum as AUGEAS, arms across chest pompously, marches to chair. SOUND CREW 3 strikes wood block as HERCULES, head high, travels around stage to EURYSTHEUS who strides center.)*

**HERCULES:** *(Proudly.)* I cleaned the Augean Stables in one day.

**EURYSTHEUS:** *(Angrily, pointing.)* Don't be smug! You are NOT done yet! Go to the island of the Amazons and bring back the jeweled belt of Hippolyta, the Amazon Queen. The Amazons are stronger than any man.

*(EURYSTHEUS swaggers to his chair.)*

**HERCULES:** *(Chin up, hands on hips and brightly.)* I am off to get the jeweled belt of Hippolyta, the Amazon Queen.

*(SOUND CREW 5 strikes gong.)*

# SCENE SEVEN
## *The Labor of the Belt of Hippolyta*

Characters: Chorus, Hercules, Tree, Amazons (3 or more), Hippolyta, Bull, Eurystheus

**CHORUS 1:** Scene Seven: The Labor of the Belt of Hippolyta

*(SOUND CREW 1 strikes triangle.)*

**CHORUS 2:** Hercules traveled to the Island of the Amazons.

*(SOUND CREW 3 strikes wood block crisply as HERCULES travels and stops up right.)*

**CHORUS 3:** He stood behind a tree to observe.

*(TREE forms and HERCULES stands behind it.)*

**HERCULES:** I want to observe these Amazons.

**CHORUS 4:** Queen Hippolyta appeared wearing the prized jeweled belt that her father gave her.

**HIPPOLYTA:** *(Proudly pointing to self.)* I am Hippolyta the Amazon Queen. *(Displaying belt to audience.)* My father gave me this beautiful belt. It is my favorite possession.

**CHORUS 1:** Hippolyta had never met a man she admired as much as her father.

**HIPPOLYTA:** *(Proudly.)* My father was brave and kind.

**CHORUS 2:** The other Amazons arrived.

*(SOUND CREW 3 strikes wood block as AMAZONS stride briskly forward forming a line on either side of HIPPOLYTA who is in center.)*

**CHORUS 3:** The Amazons were excellent horseback riders.

*(SOUND CREW 3 strikes wood block as AMAZONS led by HIPPOLYTA mime holding reins and trotting on horseback in serpentine pattern around stage.)*

**CHORUS 4:** The Amazons were excellent swimmers.

*(SOUND CREW 2, 4, and 5 shake rattles as HIPPOLYTA and AMAZONS in a line facing audience mime swimming the crawl.)*

**CHORUS 1:** The Amazons were excellent javelin throwers.

*(SOUND CREW 2 strikes drum lightly three times as HIPPOLYTA and AMAZONS face audience and mime hurling javelins to left, center, and then right of audience.)*

**CHORUS 2:** Hippolyta was the strongest and most skillful of the Amazons and also trained alone.

*(AMAZONS return to their chairs. HIPPOLYTA remains on stage.)*

**HIPPOLYTA:** *(Raising both arms.)* I Hippolyta am the strongest of the Amazons and also like to train alone.

**CHORUS 3:** Hippolyta could shoot an arrow and never miss the mark.

**HIPPOLYTA:** I can shoot an arrow and never miss the mark.

*(SOUND CREW 6 strikes high tone bell three times as HIPPOLYTA mimes shooting an arrow above audience three times—left, center, and right.)*

**CHORUS 4:** Hippolyta could run for hours and never tire.

**HIPPOLYTA:** *(Running in place.)* I can run for hours and never tire!

*(SOUND CREW 2, 4, and 5 shake rattles as HIPPOLYTA, knees high, runs in place and freezes.)*

**CHORUS 1:** Hippolyta even challenged the strongest bull.

**HIPPOLYTA:** *(Confidently, gesturing with an arm.)* Bring on the strongest bull.

*(SOUND CREW 2 rumbles drum as BULL paws ground, roars and snorts aggressively as it lumbers forward.)*

**CHORUS 2:** Hippolyta could force that bull to its knees in five seconds.

**HIPPOLYTA:** *(Assuredly, pointing at bull.)* Watch this bull fall.

*(SOUND CREW 2 rumbles drum dramatically as HIPPOLYTA mimes pushing BULL who tries to resist and SOUND CREW 2 strikes drum emphatically as BULL staggers and falls. Defeated BULL staggers to his chair.)*

**CHORUS 3:** Hercules could see that this woman WAS strong and clever.

**HERCULES:** *(Hand on chin, thinking.)* This woman IS strong and clever. How am I going to get that jeweled belt?

**CHORUS 4:** Hercules stepped up to the queen.

*(SOUND CREW 3 strikes wood block.)*

**HERCULES:** *(Gallantly.)* Queen Hippolyta, I am Hercules. I've traveled many miles to see you.

**CHORUS 1:** For days, Hippolyta and Hercules rode horseback together.

*(SOUND CREW 3 strikes wood block as HIPPOLYTA and HERCULES imitate riding horseback in serpentine pattern around stage.)*

**CHORUS 2:** Hercules and Hippolyta ran together.

*(SOUND CREW 2, 4, and 5 shake rattles as HIPPOLYTA and HERCULES knees high, face audience and run in place.)*

**CHORUS 3:** Hercules and Hippolyta tossed javelins together.

*(SOUND CREW 2 strikes drum lightly three times as HIPPOLYTA and HERCULES mime tossing three javelins.)*

**CHORUS 4:** Hippolyta admired Hercules.

**HIPPOLYTA:** Hercules, I admire you. Take my precious belt as a gift in honor of our friendship.

*(SOUND CREW 4, 5, and 6 shake handbells as HIPPOLYTA takes off belt and hands it to HERCULES.)*

**CHORUS 1:** The other Amazons ran to Queen Hippolyta and whispered.

*(SOUND CREW 2, 4, and 5 shake rattles as HERCULES steps aside and AMAZONS run to HIPPOLYTA.)*

**AMAZON 1:** *(Whispering.)* I heard Hercules came here to kill you.

**AMAZON 2:** We must fight him before he escapes with your jeweled belt.

**AMAZON 3 and 4:** We must stop him!

**CHORUS 2:** Hercules held the belt high and dodged between them. He escaped with the belt.

*(SOUND CREW 4 shakes tambourine as AMAZONS mime reaching for belt as HERCULES holds belt high and dodges in between the AMAZONS. SOUND CREW 4 slaps tambourine in the center as HERCULES holding belt higher escapes.)*

**CHORUS 3:** The Amazons shook their heads in grief.

*(SOUND CREW 5 and 6 shake rattles lightly.)*

**HIPPOLYTA:** I made a serious mistake giving that stranger my jeweled belt.

**ALL AMAZONS:** *(Bowing heads.)* We forgive you noble queen.

*(HIPPOLYTA and AMAZONS return proudly to chairs.)*

**CHORUS 4:** Hercules returned to Eurystheus.

*(SOUND CREW 3 strikes wood block as HERCULES travels around stage and EURYSTHEUS strides center.)*

**HERCULES:** *(Proudly.)* I brought back the jeweled belt of Hippolyta.

**EURYSTHEUS:** *(Grabbing the belt.)* Give me that belt! Go and bring back the golden apples from the tree of the Hesperides. They are guarded by a deadly dragon who never sleeps.

*(EURYSTHEUS swaggers to his chair.)*

**HERCULES:** *(Chin up, hands on hips and brightly.)* I am off to bring back the golden apples of Hesperides.

# SCENE EIGHT
## *The Labor of the Golden Apples of the Hesperides*

Characters: Chorus, Hercules, Dragon, Tree with Golden Apples, Hercules, Atlas, Eurystheus

**CHORUS 1:** Scene Eight: The Labor of the Golden Apples of Hesperides

*(SOUND CREW 1 strikes triangle.)*

**CHORUS 2:** Hercules traveled to the Hesperides.

*(SOUND CREW 3 strikes wood block crisply as HERCULES travels and stops up right.)*

**CHORUS 3:** Hercules gazed in wonder when he saw the tree with the golden apples.

*(SOUND CREW 6 strums tone bells low to high three times as TREE goes center and dramatically displays apples.)*

**HERCULES:** What a tree!

**CHORUS 4:** Under the golden apple tree lurked a roaring fire-breathing dragon.

**DRAGON:** *(Roaring at audience, baring teeth and slinking under tree.)* RRRRRRRRRRROAR! *(SOUND CREW 2 and 6 shake rattles and SOUND CREW 4 shakes tambourine vigorously as DRAGON roaring, snarling, and baring claws slinks on and lies under TREE.)*

**CHORUS 1:** Mighty Atlas was standing in the garden holding up the sky.

*(SOUND CREW 2 strikes drum firmly twice as ATLAS steps forward stage left straining holding up the sky on raised hands.)*

**CHORUS 2:** Atlas was the only one able to calm the dragon with his soothing song.

**ATLAS:** Only I can calm the dragon with my soothing song.

**CHORUS 3:** Atlas did not like his job holding up the heavy sky.

**ATLAS:** *(Wearily.)* I hate this job holding up this heavy sky.

**CHORUS 4:** Hercules knew the dragon could spit fire and burn him alive.

**DRAGON:** *(Roaring and lunging toward HERCULES.)* RRRRRRROAR!

**HERCULES:** This dragon could burn me alive!

**CHORUS 1:** Hercules needed Atlas to help him.

**HERCULES:** *(Going to Atlas.)* Atlas, if I hold up the sky for awhile, will you calm the dragon and get me some golden apples?

**ATLAS:** *(Enthusiastically.)* Yes, I will.

*(SOUND CREW strikes drum twice firmly—once as ATLAS removes sky from his shoulders and once when he hands sky to HERCULES, who strains lifting it up.)*

**HERCULES:** *(Straining.)* This sky IS heavy.

**CHORUS 2:** Atlas waved his arms and charmed the dragon with his song.

ATLAS: *(Waving arms and hypnotically.)* Sleep great dragon. Sleep! Sleep! Sleep! Sleep, great dragon. Deep! Deep! Deep!

*(SOUND CREW 6 strums tone bells low to high and high to low twice.)*

CHORUS 3: The dragon fell asleep.

*(SOUND CREW 5 shakes wind chimes as DRAGON snorts as if snoring and slowly collapses in deep sleep.)*

CHORUS 4: Atlas picked two apples.

*(SOUND CREW 6 strikes high tone bell once for each apple ATLAS picks.)*

CHORUS 1: Atlas did not want to take the sky back.

ATLAS: *(To audience.)* I do not want to take that heavy sky back. I'm going to TRICK Hercules. *(Going to Hercules.)* Hercules, I will deliver these apples for you. Then I will return and take the sky back.

HERCULES: All right Atlas, but first hold the sky while I put a cushion on my shoulders to relieve the pain.

CHORUS 2: Atlas put down the apples and took the sky from Hercules.

*(SOUND CREW 6 strikes two low tone bells as ATLAS sets down each apple, and SOUND CREW 2 strikes drum twice firmly—once as HERCULES hands sky to ATLAS and once as ATLAS strains lifting it up.)*

CHORUS 3: Hercules quickly picked up the apples. He returned to Eurystheus.

*(SOUND CREW 6 strikes high tone bell for each apple picked up. SOUND CREW 3 strikes wood block as HERCULES travels around stage and EURYS-THEUS strides center. DRAGON, TREE, and ATLAS return to chairs.)*

HERCULES: *(Proudly.)* Eurystheus, I have brought back the golden apples of the Hesperides.

EURYSTHEUS: *(Grabbing greedily.)* Give me those apples. Your last labor is impossible. Go to the land of the dead and bring back the three-headed guard dog Cerberus. I hope he tears you apart.

HERCULES: *(Hands on hips.)* I am off to bring back the three-headed guard dog, Cerberus.

*(SOUND CREW 5 strikes gong.)*

# SCENE NINE
## *The Labor of the Guard Dog Cerberus*

Characters: Chorus, Hermes, Athena, Hercules, Hades, Cerberus, Eurystheus

CHORUS 4: Scene Nine: The Labor of the Guard Dog Cerberus

*(SOUND CREW 1 strikes triangle.)*

CHORUS 1: Hercules had no idea how to get down into the world of the dead.

**CHORUS 2:** Athena, the goddess of wisdom, and Hermes, the messenger God, appeared and beckoned Hercules to follow them.

*(SOUND CREW 6 strikes three high tone bells as HERMES and ATHENA step forward.)*

**ATHENA:** *(With beckoning gesture.)* Follow us.

**HERMES:** *(With beckoning gesture.)* Follow us.

**ATHENA and HERMES:** To the underworld.

**CHORUS 3:** They went down a long path.

*(SOUND CREW 2, 4, and 6 shake rattles as ATHENA, HERMES and HERCULES walk downstage, then upstage and then come down center symbolizing going down to Underworld.)*

**CHORUS 4:** They arrived at the kingdom of King Hades, god of the underworld.

*(SOUND CREW 5 strikes gong three times.)*

**CHORUS 1:** King Hades appeared.

*(SOUND CREW 2 strikes drum ceremoniously to accompany HADES' majestic walk center. )*

**CHORUS 2:** Athena and Hermes introduced Hercules

**ATHENA:** King Hades, we introduce Hercules.

**HERMES:** Hercules has a favor to ask of you.

**CHORUS 3:** Hermes and Athena withdrew.

*(SOUND CREW 2, 3, and 4 shakes jingle bells as ATHENA and HERMES return to their chairs.)*

**HERCULES:** *(Bowing.)* King Hades, I come here to your land of the dead to bring the guard dog Cerberus to the land of the living. It is my final labor.

**CHORUS 4:** Hades admired Hercules.

**HADES:** Hercules, I admire you. Yes, you may bring Cerberus to the land of the living IF you can master him without using weapons.

**HERCULES:** *(Bowing head.)* Thank you King Hades. I will do so.

**CHORUS 1:** Hades called Cerberus.

**HADES:** *(Beckoning.)* Come Cerberus.

**CHORUS 2:** Cerberus snarled and bared his claws as he trotted to Hercules.

**CERBERUS:** *(Loudly.)* GRRRRRRRRR!

*(SOUND CREW 4 slaps tambourine in the center continuously as CERBERUS growling fiercely reaches out paws aggressively at HERCULES.)*

**CHORUS 3:** Hercules took Cerberus by each shoulder and stared into his eyes.

*(CERBERUS faces audience and HERCULES has back to audience as SOUND CREW 2 strikes drum once for each shoulder grasped and HERCULES, holding CERBERUS firmly, stares into his eyes.)*

**CHORUS 4:** Cerberus stared transfixed.

*(SOUND CREW 1 strikes triangle for staring.)*

**HERCULES:** *(Very assertively.)* Cerberus, I will NOT let you go until you yield to me.

**CHORUS 1:** Cerberus knew that Hercules meant it and yielded.

**CERBERUS:** *(Raising paws and pulling back.)* I yield. I yield.

**CHORUS 2:** Cerberus trotted beside Hercules as they returned to Eurystheus.

*(HADES returns to chair. SOUND CREW 3 strikes wood block as CERBERUS trots next to HERCULES. CERBERUS snarls at EURYSTHEUS as he walks center.)*

**CERBERUS:** *(Reaching paws out.)* GRRRRRRRRR!

**HERCULES:** *(Proudly.)* Eurystheus, here is Cerberus!

**EURYSTHEUS:** *(Hysterically throwing arms up and wide-eyed.)* Get that dog out of here.

**CHORUS 3:** Eurystheus ran off. He jumped into a pot.

**EURYSTHEUS:** *(Hands waving and knees high.)* Help! Help! Help!

*(SOUND CREW 3 strikes wood block rapidly as EURYSTHEUS knees high runs as POT forms center right and SOUND CREW 2 strikes drum emphatically as EURYSTHEUS jumps into POT.)*

**CHORUS 4:** Eurystheus was never heard from again.

*(POT and EURYSTHEUS return to chairs.)*

**CHORUS 1:** And Hercules, for his bravery and service to people, was led by Athena and Hermes to Mt. Olympus.

*(PROP PERSON 2 places chair center. SOUND CREW 1 strikes triangle several times as ATHENA and HERMES lead HERCULES center.)*

**CHORUS 2:** There, he was elevated to the rank of a god.

*(ATHENA places gold, laurel wreath on HERCULES' head and SOUND CREW 1 strikes triangle as HERMES and ATHENA help HERCULES stand on the chair. HERMES and ATHENA remain standing on each side of HERCULES.)*

**CHORUS 3:** Today, Hercules remains the most popular hero-god of all times. His labors that were admired by people thousands of years ago are still admired today.

*(SOUND CREW 6 strums tone bells low to high three times. Then, SOUND CREW 1 strikes triangle three times.)*

*(The play might end with the Greek dance done in the beginning. ALL CHORUS members go center stage for the finale. They should memorize this part.)*

**CHORUS 1:** "Efharisto," friends and thank you too.

*("Efharisto," pronounced Ef ha **ree** stoh, is the Greek word for thank you and literally means "good graces and joy.")*

**CHORUS 2:** For watching so kindly our myth for you.

**CHORUS 3:** From ancient Greece, it's old yet new.

**CHORUS 4:** We hope it came alive for you.

**CHORUS 1:** *(Pointing to audience.)* And here's a last tip from the Chorus your friends.

**CHORUS 2:** *(Holding up book.)* Read a book of these myths from beginning to end.

**CHORUS 3:** And study ancient Greece with its great majesty.

**CHORUS 4:** *(Making big circular gesture.)* For the more that you know, the more you'll be free.

*(CHORUS Return to their respective sides of stage to introduce the cast and crew.)*

*(To end the performance, CHORUS 1–4 introduce the performers, having them stand and say their names loudly and clearly. When all are standing, CHORUS 1–4 thank the audience and then turn toward ACTORS and raise their arms. Everyone follows, raising their arms and bringing them down together for a group bow. Performers then sit for the audience performance discussion.)*

**CHORUS:** The actors are . . .

*(SOUND CREW 6 strikes one high tone bell after each cast member stands, and introduces her- or himself. CAST and CREW remain standing after they are introduced.)*

**CHORUS:** The Sound Crew is . . .

**CHORUS:** The Chorus members are . . .

# PRODUCTION NOTES

## *Costume Suggestions*

For narrative mime presentations, all students wear black clothing—black shirts and black pants—with individual character costumes worn as additional pieces to the all-black attire. If actors play characters wearing tunics throughout the play, they need not wear black clothes as long as their clothes underneath don't show under the tunic.

**Chorus:** Use pattern for simple, knee-length, choral robe. (See "Creating Costumes, Props, and Scenery" chapter 4.) Make it from a wrinkle-free fabric. Use purple, dark blue, burgundy, dark green, off-white, or any dignified, but not overpowering, color. Might use similar or different colors for each chorus member. Tie with black or gold cord. Wear gold, store-bought, laurel leaf headpieces or make headpieces with foliage from floral-supply store. (See chapter 4, "Creating Costumes, Props, and Scenery" for making tunic and headpieces.)

**Hercules:** Dark, grape-purple tunic; gold, store-bought belt; gold, laurel wreath (worn when he's elevated to rank of Olympian god).

**Snakes:** Black men's socks with a big, yellow, felt eye and red, felt fangs; or have students in all-black clothes slither like snakes.

**Hercules' Mother:** Pink tunic; dark pink belt or sash; colorful headband, perhaps with ribbons attached.

**Mist:** Glue or tape long, white strips of crepe paper to dowels; use two dowels for each performer (see chapter 4 for making atmosphere sticks); or drape girls in white netting—to be mist.

**Priestess:** White tunic; white filmy scarf or filmy fabric attached to a headband and hanging over shoulders and back.

**Eurystheus:** Black tunic; black, tagboard crown with junk jewelry attached; silver belt.

**Trees:** Plastic greenery from floral-supply store.

**Hydra:** Red mittens; red knit caps; and black, eye masks.

**Artemis:** Light blue tunic tied with silver cord; headband with flowers attached.

**Deer of Cerynea:** Headband with tall gold horns.

**Flowers:** Plastic flowers from floral-supply store.

**Olive Tree:** Plastic greenery with small leaves from floral-supply store, or use branch from a real olive tree.

**Birds of Stymphalia:** Black or dark blue, baseball caps, perhaps staple cone-shaped beak to the visors; sunglasses.

**Athena:** Lavender tunic tied with silver cord; silver, plastic helmet.

**King Augeus:** Brown tunic, tied with black or brown cord; brown crown decorated with junk jewelry.

**River:** Five or six yards of lightweight, blue fabric that doesn't ravel cut down the middle and is manipulated by two actors—one at each end.

**Amazons:** Bright headbands of similar colors worn across the forehead in the Greek style; matching sashes or belts.

**Amazon Queen:** Bright yellow or orange tunic; gold, ornate belt with bright costume jewelry attached; yellow or orange, flamboyant headpiece (see chapter 4 for headpiece ideas).

**Tree with Golden Apples:** Green, feather boa, and two gold unbreakable Christmas balls, or use apples or tennis balls covered in gold foil.

**Dragon:** Lime green, baseball cap with tall, dragon points across the top; red knit gloves with long, lime green, pointed claws attached.

**Atlas:** Bright blue tunic, tied with white or silver cord.

**Hermes:** Lamé or similar metallic fabric tunic; three-inch wide, black, tagboard headband with cardboard or tagboard wings attached, cover wings with aluminum foil.

**Hades:** Tall, spiked, black crown of tagboard with red glitter on points; red cloak.

**Cerberus:** Three, matching, baseball caps with fierce, pointed, tall ears attached. The two actors on both ends wear black gloves creating two paws and the actor in the middle puts hands behind his or her back. Or have one student play the dog wearing a cap with ears attached as one dog head and manipulating puppets with dog heads in each hand.

*Prop Suggestions*

**Hercules' Club:** Commercial, brown plastic "caveman's club."

**Burning Branch:** Dowel with gold tinsel attached.

**Athena's Gong:** Pot lid struck with metal spoon or use a small gong with a sharp strident sound.

# STORY QUESTIONS, WRITING, ART, AND CLASSICAL CONNECTIONS (DEVELOPING LANGUAGE)

The following questions are listed scene by scene. Interpretive questions are indicated by an asterisk (*). A separate list of general and personal response questions are at the end of the section as well as a Classical Connections section with questions on words from the myths that have entered our vocabulary.

SCENE ONE: *Young Hercules and the Prediction of His Greatness*

1. What does Hercules do as a boy that shows he has unusual strength and bravery?

2. What does Hercules' mother say when she sees Hercules' extraordinary strength and bravery?

3. *How do you think Hercules feels about what he did?

SCENE TWO: *Hercules Consults the Oracle at Delphi*

1. When Hercules was eighteen, where did he go for advice and why?

2. Who gave Hercules advice and what was Hercules told to do?

3. How did Hercules feel about the advice at first?

4. What did he finally decide to do?

5. What was Hercules' distinctive weapon?

6. *Why do you think Hercules was willing to follow the advice of the oracle when he really didn't want to?

SCENE THREE: *King Eurystheus and the Labor of the Hydra of Lerna*

1. How would you describe Eurystheus?

2. *Why do you think Hercules was asked to serve a cruel master?

3. *Why do you think Eurystheus dislikes Hercules?

4. Why was it difficult to slay the Hydra?

5. How does Hercules accomplish this labor?

6. Is Eurystheus impressed that Hercules slays the Hydra? What is his attitude?

SCENE FOUR: *The Labor of the Deer of Cerynea*

1. The Goddess Artemis has four golden-horned deer. Why doesn't she have the fifth one?

2. How does Hercules get the deer?

3. What does Hercules do with the deer after he shows it to Eurystheus?

4. *Why do you think the golden-horned deer was finally eager to go to Artemis?

SCENE FIVE: *The Labor of the Birds of Stymphalia*

1. Why are the birds of Stymphalia dangerous? What do they do?

2. What happens when Hercules tries to shoot the birds with his bow and arrow?

3. How is Hercules helped in this labor?

4. What happens to the birds at the end of the labor?

5. *What do you think might have caused the birds to hate people?

SCENE SIX: *The Labor of the Augean Stables*

1. What makes King Augeas powerful?

2. What is the labor of the Augean Stables? Why is it a difficult labor?

3. What clever solution did Hercules find to complete this labor?

4. What promise did Augeas make to Hercules? Why didn't Augeas keep his promise?

5. *Think of five words to describe Augeas.

6. *What might have caused Augeas to become the kind of person he is? What might he gain from the way he acts? What might he lose from the way he acts?

SCENE SEVEN: *The Labor of the Belt of Hippolyta*

1. In what way are the Amazons exceptional?

2. What were the exceptional abilities of Hippolyta, the Amazon Queen?

3. Why was the jeweled belt the favorite possession of Hippolyta?

4. How did Hercules obtain the belt?

The Labors of Hercules  157

5. How did Hippolyta feel at first toward Hercules? Why did she feel that way? How did Hippolyta feel later about Hercules? Why?

6. *Do you approve of the way that Hercules got the jeweled belt? Explain.

## SCENE EIGHT: *The Labor of the Golden Apples of the Hesperides*

1. Why is it difficult to obtain the golden apples?

2. Who helps Hercules in this labor and how?

3. What problem does Hercules have before he can leave with the apples? How does he solve this problem?

4. What does Eurystheus say when Hercules returns with the apples?

5. Why do you think Eurystheus is so condescending to Hercules even when he gives him the valuable golden apples?

## SCENE NINE: *The Labor of the Guard Dog Cerberus*

1. Who helped Hercules get into the underworld?

2. Why did Hades agree to let Hercules take Cerberus, the guard dog, into the land of the living? What must Hercules do to get the dog?

3. How did Cerberus behave when he first went to Hercules?

4. What did Hercules do to subdue Cerberus?

5. *Why do you think Hercules was able to tame Cerberus so quickly?

6. What was the reaction of Eurystheus when Hercules brought Cerberus to him?

7. *Why do you think the dog took such an instant disliking to Eurystheus?

8. *What happened to Eurystheus at the end? Was this what you think should have happened to Eurystheus? Explain.

9. What happened to Hercules at the end? Why did he receive such a great tribute?

*General Interpretive and Personal Response Questions*

1. What other admirable qualities besides strength and bravery does Hercules have that makes him a noble hero?

2. Some say that persistence is the most important quality needed to succeed in a difficult task or endeavor. What is persistence? In what way does Hercules persist? In what tasks in your life have you shown persistence?

3. Name characters in other myths in this book who persist and finally get what they seek.

4. What heroes, leaders, artists, and athletes alive today have you heard of who have persisted to achieve their goals? What did they do that showed persistence?

5. What task or pursuit would you be willing to do with persistence even though it may at times be difficult, tedious, or unpleasant? What task or pursuit have you done or are doing now that needs persistence?

## Writing

1. Describe a labor Hercules might be given to do today to serve the world and how he would accomplish it.

2. Write a letter to Hercules and tell him why you'd like to be his friend.

3. If you were the oracle at Delphi, what three pieces of advice would you give a young person your age about living a productive life?

## Writing or Dramatizing a Scene

Take one of the following episodes from *The Labors of Hercules* and write a story or a play making the characters modern as if the story was happening today and the characters were talking in modern English. If you write a play, dramatize it for the class.

1. Instead of Hercules Consults the Oracle at Delphi, Hercules consults a TV psychic to find out what he should do for the next five years.

2. Reflecting the Labor of the Jeweled Belt of Hippolyta, have Hercules trick a rich girl into giving her car to him.

3. Instead of the Labor of the Augean Stables, Hercules must in one hour clean a man's yard that hasn't been cleaned in five years and is full of trash and weeds.

## Developing Language: Classical Connections

The following are questions on words in the myth that have entered the English language. Use the Glossary to answer these questions.

1. What does *Amazonian* mean?

2. Why is the Amazon River in South America given that name?

3. What does it mean to call something an "Augean stable"?

4. Describe a task that might be called a "Herculean task"?

5. What kind of a problem might be called a "hydra"?

6. What Internet book company is named after the Amazons? Why do you think it was called that?

7. Look through the Yellow Pages of the phone book and write names of companies that use the name Hercules and Atlas. Why do you think they do so?

## Art

- Draw your interpretation of one or more of the mythological monsters in *The Labors of Hercules?*

- Draw a picture of your favorite labor.

# The Odyssey

The *Odyssey*, with its companion work, *The Iliad*, is the first major work of literature in Western civilization and one of the greatest masterpieces of all times. It has been studied and enjoyed for more than 2,800 years.

*The Odyssey* was composed by the Greek poet, Homer, in the 8th century B.C. It consists of twenty-four episodes that tell the adventures of the Greek general and King of Ithaca Odysseus after the Greeks defeated the Trojans in the Trojan War. The war, described in *The Iliad*, occurred because the Trojan prince Paris abducted Helen, the beautiful wife of the Greek King Menealus, and brought her to Troy. The Greeks waged war to bring Helen back to Greece. During the war, the clever Greek general Odysseus devised a large wooden horse that would hold an army inside. The Trojans, thinking the horse was a gift from the gods, brought it inside their city gates. The Greeks jumped out and defeated the Trojans.

On his way home to Ithaca after the battle, Odysseus and his crew stopped on the island of the Cyclopes. The Cyclops, Polyphemus, captured the crew in his cave and began eating the sailors. Odysseus heated a wooden stake, poked Polyphemus in the eye, and they escaped. But as Odysseus set sail, Polyphemus cried out to his father, the sea god Poseidon, to never let Odysseus return to his homeland, or if he did return, not for many years. Poseidon granted Polyphemus's wish and Odysseus was made to sail the seas for ten years before he returned to Ithaca.

This play dramatizes several of the well-known adventures of Odysseus and his shipmates on their ten-year adventure home. The first scene takes place on the island of the enchantress Circe who turns Odysseus's sailors into pigs. The second scene describes three deadly sea perils Odysseus and his sailors meet. These are the beautiful Sirens, who lure sailors to their deaths by their enticing song, the mighty whirlpool Charybdis that sinks ships, and the monster Scylla who, with her many heads, devours everything. In the last scene, Odysseus finally returns home to Ithaca. The goddess Athena warns him that since he left, surly suitors have been badgering his wife Penelope to marry one of them. Athena disguises Odysseus as a beggar so he can overcome the suitors by surprise. When he travels to his palace as a beggar, only his dog recognizes that he is Odysseus, the king.

At the palace, Penelope is arranging to hold "the test of the great bow" to decide which suitor will be her bridegroom. In this difficult test, the winning suitor must shoot an arrow through six rings. No suitor passes the test, but Odysseus disguised as the "beggar" succeeds. Odysseus then declares he is Odysseus the king. Penelope gives Odysseus one final test to make sure he is her husband. Odysseus passes that test, and Odysseus is happily reunited with Penelope, and their son, Telemachus.

**Summary for the Teacher:** TV Interview with the characters in *The Odyssey*

**Goal:** To introduce the characters and story of the myth through dramatization. This is also a possible casting method.

**Materials:** Copy of the TV Interview for all students

**Procedure:** Explain that they will perform a TV Interview playing the characters in the myth telling their story. Read the TV Announcer's introduction in a low monotone. Ask students what was wrong with the way you read this and how you might make it more effective.

Cast the roles using the cast list. Choose students with animated voices that project well to play the TV Announcer and Odysseus. They will model the desired techniques and inspire other students in their playing. Before dramatizing, practice the pronunciation of the characters' names using the phonetic guide in the cast list.

Characters stand in front of the classroom with the TV Announcer sitting or standing to one side. Characters step forward in their character stance (e.g., heroic Odysseus, wickedly entrancing Circe, sprightly Hermes) when introduced. They stay in character as they speak and then step back when finished. The Announcer can use a wooden spoon or a wire whisk as a microphone. There are 18 roles in the Interview, so you may want to dramatize it twice to give all students a chance to participate. To further increase roles, use a different student as TV Announcer for each page. After dramatizing, review the characters and the story event.

# TV INTERVIEW

CAST OF CHARACTERS (18)

    TV Announcer *(enthusiastic*

    Odysseus (oh **dis** ee us)

    Sailors (3—can be played by girls and boys)

    Circe (**sir** see)

    Hermes (**her** meez)

    Scylla (**sil** ah)

    Charybdis (ka **rib** dis)

    Sirens (3 girls)

    Athena (a **thee** na)

    Telemachus (te **lem** ah kus)

    Suitors (3)

    Penelope

TV ANNOUNCER: *(Energetically.)* Today we meet the characters in the Greek myth, *The Odyssey*, composed by the Greek poet Homer in the eighth century B.C. Characters, please step forward when introduced. First meet our hero, **Odysseus** and his hardy **Sailors**. In their first adventure, they encounter the entrancing witch **Circe**, and Odysseus is helped by the fleet messenger-god **Hermes**. In a second adventure, the ship passes the island of the dangerously enticing **Sirens**. Then they come to a narrow pass and must steer their ship between two monsters—the ruthless whirlpool **Charybdis**, and ferocious **Scylla** with six heads. After ten years at sea, Odysseus finally arrives in his homeland of Ithaca. Odysseus learns that rude **Suitors** have been badgering his faithful wife to marry them. Majestic **Athena**, the goddess of wisdom, devises a plan to help Odysseus. At last, Odysseus reunites with his dignified son, Telemachus, and his gracious wife **Penelope**.

TV ANNOUNCER: Odysseus, you were made to sail the seas for ten years after your battle with the Trojans. How did this happen?

ODYSSEUS: I was a Greek general in the war against the Trojans. I had my sailors build a huge wooden horse that held one hundred sailors hidden inside. The Trojans thought the horse was a gift from the gods. They brought the horse into their city. Immediately, we Greeks sprang out and defeated the Trojans.

TV ANNOUNCER: *(Curiously.)* But why did you have to sail the seas for ten years?

ODYSSEUS: On my way home to Ithaca, we stopped on the island of the Cyclopes. The Cyclops, Polyphemus, captured us in his cave and began eating my comrades, so I heated a wooden stake and poked him in the eye. We escaped, but as we set sail, Polyphemus cried out to his father Poseidon, the sea god, to never let me return to my homeland, or if I did—to return only after many years.

TV ANNOUNCER: And so Poseidon granted the Cyclops's wish?

ODYSSEUS: Yes, and I had to sail the seas for ten years. It was very difficult. First, my sailors and I came to the island of Circe, the witch.

TV ANNOUNCER: Circe, what power do you have as a witch?

CIRCE: I have the power to turn men into pigs. I gave the sailors my magic, honeyed punch. Then I struck each one of them on the shoulder and immediately they became pigs. I tried to turn Odysseus into a pig, but he had magic protection.

TV ANNOUNCER: Hermes, you helped protect Odysseus. What did you do?

HERMES: I gave Odysseus a magic vine. The vine gave Odysseus the power to overcome Circe, and she became friendly. Circe transformed the pigs back into sailors, and they all had a wonderful feast.

TV ANNOUNCER: That experience must have been frightening.

**ODYSSEUS:** That adventure wasn't anywhere near as frightening as when we encountered the three deadly sea perils. First, we sailed past the island of the dangerous Sirens.

**TV ANNOUNCER:** Sirens, you seem to be very friendly. Why does Odysseus say you are dangerous?

**SIREN #1:** *(Too sweetly.)* We are not dangerous at all.

**SIREN #2:** *(Even more sweetly.)* How can Odysseus say we are dangerous?

**SIREN #3:** *(More sweetly still.)* We only wanted to sing to Odysseus and his sailors.

**TV ANNOUNCER:** That sounds delightful. Odysseus, what's wrong with the Sirens singing to you?

**ODYSSEUS:** *(Scowling.)* They sing to lure sailors to their island where the sailors die.

**TV ANNOUNCER:** *(Horrified.)* That's horrible! Sailors, how did you and Odysseus escape the Sirens' song?

**SAILOR # 1:** Odysseus made us put beeswax in our ears so we could not hear the Siren's song.

**SAILOR #2:** Odysseus wanted to hear the Siren's song. So, Odysseus had us tie him with rope to the mast so he could not go with the Sirens.

**SAILOR #3:** We had to row fast to escape their lures.

**TV ANNOUNCER:** *(Very interested.)* Then, what happened?

**ODYSSEUS:** Next, we met two deadly sea monsters, Charybdis and Scylla. The monsters were on either side of a narrow pass, and they destroy all sailors that sail through that pass.

**TV ANNOUNCER:** Charybdis, what makes you so evil?

**CHARYBDIS:** *(Aggressively.)* I am a whirlpool. My job is to gulp up the sea and swirl it around and around. I swallow up sailors and ships, but I can't help it. I am a whirlpool.

**TV ANNOUNCER:** *(Seriously.)* I hope I never meet you in MY boat! Scylla, why does Odysseus call YOU a monster?

**SCYLLA:** *(Fiercely.)* I have six heads. My heads are always hungry, and I eat everything in sight.

**TV ANNOUNCER:** Sailors, how did you and Odysseus get past Scylla and Charybdis?

**SAILOR #1:** We rowed fast past Scylla so she wouldn't capture any of us.

**SAILOR #2:** We were successful, except we lost one sailor. Scylla grabbed him and took him away.

**SAILOR #3:** Odysseus thought it was better to lose one sailor to Scylla than to have our whole ship sink in the whirlpool.

**TV ANNOUNCER:** *(Amazed.)* What an adventure! Odysseus, I bet you were glad when you finally got home to Ithaca.

**ODYSSEUS:** When I got home after ten years at sea, I still had a big problem. Luckily, Athena, the goddess of wisdom, helped me.

**TV ANNOUNCER:** Goddess Athena, how did you help?

**ATHENA:** I warned Odysseus that since he'd been away rude suitors were pestering his wife Penelope to marry them. I told Odysseus to disguise himself as a beggar. Then, the suitors wouldn't recognize him, and he could take them by surprise.

**TV ANNOUNCER:** Odysseus, what happened when you became a beggar?

**ODYSSEUS:** When I walked through the city as a beggar, no one recognized that I was Odysseus the king—but my old dog sniffed and rushed to me. I wanted to pet him, but I feared someone would recognize that I was Odysseus. So I sadly gestured the dog away.

**TV ANNOUNCER:** *(Shaking head sadly.)* Poor old dog! Telemachus, you are Odysseus's son. How did you feel when you first saw your father, Odysseus?

**TELEMACHUS:** *(Sincerely.)* At first I did not recognize him. Odysseus was dressed as a beggar, as you know. When he came to the palace, I ordered the servants to serve the beggar food. I was taught to be hospitable to all people.

**TV ANNOUNCER:** *(Interested.)* When did you recognize that the beggar was your father, Odysseus?

**TELEMACHUS:** After the rude suitors left that night, Odysseus removed his beggar disguise, and I knew the beggar was my father, Odysseus. It was wonderful. I had been waiting to see my father for more than ten years.

**TV ANNOUNCER:** *(Exuberantly.)* What a joyous moment! Odysseus, what happened next?

**ODYSSEUS:** I told Telemachus that I must put back my beggar disguise so I could take the suitors by surprise and get rid of them. Then, still disguised as a beggar, I went to my wife Penelope. I told Penelope that I had seen Odysseus and that he would be back with her soon.

**TV ANNOUNCER:** Penelope, how did you react?

**PENELOPE:** I did not believe the beggar when he said Odysseus would be back. Odysseus had been away so long. But I took a liking to the beggar. I told him that I was being forced to choose one of the suitors to marry. I said I would give the suitors the test of the great bow.

**TV ANNOUNCER:** *(Interested.)* What is the test of the great bow?

**PENELOPE:** It requires shooting an arrow through six rings on the top of six axes.

**TV ANNOUNCER:** Shooting an arrow through six rings! That seems impossible.

**PENELOPE:** *(Enthusiastically.)* Odysseus could do it.

**TV ANNOUNCER:** Suitors, what did you think of this contest?

**SUITOR #1:** *(Confidently.)* I thought if Odysseus could shoot an arrow through the rings so could I.

**SUITOR #2:** *(More confidently.)* I am a super marksman. I knew I could do it.

**BIGGEST BULLY SUITOR:** *(Boastfully.)* Everyone knows that I am the strongest suitor of all. I was positive I could do it.

**TV ANNOUNCER:** Telemachus, which one of the suitors succeeded?

**TELEMACHUS:** None of them. And then my father, still disguised as a beggar, asked to shoot the arrow. And he succeeded!

**TV ANNOUNCER:** *(Exuberantly.)* How exciting, and then Odysseus what did you do?

**ODYSSEUS:** *(Excitedly.)* I leaped to the center of the room and removed my beggar's disguise. The suitors saw that I was Odysseus, the king, and they all left hastily.

**TV ANNOUNCER:** And so Penelope, your family was reunited.

**PENELOPE:** Not yet. I needed to give this man one more test to make sure he was Odysseus. I told the man to rest and said I would have Odysseus's bed moved to another room for him.

**ODYSSEUS:** And I told Penelope that the bed could never be moved because I had made it. One of the bedposts is the trunk of a tree with roots deep in the earth.

**PENELOPE:** I then knew that this man was my husband Odysseus.

**TV ANNOUNCER:** What a remarkable story. After all those years, the family of Odysseus, Penelope, and Telemachus was finally reunited. Thank you, characters for sharing your exciting story. I can see why the book, *The Odyssey,* by Homer is still considered one of the greatest masterpieces of all times. I bet many of you in the audience would enjoy reading the complete book with ALL of the adventures of Odysseus. I know that the minute I leave the studio I am going to my library to check out the complete *Odyssey.* And I look forward to many nights of reading pleasure.

# ACTING EXERCISES

Use the following exercises to involve all students in experiencing the characters in the story and to develop stage speech and acting skills to dramatize the play.

## Practicing Effective Stage Speech Using the Script

**Goal:** To practice the stage-speaking skills using introductory verse from the script.
**Procedure:** First, discuss and practice the four stage-speaking skills. (See chapter 1, "The Four Stage-Speaking Principles.") Then, recite each line of the following introduction modeling the good speaking skills using gestures and then the students recite it with you. (This is a good vocal warm-up to use before any rehearsal or recite opening dialogue from the scene you are rehearsing.)

*(Very energetically.)* Welcome audience, and "yas sas" or to your health too.

*(Pointing on "you.")* Today we'll act a myth for you.

*(Arms down on "old," and up on "new.")* From ancient Greece, it's old yet new.

*(Opening arms up colorfully.)* We'll make it come alive for you.

*(Gesturing to audience.)* So watch our play, *The Odyssey.*

*(Raising arms up.)* And wondrous feats you will see.

## Developing Majestic Bearing

**Goal:** To stand, sit and move with dignity, nobility, and majesty.
**Acting Principles:** Belief, Movement.
**Materials:** Drum (optional)
**Procedure:** Tell students that Odysseus, Circe, the Sirens, Athena, Telemachus, and Penelope have a royal, commanding stance. Explain that they sit and stand erectly with excellent posture. Model poor posture by slouching, then leaning on one foot, shifting from one foot to another, and putting your hands in your pockets. As you do these, ask what was wrong with your posture if you wanted to convey a royal stance? Then, stand with a royal bearing. Have the students do the following majestic bearing activity.

- Sit with head up, shoulders back, feet together and firmly on the ground.

- Place your hands on each side of the chair to help lift you. Then keeping your head up, press your hands on a chair to help lift you, and slowly rise.

- Walk slowly with head up, shoulders back, and hands by your sides perhaps to the accompaniment of a steady majestic drum beat.

• Finally, stand with your feet planted firmly on the floor, hands by your sides, shoulders back, and head looking slightly up to the back wall of the auditorium. Lift your arms up and out in a majestic gesture showing that you are ready to lead your people. Freeze.

## Circle Walk Character Transformation

**Goal:** To develop creative flexibility and to experience the characters' movement style.

**Acting Principles:** Belief, Control, Movement.

**Materials:** Use a wood block to create a beat and pitch that matches the pace and style of each character—tapping lightly and quickly for Hermes and the dog, then tapping more heavily and slowly for the suitors and Odysseus as the old beggar.

**Procedure:** Students form a circle and begin by walking to the beat of the drum. Students transform from one character to another as they walk in the circle. Perhaps divide the class into two groups with one performing all of the actions while the other group observes, and then reverse the process. Use a drum or wood block struck at different tempos to accompany each action.

• Walk as yourself.

• Move briskly, as Odysseus ready to rescue your sailors.

• Walk stooped, as Odysseus disguised as an old beggar.

• Walk as a tired, famished sailor searching the island for food and shelter.

• Slink as a snarling wolf or lion threatening the sailors.

• Stride as Circe, leading the sailors to the pigsty.

• Leap as Hermes, to stop Odysseus from getting into danger.

• Trot as the old dog delighted to see his master.

• Glide as Athena, magically appearing in the mist.

• Swagger as a suitor to bully the servants.

• Move majestically as a god or goddess.

## Miming the Characters' Situations

**Goal:** To develop the imagination and pantomime skills that communicate the action clearly and to warm-up to rehearse the play.

**Acting Principles:** Belief, Movement, Control.

**Materials:** Bell.

**Procedure:** Divide the class into Group One and Group Two. Each group does every other one of the following scenarios unless the exercise specifically indicates female or male. All actions are done "in place" and end in a freeze. Use a bell to begin and end each pantomime. Perhaps do these as warm-ups for the scenes you are rehearsing that day.

Scene One: *Odysseus and his Sailors Meet the Witch Circe*

- Become sailors rowing. Pull arms into the body and lean back so both arms and back are doing the stroke. Feel the heavy water as you pull through it with your oars. Put effort and muscle into the rowing. Freeze.

- Girls: Become Circe. Stand with majestic confidence. Strum your lyre. Smile sweetly as you gesture the sailors into your house. Mix a honeyed punch in a big glass bowl set on a table. Turn your back and drop in an evil potion, mixing it well. Pick up a ladle and ladle punch into three glasses. Smile and hand the drinks to the sailors. Raise your wand and strike each sailor's shoulder firmly to turn them into pigs. Freeze.

- Become a sailor. You are hot and thirsty. Circe hands you a glass of cold, orange, honeyed punch. See the size of the glass and feel its weight. Take the cold frosty glass. Look at the delicious orange punch. Bring the frosty cold glass to your lips. Take a big drink. Taste the sweet cool orange juices. Swallow. Lick the sweet juices off of your lips. Smile happily as you set the glass down on the table. Freeze.

- Now, feel yourself being struck sharply on the shoulder by Circe's wand. Horrified, you are becoming a pig. Examine your thick, pink skin covered with sharp bristles. Examine your cloven hooves. Wiggle your little pig ears and your large snout. Squint and stare with your sharp beady eyes. Exclaim in horror, "I'm a pig. I'm a pig!"

- Girls: Become a graceful nymph. Spin lightly, bow, and serve the sailors food on large trays. Freeze.

- Boys: Become the cautious leading sailor. Observe Circe carefully. Step aside and observe her suspiciously from a distance. Freeze.

Scene Two: *Odysseus and his Sailors Meet Three Deadly Sea Perils*

- Girls: Become a Siren. Smile and beckon the sailors to lure them to your deadly island. Freeze enticingly.

- Boys: Become Odysseus with your arms tied tight to the mast. Hear the beautiful Sirens' song. Struggle to get free. Freeze.

- Become the mighty whirlpool Charybdis. Swirl an arm in circles. Begin high and go faster and faster as you move down trying to suck a ship into your treacherous waters. Freeze pulling a great ship into your depths.

- Become Scylla. Lunge forward with your long arms and ravenous huge heads. Grab all the food in sight and push it between your strong ferocious teeth. Hiss menacingly. Freeze.

Scene Three: *Odysseus Returns to His Homeland of Ithaca*
(In this scene girls can play male roles.)

- Become a majestic goddess or god. Whisk the fog away. Freeze.

- Become Odysseus, look all around in the fog. Squint trying to recognize where you are. Freeze.

- Become Odysseus. See your faithful dog come to you. Reach to pet him. Realize someone might recognize who you are and sadly gesture your dog away. Freeze.

- Become Odysseus's faithful old dog. Trot eagerly in place to Odysseus. See Odysseus gesture you away. Whimper and trot in place sadly back to your doghouse.

- Become the biggest bully suitor. Grab a bunch of grapes. Pop them greedily in your mouth. See the beggar. Look at him with haughty disdain. Freeze.

- Become Prince Telemachus. Rise majestically and gesture hospitably to the beggar to sit. Freeze.

- Become Telemachus majestically carrying the long great bow. Freeze.

- Become Odysseus. Pick up the large heavy bow. Show exertion as you pull the long arrow taut to get a strong action. Aim carefully. Release the arrow. Shoot the arrow perfectly through the rings. Freeze.

- Become Penelope, Odysseus, or Telemachus poised and ready to lead your nation. Freeze.

## Motivated Dialogue

**Goal:** To speak purposefully.
**Acting Principles:** Belief, Voice, and Movement.
**Materials:** Bell.
**Procedure:** Tell students that when you ring the bell, they will rise and become different characters saying their dialogue with a purpose. Boys play male roles and girls, female roles—or alternate boys and girls. Use a bell to start and stop action.

**ODYSSEUS:** *(To rescue your sailors.)* I must go to Circe's house.

**LEADING SAILOR:** *(To size up the situation.)* I am suspicious of this woman.

**CIRCE:** *(To humiliate the sailors.)* Into the pigsty.

**HERMES:** *(To help Odysseus.)* Wear this magic vine.

**SIRENS:** *(To seduce Odysseus.)* Come to us, great Odysseus.

**ATHENA:** *(To help and protect Odysseus.)* I must disguise you.

**TELEMACHUS:** *(To befriend the beggar.)* Welcome, stranger.

**PENELOPE:** *(To comfort the stranger.)* Rest now, stranger.

## Becoming Odysseus

**Goal:** To develop creative flexibility and to involve all students in experiencing and portraying the central character Odysseus in key moments in the play.
**Acting Principles:** Belief, Voice, and Movement.
**Materials:** Use a bell to begin and end each scenario.
**Procedure:** Both girls and boys act these scenarios. Divide the class into two groups. Each group dramatizes every other Odysseus scenario ending in a freeze. First read each scenario so they are familiar with it, and then coach them through it emphasizing dramatic character speech. Ring the bell to start and stop each action.

- Become Odysseus determined to save his sailors. Say forcefully, "I must go to Circe's house." Freeze.

- Become Odysseus plotting to subdue Circe. Swallow her punch. Then, raise your arms to overcome Circe. Say forcefully, "You must take an oath." Freeze.

- Become Odysseus concerned when you hear of the three deadly sea perils. Ask Circe, "What can I do?" Freeze.

- Become Odysseus tied to the mast. Hear the Sirens' song. Pull to get free to go with the Sirens. Say, "Release me. Release me." Freeze.

- Become Odysseus. Recognize your homeland of Ithaca after being away for ten years. Say, "I'm finally back home in Ithaca." Freeze.

- Become Odysseus disguising yourself as a beggar to fool the suitors. Stoop and walk in place to trick people into thinking you're a very old man. Say, "No one must recognize me!" Freeze.

- Become Odysseus. See your faithful old dog rush to greet you. Sadly shake your head and gesture the poor dog away. Freeze.

- Become Odysseus. Lift the heavy bow, aim carefully at all of the rings, shoot the arrow through. Freeze. Throw off your beggar disguise. Say triumphantly, "Odysseus the king is home!" Freeze.

# THE ODYSSEY
Adapted from a version by Homer

CAST OF CHARACTERS (In order of appearance)

CHORUS 1 Leader, very responsible, strong voice

CHORUS 2, 3, 4 Strong voices, ability to follow and pick up cues

ODYSSEUS (oh **dis** ee us) Leading role; heroic leader; strong voice, requires line memorization

SAILORS 6 or more—can be played by girls and boys

LEADING SAILOR Played by one of the Sailors

PINE TREES (3 or more)

WOLF

LION

CIRCE (**sir** see) Assertive, bewitching; requires stage presence and line memorization

HERMES (**her** meez) Helpful, lively; requires minimal line memorization

NYMPHS (3) Graceful

PROP PERSON (1 or more)

SIRENS (3 or more) Graceful, wickedly enchanting

FLOWERS (3 or more)

SCYLLA (**sil** ah) (2) Fierce, ravenous

CHARYBDIS (ka **rib** dis) (2 or 3) Ruthless, powerful

Fog (2)

ATHENA (a **thee** na) Commanding, majestic; requires minimal line memorization

TELEMACHUS (te **lem** ah kus) Gallant, assertive; an important role; requires line memorization

DOG OLD loving, and still lively

SUITOR #1 Rude and belligerent, strong voice

SUITOR #2 Ruder and more belligerent, very strong voice

BIGGEST BULLY SUITOR Rudest and most belligerent, the strongest voice

SERVANTS (2)

PENELOPE Majestic, elegant, mature; an important role; requires line memorization

RINGS (5 to 8) Use the number needed allowing for size of stage and class.

*Sound Crew*

SOUND CREW 1 triangle, small drum

SOUND CREW 2 jingle bells, drum, rattle

SOUND CREW 3 wood block, rattle

SOUND CREW 4 tambourine, jingle bells, rattle

SOUND CREW 5 jingle bells, handbell, rattles, wind chimes, guiro, gong

SOUND CREW 6 tone bells, handbell

## Basic Stage Setup

The actors sit in chairs arranged in a semicircle in view of the audience. Two Chorus members stand on each side of the stage. Costumes and props are stored under the actors' chairs. The Chorus and characters wearing tunics throughout the play wear their tunics

The Sound Crew sits with instruments on a table or two to the right or left of the stage area and in view of the audience. Tables are set so that the Crew can see the stage action.

## Stage Setup

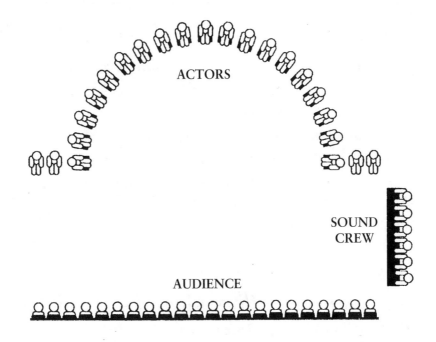

NOTE: Chairs to represent the boat are in the center of the semicircle and a foot or so forward from the chairs of the other actors. Space is left in the semicircle so the chairs can be put into the semicircle in Scene Three when no boat is needed. Chairs face sideways to the audience. ODYSSEUS sits in the first chair facing stage right. The LEADING SAILOR sits behind him with the other SAILORS following. For a simpler way to stage the boat, have the sailors stand in this direction and mime rowing. The vine wreath that HERMES gives ODYSSEUS is placed downstage center. CIRCE'S chair is set center stage right with her wand under it. Down left is the pigsty.

*The play might begin with a Greek dance. (See Chapter 5 for dance instructions and music suggestions. If doing the dance, place the chairs and the vine wreath after the dance.)*

# PROLOGUE

*(SOUND CREW 1 strikes triangle three times slowly to signal the play will begin.)*

**CHORUS 1:** *(Very energetically.)* Welcome audience, and "yas sas" or to your health too.

*("Yas sas" is Greek for "to your health" and is used for both hello and good-bye.)*

**CHORUS 2:** *(Pointing on "you.")* Today we'll act a myth for you.

**CHORUS 3:** *(Arms down on "old," and up on "new.")* From ancient Greece, it's old yet new.

**CHORUS 4:** *(Opening arms up colorfully.)* We'll make it come alive for you.

**CHORUS 1:** *(Gesturing to audience.)* So watch our myth, *The Odyssey*

**CHORUS 2:** *(Excitedly.)* And wondrous feats you will see.

**CHORUS 1:** *(Clearly and emphatically.)* The Odyssey

*(SOUND CREW 1 strikes triangle.)*

**CHORUS 2:** *(Slowly and clearly.)* An ancient Greek epic based on a version by the Greek poet Homer from the 8th century B.C.

*(SOUND CREW 1 strikes triangle.)*

# SCENE ONE

## *Odysseus and His Sailors Meet the Witch Circe*

CHARACTERS: Chorus, Odysseus, Sailors, Leading Sailor, Prop Person, Pine Trees, Wolf, Lion, Circe, Nymphs

**CHORUS 3:** *(Slowly, energetically.)* Scene One: Odysseus and his Sailors Meet the Witch Circe

*(SOUND CREW 1 strikes triangle.)*

**CHORUS 4:** In this scene, the hero Odysseus and his sailors have lost their way on their sea voyage. They row to an unknown island.

**ODYSSEUS:** *(Strongly.)* Row, row, row, ROW!

*(SOUND CREW 3 strikes wood block four times as SAILORS row—showing exertion and putting muscle into it, and in unison following the SAILOR in front of them.)*

**CHORUS 1:** Odysseus climbed out. The crew rose to attention.

(*SOUND CREW 1 strikes triangle once as ODYSSEUS climbs out and again when the SAILORS stand with military attention.*)

ODYSSEUS: (*Assertively, facing audience.*) We must explore the island for help.

CHORUS 2: Odysseus sent the sailors with his leading sailor through the pine woods.

(*PINE TREES form upstage and downstage. SOUND CREW 1 strikes small drum as SAILORS follow LEADING SAILOR in serpentine pattern around the PINES. ODYSSEUS sits in boat.*)

CHORUS 3: In the clearing, they saw a smooth stone house.

(*SOUND CREW 1 strikes triangle. PINE TREES return to chairs.*)

CHORUS 4: A wolf and lion prowled in front of the house. The sailors cringed in fear as the animals circled the sailors.

(*SOUND CREW 5 strikes guiro as WOLF and LION prowl menacingly back and forth downstage and SOUND CREW 2, 3, and 4 shake rattles as SAILORS cringe, and WOLF and LION circle them. WOLF and LION return to their chairs.*)

CHORUS 1: A beautiful lady sat inside the house.

(*SOUND CREW 1 strikes triangle as CIRCE holding her lyre strides majestically and sits.*)

CHORUS 2: From inside came the sound of melodious music.

(*SOUND CREW 6 strums tone bells low to high once as CIRCE sits in chair and strums lyre once.*)

CHORUS 3: A woman was playing a lyre.

(*SOUND CREW 6 strums tone bells low to high three times as CIRCE strums lyre three times.*)

CHORUS 4: Reassured, they called . . .

CREW: (*Cheerfully and loudly.*) Good evening, lady.

CHORUS 1: Only the leader stood aside suspicious.

(*SOUND CREW 1 strikes triangle as LEADING SAILOR steps downstage right.*)

LEADING SAILOR: (*To audience.*) I'm SUSPICIOUS of this woman. I sense a TRAP!

CHORUS 2: The lady set down her lyre.

(*SOUND CREW 1 strikes triangle as CIRCE sets lyre on chair.*)

CHORUS 3: She opened the door and gestured them inside.

(*SOUND CREW 5 strikes guiro for opening the door.*)

CIRCE: (*Exuberantly with sweeping gesture.*) WELCOME, I am Circe, the lady of these halls. You look thirsty. Let me make you my HONEYED PUNCH.

CHORUS 4: She mixed a HONEYED PUNCH.

(*SOUND CREW 2, 3, and 4 shake rattles as CIRCE facing audience mixes.*)

CHORUS 1: She turned her back and dropped in an evil potion stirring it well.

*(SOUND CREW 6 strikes one low tone bell emphatically as CIRCE turns and drops potion in. SOUND CREW 2, 3, and 4 shake rattles for stirring. Then, CIRCE ladles punch into imaginary cups.)*

**CHORUS 2:** The sailors swallowed the punch.

*(SOUND CREW 1 strikes triangle as CIRCE hands drinks on imaginary tray to SAILORS who drink.)*

**CHORUS 3:** They yawned and drooped drowsily.

*(SOUND CREW 3, 4, and 5 shake rattles as SAILORS yawn and slump forward drowsily.)*

**CHORUS 4:** Then, Circe grabbed a wand and struck each sailor on the shoulder.

*(SOUND CREW 3 strikes wood block each time CIRCE strikes each shoulder.)*

**CIRCE:** *(Triumphantly and pointing down.)* DOWN and into the PIGSTY.

**CHORUS 1:** The sailors got down. They snorted loudly and shuffled into the PIGSTY.

*(SOUND CREW 5 strikes guiro as SAILORS now PIGS snort loudly and shuffle to the sty.)*

**CHORUS 2:** The sailors had become PIGS. They wailed, wanting to be human again.

**SAILORS:** *(Wailing loudly and begging and holding up hooves.)* Oh please, Circe, let us be HUMAN again.

**CHORUS 3:** But Circe tossed acorns and berries, food for pigs. And the pigs snorted for the food and began to roll in the mud.

*(SOUND CREW 2, 4, and 5 shake rattles for tossing food as PIGS snort loudly and roll exuberantly.)*

**CHORUS 4:** The leader ran to the ship with arms waving.

*(SOUND CREW 3 strikes wood block quickly at running pace.)*

**ODYSSEUS:** *(Alarmed.)* What's the matter? What happened to the SAILORS?

**LEADING SAILOR:** *(Eyes wide and gesturing toward Circe's house.)* The wicked Circe gave them an EVIL POTION, and they turned into PIGS!

**ODYSSEUS:** *(Determined, hands on hips, and to audience.)* I MUST go to Circe's house.

**LEADER:** Odysseus, I beg you not to go. You too will be made into a PIG.

**ODYSSEUS:** *(More determined, raising fist.)* No, I MUST go.

**CHORUS 1:** Odysseus went into the pine woods toward the smooth, stone house.

*(SOUND CREW 1 strikes small drum for walking as PINES form and ODYSSEUS walks among them.)*

**CHORUS 2:** Suddenly, Hermes, the messenger god, flew onto the path.

*(PINES sit. SOUND CREW 2, 4, and 5 shake jingle bells as HERMES flies in and leaps to center.)*

**CHORUS 3:** Hermes held up a hand.

*(SOUND CREW 1 strikes triangle.)*

**HERMES:** Odysseus, you will become a PIG if you go into Circe's house.

**CHORUS 4:** Hermes handed Odysseus a magic vine.

*(SOUND CREW 6 strikes high tone bell as HERMES picks up vine.)*

**HERMES:** *(Handing vine to ODYSSEUS.)* Wear this magic vine into Circe's house. *(ODYSSEUS puts vine on his head.)* Then you can drink her evil potion, and it will not hurt you. *(Miming striking with wand, raising arms and kneeling.)* When she strikes you with her wand, raise your arms high, and she will kneel to you.

**CHORUS 1:** Hermes flew off.

*(SOUND CREW 2, 4, and 5 shake jingle bells for flying.)*

**CHORUS 2:** Odysseus walked to Circe's house, and his heart beat hard.

*(SOUND CREW 2 strikes drum in heart-beat rhythm.)*

**CHORUS 3:** The lion and wolf circled Odysseus, but Odysseus firmly gestured them away.

*(SOUND CREW 5 strikes guiro as LION and WOLF circle, and ODYSSEUS assertively gestures them away.)*

**CHORUS 4:** Odysseus called.

**ODYSSEUS:** *(Loudly, pleasantly.)* Good evening, lady!

**CHORUS 1:** Circe opened the door. She introduced herself and gestured him inside.

*(SOUND CREW 5 strikes guiro for opening the door.)*

**CIRCE:** *(Exuberantly with sweeping gesture.)* WELCOME, I am Circe, the lady of these halls. You look thirsty. Let me make you my honeyed punch.

**CHORUS 2:** Again, Circe mixed a honeyed punch.

*(SOUND CREW 2, 3, and 4 shake rattles as CIRCE mixes.)*

**CHORUS 3:** Again, she turned her back and dropped in an evil potion stirring it well.

*(SOUND CREW 6 strikes one low note on tone bells emphatically as CIRCE turns and drops potion in. SOUND CREW 2, 3, and 4 shake rattles as CIRCE facing audience stirs potion in and then ladles it into a cup.)*

**CIRCE:** *(Smiling and handing punch to Odysseus.)* Drink my special honeyed punch.

**CHORUS 4:** The minute Odysseus drank, Circe grabbed her wand and struck his shoulder.

*(SOUND CREW 3 strikes wood block.)*

**CIRCE:** *(Triumphantly and pointing down.)* Down and into the pigsty.

**CHORUS 1:** But Odysseus thrust his arms up, and Circe kneeled and cried out.

*(SOUND CREW 5 strikes gong as ODYSSEUS thrusts arms up and CIRCE falls on her knees.)*

**CIRCE:** *(Raising hands up.)* Stop! Stop! You must be Odysseus. Hermes warned me that someday Odysseus would overcome me. Now, let us show that we trust each other.

**CHORUS 2:** Odysseus first demanded that Circe take an oath.

**ODYSSEUS:** *(Strongly and sternly.)* You must take an oath that you will NEVER trick or harm me.

**CIRCE:** *(Sincerely bowing head.)* I vow I will never trick or harm you.

**CHORUS 3:** Then, graceful Nymphs brought Odysseus a delectable meal of cheeses, fruit, and bread.

*(CIRCE stands. SOUND CREW 2 and 4 shake jingle bells and SOUND CREW 5 and 6 shake hand bells as NYMPHS spin gracefully bow, and mime carrying trays. NYMPHS kneel on both sides of ODYSSEUS.)*

**CHORUS 4:** But Odysseus stared at the food.

**CIRCE:** *(Gesturing toward the food.)* Eat up Odysseus.

**ODYSSEUS:** *(Frowning.)* Circe, how can I EAT while my COMRADES are in your PIGSTY?

*(NYMPHS return to their chairs.)*

**CHORUS 1:** Circe took her wand and strode to the pigsty and flung open the pens.

*(SOUND CREW 3 strikes wood block as CIRCE assertively grabs wand and strides.)*

**CHORUS 2:** She touched each pig on the shoulder with the wand.

*(SOUND CREW 3 strikes wood block for each shoulder struck.)*

**CHORUS 3:** The sailors became human again and inspected themselves happily.

*(SOUND CREW 6 strums tone bells low to high three times for happy transformation.)*

**CHORUS 4:** The sailors thanked Odysseus.

**SAILORS:** *(Very gratefully.)* Thank you, Odysseus.

**CIRCE:** *(Enthusiastically.)* Odysseus, go and get the rest of your crew, and we'll have a GREAT FEAST.

**CHORUS 1:** Odysseus returned quickly to the ship and told the leading sailor what happened.

*(SOUND CREW 3 strikes wood block for quick walking.)*

**ODYSSEUS:** *(Enthusiastically.)* Hermes helped me transform Circe into a KIND HELPFUL person.

**CHORUS 2:** The overjoyed sailor returned with Odysseus.

*(SOUND CREW 3 strikes wood block for quick walking.)*

**CHORUS 3:** Circe now welcomed them with honest friendliness.

**CIRCE:** We will have a WONDERFUL FEAST!

**CHORUS 4:** The Nymphs brought delicious food and drinks.

*(SOUND CREW 2 and 4 shake jingle bells and SOUND CREW 5 and 6 shake handbells as NYMPHS spin gracefully, bow and serve food on imaginary trays.)*

**CHORUS 1:** Circe strummed delightful music on her lyre.

*(SOUND CREW 6 strums tone bells low to high three times as CIRCE standing to the side strums lyre three times. NYMPHS kneel on both sides of the SAILORS with ODYSSEUS in the center. They mime eating and drinking, creating a festive stage picture.)*

**CHORUS 2:** Odysseus and his crew stayed one year on the island with Circe for she treated them graciously and with splendor.

*(CIRCE, NYMPHS, SAILORS, and ODYSSEUS freeze in festive pose of eating, drinking, and toasting. They hold pose until after the third strike of the triangle at the end of the scene.)*

**CHORUS 3:** *(Slowly and clearly.)* And THAT is the adventure of Odysseus and his sailors on the island of the witch Circe.

*(SOUND CREW 1 strikes triangle three times. On the third strike, ACTORS break the freeze and return to their chairs.)*

# SCENE TWO
## Odysseus and His Sailors Meet Three Deadly Sea Perils

CHARACTERS: Chorus, Odysseus, Circe, Sailors, Sirens, Flowers, Scylla, Charybdis

NOTE: *In this scene, the boat changes position facing the audience and going from upstage to downstage. ODYSSEUS sits alone in the chair farthest down stage. The other SAILORS sit in double rows of chairs behind him. The LEADING SAILOR sits directly behind ODYSSEUS with one SAILOR next to him, two others sit behind them, and so forth. Or as in previous scene, stage the boat with ODYSSEUS and SAILORS standing in this position. The SIRENS and SCYLLA will appear on stage right, CHARYBDIS, on stage left.*

**CHORUS 4:** Scene Two. Odysseus and His Sailors Meet Three Deadly Sea Perils

*(SOUND CREW 1 strikes triangle continually giving SAILORS time to move their chairs quickly and quietly to new boat position. ODYSSEUS stands outside the boat, stage left [on shore] with CIRCE.)*

**CHORUS 1:** The enchantress Circe warns Odysseus of three great perils before him.

**CIRCE:** *(Urgently.)* Odysseus, you will meet THREE great perils when you sail from this island. FIRST, you will pass the island of the DEADLY SIRENS. THEN, you will pass CHARYBDIS, the whirlpool, and SCYLLA, the sea monster. They could KILL you.

ODYSSEUS: *(Frowning and very concerned.)* What can I do about these perils?

CIRCE: The beautiful SIRENS lure sailors to their death by their song. *(Shaking head and gesturing negatively.)* Do NOT LISTEN to their song.

ODYSSEUS: *(Urgently.)* What about Charybdis, the whirlpool?

CIRCE: *(Creating a pass with arms.)* Charybdis is so powerful that its swirling waters can pull whole ships down into the sea. *(Gesturing negatively.)* You MUST AVOID Charybdis.

*(SOUND CREW 2 rumbles the drum building the volume during the following "CHARYBDIS" sequence as the CHORUS builds the volume too.)*

CHORUS 1–4: *(In strong warning voice.)* AVOID Charybdis.

*(SOUND CREW 2 strikes drum rapidly and loudly.)*

CHORUS 1–4: *(Louder.)* CHARYBDIS!

*(SOUND CREW 2 strikes drum more rapidly and louder.)*

CHORUS 1–4: *(Louder still.)* CHARYBDIS!

*(SOUND CREW 2 strikes drum even more rapidly and louder still.)*

CHORUS 1–4: *(Loudest and explosively.)* CHARYBDIS!

*(SOUND CREW 2 strikes drum rapidly and very loudly and then strikes it emphatically in the center, to end the sequence.)*

CIRCE: *(Gesturing stage right.)* On the other side is the sea monster Scylla. *(Holding up six fingers.)* Scylla has SIX HEADS and *(Miming grabbing and devouring.)* grabs sailors and DEVOURS them. BEWARE SCYLLA!

*(SOUND CREW 4 shakes the tambourine increasingly vigorously during the next sequence as was done for the previous sequence.)*

CHORUS 1–4: *(In strong warning voice, and hissing.)* BEWARE SCYLLA!

*(SOUND CREW 4 shakes tambourine more vigorously.)*

CHORUS 1–4: *(Hissing louder.)* SCYLLA!

*(SOUND CREW 4 shakes tambourine more vigorously still.)*

CHORUS 1–4: *(Hissing and still louder.)* SCYLLA!

*(SOUND CREW 4 shakes tambourine even more vigorously.)*

CHORUS 1–4: *(Hissing and loudest.)* SCYLLA!

*(SOUND CREW 4 shakes tambourine most vigorously and slaps it in the center emphatically.)*

CHORUS 2: Odysseus asked Circe how to avoid the whirlpool, Charybdis, and the sea monster, Scylla.

ODYSSEUS: *(Intently and very concerned.)* HOW can I avoid Charybdis and Scylla?

CIRCE: *(Assertively.)* Stay away from CHARYBDIS AT ALL COSTS. Hug Scylla's side and row by at top speed.

CHORUS 3: Odysseus thanked Circe and bid her good-bye.

ODYSSEUS: *(Bowing gratefully.)* Good-bye Circe, and thank you.

*(CIRCE returns to chair.)*

**CHORUS 4:** Odysseus got in the boat. The sailors took up their oars and rowed in rhythm.

**ODYSSEUS:** Row, row, row, ROW!

*(SOUND CREW 3 strikes wood block four times as SAILORS pull their arms slowly and strongly in unison to the "Row," of ODYSSEUS.)*

**CHORUS 1:** Soon, they saw the field of FLOWERS on the island of the SIRENS.

*(SOUND CREW 6 strums tone bells low to high three times as FLOWERS kneel downstage right.)*

**CHORUS 2:** Odysseus warned the crew to steer clear of the Sirens.

**ODYSSEUS:** *(Assertively.)* STEER CLEAR of the SIRENS. They lure sailors to their deaths with their song.

**CHORUS 3:** Odysseus took beeswax from his pocket and broke it apart.

*(SOUND CREW 6 strikes high tone bell as ODYSSEUS breaks beeswax apart.)*

**ODYSSEUS:** When the Sirens appear, put this beeswax in your ears so you can't hear the Siren's song.

*(SOUND CREW 6 strikes high tone bell each time ODYSSEUS hands a SAILOR beeswax. SAILORS don't put beeswax in their ears yet.)*

**CHORUS 4:** Odysseus wanted to hear the Sirens' song.

**ODYSSEUS:** *(Very determined.)* I want to hear the Siren's song.

**SAILORS:** *(Loudly, shaking heads and gesturing negatively.)* NO! NO! NO! NO!

**CHORUS 1:** Odysseus commanded the crew to bind him to the mast.

**ODYSSEUS:** *(Firmly.)* Bind me to the mast. If I struggle to go with the Sirens, bind me tighter.

**CHORUS 2:** The Leading Sailor bound Odysseus to the mast.

*(SOUND CREW 5 strikes guiro three times as LEADING SAILOR puts ODYSSEUS'S hands behind his back and mimes tying ODYSSEUS to the mast.)*

**CHORUS 3:** Odysseus saw the Sirens appearing.

**ODYSSEUS:** *(Quickly and assertively.)* NOW, put the beeswax in your ears.

**CHORUS 4:** The sailors put the beeswax in their ears.

*(SOUND CREW 6 strikes high tone bell as each SAILOR puts beeswax in his ears.)*

**CHORUS 1:** The Sirens glided into the field of flowers.

*(SOUND CREW 6 strums tone bells low to high as SIRENS lift their arms up and glide gracefully behind FLOWERS. SIRENS reach out arms enticingly and freeze.)*

**CHORUS 2:** The Sirens burst out in song.

*(SOUND CREW 6 strums tone bells low to high.)*

**SIRENS:** *(Beckoning with both arms enticingly.)* Come to us great Odysseus. We know the secrets of day and night.

*(SOUND CREW 6 strums tone bells low to high.)*

**SIRENS:** *(Beckoning enticingly.)* Come to us great Odysseus. *(Raising arms up and freezing.)* We'll bring you great delight.

*(SOUND CREW 6 strums tone bells low to high as SIRENS reach arms up gracefully, freeze, and then slowly, gracefully lower them.)*

**CHORUS 3:** Odysseus yearned to go with the Sirens and called out . . .

**ODYSSEUS:** *(Struggling to get free.)* Release me! Release me!

**CHORUS 4:** The sailor tied Odysseus tighter as he continued to struggle.

*(SOUND CREW 5 strikes guiro three times as LEADING SAILOR mimes tying ODYSSEUS'S hands tighter.)*

**ODYSSEUS:** *(Struggling more and louder.)* RELEASE ME! RELEASE ME!

**CHORUS 1:** The Sirens kept singing.

**SIRENS:** *(Beckoning enticingly and moving dreamily backwards to their chairs.)* Come to us great Odysseus. We know the secrets of day and night.

*(SOUND CREW 6 strums tone bells low to high as SIRENS step back as if boat is passing by their island.)*

**SIRENS:** *(Beckoning enticingly and continuing to move back.)* Come to us great Odysseus. *(Raising arms up.)* We'll bring you great delight.

*(SOUND CREW 6 strums tone bells low to high as SIRENS freeze and then continue stepping back, and ethereally gliding, return to their chairs.)*

**CHORUS 2:** The sailors rowed fast and passed the island.

*(FLOWERS return to their chairs.)*

**ODYSSEUS:** *(Still at mast and more urgently than previously.)* ROW, ROW, ROW, ROW!

*(SOUND CREW 3 strikes wood block four times as SAILORS pull their arms strenuously and more quickly and strongly to the urgent "ROW" of ODYSSEUS.)*

**CHORUS 3:** The sailor untied Odysseus.

*(SOUND CREW 5 strikes guiro three times as SAILOR mimes untying and releasing ODYSSEUS.)*

**CHORUS 4:** The crew took the beeswax out of their ears.

*(SOUND CREW 6 strikes high tone bell for each SAILOR removing beeswax from their ears.)*

**CHORUS 1:** BUT the ANGER of Charybdis and Scylla were soon upon them.

**CHORUS 2:** The sea began to rumble.

*(SOUND CREW 2 strikes large drum throughout the following sequence in a background rumble to create suspense but not so loudly as to prevent the audience from hearing the dialogue.)*

**CHORUS 3:** Odysseus knew this was THE most dangerous pass in the seven seas.

**CHORUS 4:** They MUST steer the ship by Charybdis and Scylla.

**CHORUS 1:** They must AT ALL COSTS avoid the WHIRLPOOL, CHARYBDIS. *(Swirling arm and imitating whirlpool pulling down.)* Her swirling waters could suck their whole ship down and drown them all.

**ODYSSEUS:** *(Seriously.)* Crew, we are approaching the WHIRLPOOL CHARYBDIS. We must avoid CHARYBDIS at all costs. She could drown us all.

**CHORUS 2:** *(Dramatically.)* THEN, CHARYBDIS the whirlpool APPEARED swirling its waters closer and closer to the boat.

*(SOUND CREW 2 strikes drum emphatically in the center as CHARYBDIS actors leap forward creating the whirlpool and swirl closer and closer to the boat. SAILORS lean away hands up, mouths and eyes wide open in fear.)*

*(CHORUS 1 now leads ALL CHORUS and all ACTORS in chairs in the following CHARYBDIS sequence.)*

**CHORUS 1 leading ALL CHORUS AND ACTORS:** *(In menacing voice.)* Charybdis.

*(SOUND CREW 2 strikes drum rapidly and loudly as CHARYBDIS swirl a few feet away from the boat. SAILORS, wide-eyed, lean back.)*

**CHORUS 1 leading ALL CHORUS AND ACTORS:** *(Louder.)* CHARYBDIS.

*(SOUND CREW 2 strikes drum more rapidly and louder as CHARYBDIS ACTORS continue swirling moving closer to the boat. SAILORS, still wide-eyed, lean back farther and raise hands up.)*

**CHORUS 1 leading ALL CHORUS AND ACTORS:** *(Louder still.)* CHARYBDIS.

*(SOUND CREW 2 strikes drum even more rapidly and louder as CHARYBDIS ACTORS swirl most rapidly and SAILORS lean away even farther raising arms above their heads.)*

**CHORUS 1 leading ALL CHORUS AND ACTORS:** *(Loudest and explosively.)* CHARYBDIS!

*(SOUND CREW 2 strikes drum most rapidly and loudly and strikes it emphatically in the center as CHARYBDIS ACTORS swirl directly above the boat and SAILORS lean to the side and cover their heads with their hands as if about to be engulfed.)*

**ODYSSEUS:** *(Loudly and most urgently.)* Watch out! Watch out! ROW, ROW, ROW, ROW!

*(SOUND CREW 3 strikes wood block as ODYSSEUS and SAILORS now row sideways moving chairs toward stage right to avoid CHARYBDIS. CHARYBDIS steps back as boat rows away and still swirling return to their chairs.)*

CHORUS 3: Then, on the other side LEAPED SCYLLA, the man-eating monster with six vicious heads!

*(SOUND CREW 4 shakes tambourine vigorously and slaps it in the center as the SCYLLAS leap forward aggressively and crouch, baring teeth and hissing.)*

ODYSSEUS: *(Loudly.)* Here comes Scylla! Watch those six VICIOUS HEADS.

*(The following "SCYLLA" sequence builds becoming increasingly louder as the SCYLLAS pop forward each of its six heads every time "SCYLLA" is said.)*

CHORUS 4: Each of Scylla's six vicious heads hissed and popped forward.

CHORUS 1 leading ALL CHORUS and ACTORS: *(Thrusting forward maliciously and loudly.)* SCYLLA!

*(SOUND CREW 4 shakes tambourine and SOUND CREW 2, 3 and 5 shake rattles vigorously.)*

CHORUS 1 leading ALL CHORUS and ACTORS: *(Thrusting forward maliciously and louder.)* SCYLLA!

*(SOUND CREW 4 shakes tambourine and SOUND CREW 2, 3, and 5 shake rattles more vigorously.)*

CHORUS 1 leading ALL CHORUS and ACTORS: *(Thrusting forward maliciously and louder still.)* SCYLLA!

*(SOUND CREW 4 shakes tambourine and SOUND CREW 2, 3, and 5 shake rattles even more vigorously.)*

CHORUS 1 leading ALL CHORUS and ACTORS: *(Thrusting forward maliciously and louder still.)* SCYLLA!

*(SOUND CREW 4 shakes tambourine and SOUND CREW 2, 3, and 5 shake rattles even more vigorously.)*

CHORUS 1 leading ALL CHORUS and ACTORS: SCYLLA *(Thrusting forward maliciously and even louder.)* SCYLLA!

CHORUS 1 leading ALL CHORUS and ACTORS: *(Thrusting forward maliciously and loudest of all.)* SCYLLA!

*(SOUND CREW 4 shakes tambourine most vigorously and slaps it in the center as SCYLLAS do a karate kick and freeze sideways to the audience for a count of three with foot, if necessary, on the floor but out in karate kick pose.)*

ODYSSEUS: *(Urgently.)* CREW, ROW PAST SCYLLA FAST!

ODYSSEUS: *(Very forcefully and urgently.)* ROW, ROW, ROW, ROW!

*(SOUND CREW 3 strikes wood block as SAILORS pull arms strongly and row in unison to the "ROW" of ODYSSEUS.)*

CHORUS 1: The crew rowed hard, but Scylla snatched and carried one sailor away.

*(SOUND CREW 2 strikes drum slowly and ominously like a funeral dirge as SCYLLAS crouched and menacing move slowly and relentlessly to the boat.*

*SCYLLAS tap ONE SAILOR on the shoulder and slowly herd SAILOR with head covered back to the semicircle where he kneels with back to the audience until the end of the scene.)*

**CHORUS 2:** Odysseus and his sailors continued on their journey.

**ODYSSEUS:** Row, row, row, ROW!

*(SOUND CREW 3 strikes wood block four times as SAILORS pull their arms slowly and strongly in unison to the "Row," of ODYSSEUS.)*

**CHORUS 3:** Odysseus congratulated the sailors for their bravery.

**ODYSSEUS:** *(Enthusiastically.)* You were brave. We managed to steer past the three most deadly perils in the Seven Seas.

**CREW:** Thank you, Odysseus, for your wise leadership.

*(ODYSSEUS sits and ODYSSEUS and SAILORS freeze in rowing pose.)*

**CHORUS 4:** And THAT is the adventure of Odysseus and his sailors and their triumph over the three deadly sea perils.

*(SOUND CREW 1 strikes triangle three times. On third strike, ODYSSEUS and sailors break the "rowing" freeze. Then SOUND CREW ONE strikes triangle slowly and continually to give ODYSSEUS and SAILORS time to quickly move their chairs into places left for them in the semicircle. There is no boat in Scene Three.)*

# SCENE THREE
## *Return to Ithaca*

CHARACTERS: Odysseus, Fog, Athena, Dog, Telemachus, Suitor #1, Suitor #2, Biggest Bully Suitor, Servants, Penelope, Rings

**CHORUS 1:** Scene Three. Odysseus Returns to His Homeland of Ithaca

*(SOUND CREW 1 strikes triangle.)*

**CHORUS 2:** After ten years of adventures, Odysseus arrives in his homeland of Ithaca. Ithaca is covered in fog.

*(SOUND CREW 5 shakes wind chimes as FOG ACTORS hold up netting across down stage. ODYSSEUS stands behind FOG.)*

**CHORUS 3:** Odysseus squinted and looked all around. In the dense fog, he couldn't tell where he was. Odysseus also didn't know that since he'd been away rude suitors have been bullying his wife Penelope to marry them.

*(SOUND CREW 5 shakes wind chimes as ODYSSEUS, confused, squints looking out and around.)*

**CHORUS 4:** The goddess Athena arrives.

*(SOUND CREW 2, 4, and 5 shake jingle bells as ATHENA majestically goes center to ODYSSEUS.)*

ODYSSEUS: (*Looking confused.*) Goddess Athena, this place is covered in fog. Where am I?

CHORUS 1: Goddess Athena whisked the fog away.

> (*SOUND CREW 5 shakes wind chimes as ATHENA sweeps fog away with arms. FOG lifts netting over the heads of ATHENA and ODYSSEUS who bend down so as not to be hit by it. FOG takes netting to their chairs.*

ATHENA: (*Exuberantly.*) NOW, do you recognize your HOMELAND, ITHACA!

> (*SOUND CREW 1 strikes triangle.*)

ODYSSEUS: (*Enthusiastically looking around.*) I am FINALLY BACK HOME IN ITHACA after ten years.

> (*SOUND CREW 1 strikes triangle.*)

ATHENA: (*Assertively and slowly.*) Odysseus, I MUST DISGUISE you as a BEGGAR. RUDE SUITORS have been BADGERING YOUR WIFE PENELOPE to marry them. If you are a beggar, the suitors will not recognize you, and you can take them by surprise.

CHORUS 2: Athena held out a beggar disguise.

> (*PROP PERSON hands ATHENA disguise in a way that she can easily hand it to ODYSSEUS and he can easily put it on.*)

ATHENA: (*Handing disguise to Odysseus.*) Wear this disguise and walk like an old man.

> (*SOUND CREW 6 strikes two high tone bells slowly and continuously as ODYSSEUS puts on disguise and stoops over like an old man.*)

CHORUS 3: Athena disappeared.

> (*SOUND CREW 2, 4, and 5 shake jingle bells as ATHENA nods meaningfully at ODYSSEUS and then regally returns to her chair.*)

CHORUS 4: Stooped like an old man, Odysseus walked slowly to the palace.

> (*SOUND CREW 3 strikes wood block as ODYSSEUS walking slowly circles stage once or twice symbolizing going a distance.*)

CHORUS 1: NO ONE recognized that this BEGGAR was KING ODYSSEUS returned after ten years.

> (*SOUND CREW 3 continues striking wood block as ODYSSEUS continues walking.*)

CHORUS 2: Suddenly, a sad old dog trotted to Odysseus.

> (*ODYSSEUS stops upstage right. SOUND CREW 3 strikes wood block as DOG trots to ODYSSEUS.*)

CHORUS 3: The dog sniffed and looked up eagerly at the beggar.

CHORUS 4: THIS was ODYSSEUS'S OLD DOG. His dog was the ONLY ONE to recognize that the beggar was Odysseus.

CHORUS 1: Odysseus loved his dog, and reached to pet him. But, fearing someone might recognize he was King Odysseus, he sadly gestured his dog away.

*(ODYSSEUS smiles at DOG and then sadly gestures DOG away. DOG tilts head and looks longingly at ODYSSEUS. Then, SOUND CREW 3 strikes wood block as DOG sadly trots to his chair and sits.)*

**CHORUS 2:** Odysseus continued his journey to the palace.

*(SOUND CREW 3 strikes wood block as ODYSSEUS continues circling the stage.)*

**CHORUS 3:** Finally, he arrived at the palace. He opened the door and went inside.

*(SOUND CREW 1 strikes triangle once when ODYSSEUS arrives at the palace and again as ODYSSEUS mimes opening the door.)*

**CHORUS 4:** Two suitors stood with a foot on the furniture.

*(SOUND CREW 1 strikes small drum once as SUITOR #1 puts foot boorishly on chair and again as SUITOR #2 puts a foot on a chair.)*

**CHORUS 1:** The biggest bully was greedily eating grapes.

*(SOUND CREW 2 and 4 shakes rattles as BIGGEST BULLY SUITOR mimes tipping head back, popping grapes into mouth, and wiping mouth on sleeve.)*

**CHORUS 2:** The suitors insulted the beggar.

**SUITOR #1:** *(Loudly, hands on hips.)* What are YOU doing here old man?

**SUITOR #2:** *(Louder, raising fist.)* BEGGARS don't belong in THIS fine hall.

**BIGGEST BULLY SUITOR:** *(Loudest and pointing.)* GO BACK where you belong!

**CHORUS 3:** But Prince Telemachus, Odysseus's son, rose and gestured Odysseus to sit.

**TELEMACHUS:** *(Gesturing Odysseus to chair.)* WELCOME, stranger. *(Gesturing to Servants.)* Bring this stranger a chair to rest. *(SERVANT brings chair center for ODYSSEUS.)* Now, serve this stranger meat and bread. We are hospitable to ALL in King Odysseus's house.

*(Other SERVANTS bring food to ODYSSEUS, and place it on imaginary table in front of ODYSSEUS.)*

**ODYSSEUS:** *(To Telemachus.)* Thank you, young gentleman.

**TELEMACHUS:** You are welcome. I am Telemachus, son of Odysseus, the king. My father Odysseus has been away for ten years, but he taught me to be hospitable.

**CHORUS 4:** The beggar ate and thanked Telemachus.

**ODYSSEUS:** *(Bowing head.)* I appreciate your hospitality.

**CHORUS 1:** The suitors snatched the palace food and devoured it.

*(SOUND CREW 2 and 4 shake rattles as SUITORS mime greedily grabbing and chomping with mouths open.)*

**CHORUS 2:** Finally, at midnight, the suitors swaggered out of the hall.

*(SOUND CREW 4 shakes tambourine slapping it in the center to create swaggering walk.)*

**CHORUS 3:** Odysseus and Telemachus were alone. Then Odysseus removed his beggar disguise.

*(SOUND CREW 6 strikes two high tone bells successively as ODYSSEUS takes down hood of disguise revealing who he is.)*

**ODYSSEUS:** *(Standing regally.)* Telemachus, I am your father King Odysseus. I have waited ten years for this day.

**TELEMACHUS:** *(Joyfully.)* Father, I have been awaiting your return too. I am overjoyed to see you.

*(ODYSSEUS and TELEMACHUS give a vigorous handshake.)*

**CHORUS 4:** Then, Odysseus and Telemachus planned how to overcome the surly suitors.

**ODYSSEUS:** I will put on my beggar disguise so the suitors will not recognize me, and I can take them by surprise.

*(SOUND CREW 6 strikes two high tone bells as ODYSSEUS puts hood over his head.)*

**ODYSSEUS:** Take me to my wife Penelope. I will keep my disguise. But I have news to give her of Odysseus that may give her hope.

**CHORUS 1:** Telemachus led Odysseus to Penelope.

*(PENELOPE walks regally to right center.)*

**TELEMACHUS:** Mother, this beggar has news of my father, Odysseus. *(Bowing head.)* I will leave you to question him.

*(TELEMACHUS returns to his chair.)*

**PENELOPE:** Please tell me what you know of my husband, Odysseus.

**ODYSSEUS:** I met Odysseus. He spoke only of his wife, Penelope, and their son.

**PENELOPE:** Thank you for these kind words, but after ten years, I believe Odysseus is dead.

**ODYSSEUS:** *(Bowing head.)* Noble lady, I KNOW that Odysseus is alive and will be at the palace soon.

**PENELOPE:** *(Longingly and looking out thoughtfully.)* If only that were true. *(Sadly shaking head.)* I must choose a new husband tonight from those rude suitors.

**ODYSSEUS:** How will you choose?

**PENELOPE:** I will give the suitors the test of the great bow. The winning suitor must be able to shoot an arrow through six rings.

**ODYSSEUS:** Shoot an ARROW through SIX RINGS! That test seems impossible.

**PENELOPE:** *(Proudly.)* Odysseus could do it.

**ODYSSEUS:** Have the contest immediately! I guarantee that before the contest is over, Odysseus will be home.

**PENELOPE:** *(Shaking head.)* If only I could believe that. *(Graciously.)* Please come and observe the contest.

**ODYSSEUS:** *(Bowing head.)* Noble lady I will.

**CHORUS 2:** That night Penelope and Telemachus went to the great hall.

**CHORUS 3:** Telemachus carried the great bow and an arrow.

*(SOUND CREW 6 strikes high tone bell several times as TELEMACHUS mimes holding large heavy bow and arrow.)*

**CHORUS 4:** The suitors arrived.

*(SOUND CREW 4 shakes tambourine to create swaggering walk as SUITORS swagger to upstage left and stay grouped together.)*

**CHORUS 1:** Penelope announced how she would choose her husband from the suitors.

**PENELOPE:** I promise to marry the man who can shoot an arrow through six rings. Now, I will leave you to carry on the contest.

*(PENELOPE regally returns to chair.)*

**CHORUS 2:** The servants set up six rings in a row.

*(SOUND CREW 6 strikes high tone bell each time as the actors playing the SIX RINGS one by one make a straight line along downstage facing stage left. Each RING kneels sideways to the audience and makes a circle above their heads with their arms.)*

**CHORUS 3:** The first suitor swaggered up to make the attempt.

*(SOUND CREW 4 shakes tambourine as SUITOR # 1 swaggers stage right behind RINGS. TELEMACHUS mimes handing SUITOR heavy bow and arrow.)*

**CHORUS 4:** This suitor lacked the strength even to pull the taut string.

**SUITOR #1:** *(Grunting, straining, and irritated.)* This bow will be the end of me.

*(SOUND CREW 5 strikes gong to indicate failure as SUITOR #1 puts bow and arrow down.)*

*(SOUND CREW 4 shakes tambourine as SUITOR # 2 swaggers up to same position.)*

**CHORUS 2:** The second suitor's arrow fell limply from the bow.

**SUITOR #2:** *(Pulling string and more irritated than SUITOR 1.)* This test is IMPOSSIBLE.

*(SOUND CREW 5 strikes gong as SUITOR #2, depressed, looks at arrow fallen onto floor.)*

**CHORUS 3:** The biggest bully swaggered forward.

*(SOUND CREW 4 shakes tambourine as BIGGEST BULLY swaggers to same position.)*

**BIGGEST BULLY SUITOR:** *(Sneering.)* You are all TOO WEAK! Let ME try.

**CHORUS 4:** Puffing and straining, the bully shot the arrow into the ceiling.

**BIGGEST BULLY:** *(Furiously pointing at RINGS.)* Leave the rings there tonight. I'll try tomorrow.

*(SOUND CREW 5 strikes gong to indicate failure.)*

**CHORUS 1:** Then, the beggar stepped forward.

**ODYSSEUS:** Let me try my hand at that bow.

**SUITOR #1:** *(Loudly, sneering, with hands on hips.)* Go away, beggar.

**SUITOR #2:** *(Louder, sneering more, and raising fist.)* This contest ISN'T for beggars.

**BIGGEST BULLY:** *(Loudest, sneering most, and pointing.)* WHO do you think you are!

**TELEMACHUS:** *(Picking up bow and handing it to Odysseus.)* Let him try! All contestants are welcome! *(To Odysseus.)* Good luck to you.

**ODYSSEUS:** Thank you for your support, young prince.

**CHORUS 2:** Odysseus picked up the arrow and put it in the bow. He drew the string aiming toward the rings.

*(SOUND CREW 6 strikes high tone bell as ODYSSEUS carefully aims.)*

**CHORUS 3:** The arrow sang sweetly as it flashed through the six rings.

*(ODYSSEUS shoots arrow. SOUND CREW 6 strikes high tone bell as each RING in turn opens out its arms as if the arrow is flashing through it. RINGS sit.)*

**CHORUS 4:** Odysseus threw off his disguise and leaped triumphantly into the center of the room.

*(SOUND CREW 2 and 4 shake jingle bells and SOUND CREW 5 and 6 shake handbells as ODYSSEUS leaps center stage and freezes with arms raised triumphantly.)*

**CHORUS 1:** The suitors recognized Odysseus the king and threw up their hands in alarm.

**SUITOR #1:** *(Alarmed and stepping back.)* Odysseus is back!

**SUITOR #2:** *(More alarmed and stepping back.)* Bad luck!

**BIGGEST BULLY SUITOR #3:** *(Wide-eyed and most alarmed.)* We must withdraw quickly.

**CHORUS 2:** The suitors left the hall in haste.

*(SOUND CREW 3 strikes wood block for rapid withdrawal.)*

**CHORUS 3:** Now, Penelope joined Odysseus and Telemachus in the hall.

**TELEMACHUS:** *(To Penelope, exuberantly.)* Odysseus has returned.

**PENELOPE:** *(Looking at Odysseus.)* It just cannot be. I still cannot believe it.

**TELEMACHUS:** You should have seen this man shoot an arrow through all six rings.

**PENELOPE:** No one but Odysseus could do that. Still I'm doubtful.

**TELEMACHUS:** Will you not look carefully and question the man?

**CHORUS 3:** Penelope could see the man looked like Odysseus. But she needed to give him a final test to see if he truly was her husband, Odysseus.

**PENELOPE:** Please rest now after your hard contest. You may sleep in the bed of Odysseus. I will have a servant move it to another room.

**CHORUS 4:** Odysseus jumped up.

**ODYSSEUS:** *(Frowning and assertively.)* That bed cannot be moved! I made that bed. One bedpost is the trunk of a tree that's rooted deep in the earth. No one could EVER move that bed.

**PENELOPE:** *(Exuberantly joyful.)* You are right, Odysseus. That bed can NEVER be moved. You MUST BE my husband, Odysseus.

**CHORUS 1:** Penelope placed the crown of Odysseus on his head.

*(PROP PERSON hands crown to PENELOPE who puts it on Odysseus's head.)*

**CHORUS 1:** Now, Odysseus, Penelope, and Telemachus stood together.

*(ODYSSEUS stands between PENELOPE and TELEMACHUS.)*

**CHORUS 2:** They looked out thinking of their future together and that of their country of Ithaca.

*(SOUND CREW 6 strums tone bells low to high three times as ODYSSEUS, PENELOPE, and TELEMACHUS look out slightly over heads of audience and freeze in the pose.)*

**CHORUS 3:** *(Gesturing toward Odysseus, Penelope, and Telemachus.)* And that is the story of the adventures of Odysseus and his return to his homeland, Ithaca.

*(ODYSSEUS, PENELOPE, and TELEMACHUS hold the pose until after SOUND CREW 1 strikes triangle three times.)*

# EPILOGUE

*(ALL CHORUS members go center stage for the finale.)*

NOTE: *They should memorize this part.*

**CHORUS 1:** "Efharisto," friends, and thank you too.

*("Efharisto," pronounced* Ef ha **ree** stoh, *is Greek for thank you and literally means good graces and joy).*

**CHORUS 2:** For watching so kindly our myth for you

**CHORUS 3:** From ancient Greece, it's old yet new.

**CHORUS 4:** We hope it came alive for you.

**CHORUS 1:** *(Pointing to audience.)* And here's a last tip from the chorus your friends.

**CHORUS 2:** *(Holding up book.)* Read a book of these myths from beginning to end.

**CHORUS 3:** And study ancient Greece with its great majesty.

**CHORUS 4:** *(Making big circular gesture.)* For the more that you know, the more you'll be free.

*(CHORUS return to their respective sides of stage to introduce the cast and crew)*

*(To end the performance, CHORUS 1-4 introduce the performers, having them stand and say their names loudly and clearly. When all are standing, CHORUS 1-4 thank the audience and then turn toward ACTORS and raise arms. Everyone follows, raising their arms and bringing them down together for a group bow. Performers then sit for the audience performance discussion.)*

**CHORUS 1:** The Actors are . . .

*(SOUND CREW 6 strikes one high tone bell after each cast member stands, and introduces her or himself. CAST and CREW remain standing after they are introduced.)*

**CHORUS 2:** The Sound Crew is . . .

**CHORUS 3:** The Chorus members are . . .

# PRODUCTION NOTES

## *Costume Suggestions*

For narrative mime presentations students wear all black clothing—black shirts and black shorts, pants, or skirts—with individual character costumes worn as additional pieces to the all-black attire. If actors play characters wearing tunics throughout the play, they need not wear black clothes as long as the clothes underneath aren't visible under the tunic. If possible, students should perform the play barefoot.

**Chorus:** Use pattern for simple knee-length choral robe. (See chapter 4, "Creating Costumes, Props and Scenery.") Make it from a cotton-polyester blend or similar fabric. Might be purple, dark blue, burgundy, dark green, off-white, or any dignified but not overpowering color. Might be similar or different colors for each chorus member. Tie with black cord. Wear gold, store-bought, laurel-leaf headpieces or make headpieces with foliage from floral-supply store. (See chapter 4, "Creating Costumes, Props, and Scenery," for making tunic and headpieces.)

**Odysseus:** White knee-length tunic; gold belt. For beggar disguise—black, hooded sweatshirt cut down the middle. At the end of the play when Odysseus resumes the kingship—gold, store-bought, laurel wreath.

**Sailors:** Similar red headbands.

**Pine Trees:** Dark green feather boas, or branches resembling a pine tree from a floral-supply store, or real pine branches.

**Wolf:** Brown or gray baseball cap with long, pointed ears attached.

**Lion:** Yellow baseball cap with lion ears and yellow yarn for mane attached.

**Circe:** Long, red tunic; bright-colored belt; flamboyant, multicolored, or decorated, wide headband worn in the Greek style around the head.

**Hermes:** Lamé—or similar, metallic fabric—knee-length tunic with silver belt; three-inch wide, black, tagboard headband with cardboard or tagboard wings covered with aluminum foil attached.

**Nymphs:** Matching colorful headbands worn Greek style around the head, bright-colored belts.

**Sirens:** Elasticized headbands with artificial flowers attached and with filmy scarves of pastel colors tied to headband to create dreamy, alluring look.

**Flowers:** Plastic flowers of different, bright colors from floral-supply store.

**Scylla:** Black men's socks with felt yellow eyes and red felt fangs; red, knit hats and black eye masks. (Two actors play the six-headed monster using their two hands as puppet heads and their own head with knit cap and eye mask to create the six-headed monster.)

**Charybdis:** Atmosphere sticks with black, red, deep blue, and purple streamers attached. Two sticks for each Charybdis actor. (See chapter 4, "Creating Costumes, Props and Scenery" for creating atmosphere sticks.)

**Fog:** Three or four yards of white, nylon netting.

**Athena:** Long, yellow tunic; silver, store-bought, plastic helmet; gold belt.

**Telemachus:** Deep purple, knee-length tunic; silver cord for belt; narrow, sawtooth, silver crown.

**Dog:** Black baseball cap with felt dog ears attached.

**Suitors:** Black or brown tagboard crowns with gaudy junk jewelry. The Biggest Bully has the tallest one.

**Servants:** Headbands of the same color worn around the forehead, in the Greek style.

**Penelope:** Long, light blue tunic; gold or jeweled belt; gold, store-bought tiara.

**Rings:** No costume other than black clothing is necessary.

## Prop Suggestions

**Lyre:** Use a simple lyre design and make of foam core. The finished lyre should be about 18 inches long. (See chapter 4, "Creating Costumes, Props and Scenery" for lyre instructions.)

**Wand:** Dowel with ribbons attached, or a commercial wand.

**Magic Wreath:** Green plastic leaves attached to an elasticized headband and worn in the Greek style around the head.

# STORY QUESTIONS, WRITING, ART, AND CLASSICAL CONNECTIONS (DEVELOPING LANGUAGE)

The following questions are listed scene by scene. Interpretive questions are indicated by an asterisk (*). A separate list of general interpretive and personal response questions are at the end of the section as well as a Classical Connections section with questions on words from the myths that have entered our vocabulary. Students might consult the Glossary for answers to the Classical Connections questions.

SCENE ONE: *Odysseus and His Sailors Meet the Witch Circe*

1. Why did Odysseus send his sailors to explore the island of Circe?

2. What did the sailors find?

3. What frightened the sailors when they first arrived at Circe's house?

4. Why do you think most of the sailors went eagerly inside Circe's house?

5. Do you think most people in that circumstance would go inside Circe's house? Explain why or why not.

6. The word *circumspect* means "cautious or prudent" and comes from two Latin words, *circum*, meaning "around" and *spectere*, "to look." Which character in this scene is circumspect? What does he or she do that shows he or she is circumspect?

7. What happened to the sailors when they went inside Circe's house?

8. *What did Circe do to the sailors that showed her lack of hospitality?

9. *Why do you think Circe took this action against the sailors?

10. What did the Leading Sailor do when he saw what happened to the other sailors?

11. *What heroic action did Odysseus take when he discovered what happened to his sailors? What made his action heroic?

12. Who helped Odysseus resist Circe's evil powers, and what did that character do to help?

13. What did Circe try to do to Odysseus? Why wasn't she successful?

14. How did Circe react to Odysseus's successful action against her evil powers?

15. Why wouldn't Odysseus eat the food that the Nymphs first served him?

16. What did Odysseus make Circe promise before he would become her friend?

17. Why were the sailors grateful to Odysseus?

18. What did Circe do at the end of the scene to show her friendship and hospitality?

19. Why did Odysseus and his sailors stay on the island of Circe for a year?

20. *What did Odysseus do in this scene that showed he was a strong leader?

SCENE TWO: *Odysseus and His Crew Meet Three Deadly Sea Perils*

1. Who warns Odysseus of the three deadly sea perils before him?

2. Describe the three sea perils.

3. What did Circe tell Odysseus to do to resist the Sirens?

4. What did Circe tell Odysseus to do to get past Scylla and Charybdis?

5. What did Odysseus give his sailors so they would not hear the Sirens' song?

6. *Why do you think Odysseus wanted to hear the Sirens' song when he knew it was dangerous?

7. What did Odysseus tell his sailors to do so that he would not go to the Sirens? What did the Sirens say in their song to lure the sailors to their island?

8. *Why did Odysseus yell "Release me, release me!"?

9. What did the sailors do when Odysseus begged to be released?

10. * The whirlpool, Charybdis, says that it can't help sinking ships because it is a whirlpool. What is a whirlpool?

11. *What other natural phenomena besides whirlpools should people be wary of?

12. How do Odysseus and his sailors try to escape Scylla and Charybdis?

13. *Do Odysseus and his sailors succeed in escaping Scylla and Charybdis? Explain.

14. *Do you think it was good that Odysseus knew of the three deadly perils before he encountered them? Explain.

15. Why is it important to have a strong leader in times of danger?


SCENE THREE: *Return to Ithaca*

1. How many years was Odysseus away from his homeland of Ithaca?

2. Why doesn't Odysseus recognize Ithaca when he first arrives there?

3. How does Odysseus finally recognize that he is in Ithaca?

4. Who helps Odysseus on his return, and why does this character tell him to disguise himself as a beggar?

5. *Why is it clever for Odysseus to be disguised as a beggar, rather than say a farmer or a musician?

6. *How do you think Odysseus's dog recognized him on his way to the palace? Why do you think no one else recognized him?

7. *Why do you think the poet Homer included a dog in this story? What does Odysseus's reaction to his dog tell you about Odysseus?

8. *Hospitality or being kind and respectful to others is considered important behavior for all Greeks. Which characters in this scene are not hospitable? What do they do that show their lack of respect and courtesy?

9. *Which characters show they are hospitable? What do they do to show their generosity and respect?

10. How did Odysseus's son, Telemachus, react to the beggar when he first arrived at the palace?

11. How did Telemachus discover the beggar was his father, Odysseus?

12. *Why do you think Odysseus hid his true feelings toward the suitors even when they mocked him?

13. How did Penelope react when the beggar told her that he had seen her husband Odysseus and that he would return to the palace soon?

14. *Many have described Penelope as gracious. What does the word *gracious* mean? What does Penelope do that shows she is gracious?

15. Why didn't Penelope believe the beggar when he said that Odysseus would be back in the palace soon?

16. *Why do you think Penelope "took a liking" to the beggar?

17. *Why do you think Penelope gave the suitors the test of the great bow rather than another test to determine who would be her bridegroom?

18. What is the test of the great bow?

19. What were the results of the test of the great bow?

20. Why did the suitors hastily leave the hall after the test of the great bow?

21. What final test did Penelope give to Odysseus to make sure that he really was her husband?

22. How did Odysseus pass the final test and prove he was Odysseus and her husband?

23. What does the play say that Odysseus, Penelope, and Telemachus are thinking at the end of the story?

## General Interpretive Questions

1. Odysseus made his journey by sea. Why might a sea journey be more dangerous than a land journey? What type of land journey might be equally as dangerous and why?

2. Name two instances in which Odysseus faced a challenge that seemed insurmountable and tell how he surmounted it. Then, describe a challenge that you had in your life that seemed insurmountable and tell how you surmounted it.

3. What do you think is the most dramatic scene in this story?

4. Describe two incidents in which Odysseus uses cleverness or intelligence rather than brute force to achieve his objectives? Why is it better in general to use intelligence rather than brute force?

5. Odysseus was helped by a god, Hermes, and a goddess, Athena in this story. In what way did each of them help Odysseus? Why do you think they wanted to help him?

6. Odysseus was brave, intelligent, clever, and kind—all qualities Greeks admired. Name incidents in which Odysseus shows these traits.

7. *The Odyssey* has been used for hundreds of years to teach young Greeks how to behave to lead a good and noble life. What might a young Greek learn from the bad and good characters on the right and wrong ways to behave?

## Writing

1. Write a dramatization of a modern-day adventure in which Odysseus escapes danger by a clever trick. Have someone help him or have him do it on his own. Perform your dramatizations.

2. Write five sentences describing what Odysseus does that makes him a hero.

3. Compare the character of the Sirens and the character of Penelope. What might people say is attractive and unattractive about the Sirens and about Penelope?

## Research

1. Find and copy artworks based on *The Odyssey*. Give a report on the painting or art object you copied and then display the art in the room.

2. Listen to the Sirens No 3 from *Nocturnes for Orchestra* by Claude Debussy, a French composer who lived from 1862 to 1918. Write words that come to mind as you listen to the music. Then tell whether the music conveys any of the luring qualities of the Sirens.

*Developing Language: Classical Connections*

The following are questions on words in the myth that have entered the English language. Use the Glossary to answer these questions.

1. Which character in this play is connected to the word *athenaeum*? What is an athenaeum?

2. What does it mean to be between Scylla and Charybdis? In what way was Odysseus between Scylla and Charybdis?

3. What kind of a person is Circe?

4. What type of a woman is a Siren? What is a "Siren song"?

5. Why do we call a loud, warning noise of a fire engine or ambulance a siren?

6. What kind of woman might be called a Penelope?

7. What might a headline in the travel section of a newspaper mean when it says, "Traveler Makes an African Odyssey"? Why might a recreational vehicle be called "The Odyssey"?

8. Why might a temple in Athens be dedicated to the goddess Athena?

## Art

• Draw a picture of Odysseus bound to the mast, draw a picture of the Sirens, or draw both in the same picture.

• Draw your interpretation of Scylla or Charybdis, or both.

• Draw Odysseus and his old dog.

• Design a book jacket for *The Odyssey*.

# The Myth of Orpheus and Eurydice or Descent into the Underworld

The myth of Orpheus and Eurydice is depicted in films, paintings, dances, and an operetta. This play is based on the version by the Roman poet Ovid from his book of love story–poems, *The Metamorphosis*, written in the 8th century. According to the story, Orpheus was the greatest musician the world has ever known. His mother was Calliope, muse of the beautiful voice, and his father, Apollo, god of music and light. Orpheus played his lyre so wonderfully that people, animals, and even the brooks and trees were entranced. His music so enchanted the wood nymph Eurydice that she danced to Orpheus, and soon they were to be married. However, on their wedding day, Hymen, the marriage god, could not light the wedding torch (a very bad omen) and the following day, Eurydice was bitten by a snake and taken by Hermes, the messenger god, to the underworld.

Orpheus could not live without Eurydice and undertook a journey to the underworld to convince King Hades to let Eurydice return to the land of the living. On his journey Orpheus met powerful obstacles. Each time he played his lyre to overcome them. First he played a boating song that enticed the cranky boatman, Charon, who ferries dead souls to the underworld. He was so taken with the music that he let Orpheus, a living person, proceed. Then, Orpheus played a lullaby and lulled the vicious, three-headed, guard dog, Cerberus; and Orpheus was able to proceed through the entrance gates to the world below.

In the underworld, he met miserable sinners condemned to eternal punishment. There was Tantalus, who boiled up his son and served him up at a banquet; Sisyphus, who defied the god Zeus; and the daughters of King Danaus, who murdered their husbands on their wedding nights.

Orpheus finally reached King Hades and his wife, Queen Persephone. Hades at first was angry that Orpheus, a living soul, had entered his underworld. But when Orpheus played his lyre, Queen Persephone wept and Hades agreed to let Eurydice go back to the land of the living, but there was one condition. Eurydice must follow Orpheus, and he must not look back at her until they both arrived in the world above. Orpheus agreed, but just as he was about to step into the land above, he looked back to make sure Eurydice was there, and Hermes led Eurydice back to the world below. Orpheus knew that now Eurydice would never join him in this world, and he died of grief. Hermes then escorted Orpheus to Eurydice in the underworld. There, Orpheus and Eurydice were united forever in the Elysian fields, a golden place of pleasure and joy where all good souls go.

**To the Teacher:** TV Interview with the Characters in *The Myth of Orpheus and Eurydice or Descent to the Underworld*

**Goal:** To introduce the characters and story of the myth through dramatization. This may also be used as a possible casting method.

**Materials:** Copy of the TV Interview for all students, or students might share copies.

**Procedure:** Explain that they will perform a TV Interview playing the characters in the myth telling their story. Read the TV Announcer's introduction in a low monotone. Ask students what was wrong with the way you read it and how you might make it more effective.

Cast the roles using the cast list. Choose students with animated, projected voices to play the TV Announcer, Orpheus, Calliope, and Apollo. They will be able to model the techniques desired and to inspire the other students in their playing. Before dramatizing, practice the pronunciation of the characters' names using the phonetic guide in the cast list.

Characters stand in front of the classroom with the TV Announcer sitting or standing to one side. Characters step forward when introduced and when speaking and step back when finished. Students might wear signs with their character names to identify them. Use a wooden spoon or a wire whisk as a microphone. There are 14 roles in the interview, so perhaps dramatize it twice to give all students a chance to participate. To further increase roles, use a different student as interviewer for each page. After dramatizing, review the characters and the events of the story.

# TV INTERVIEW

CAST OF CHARACTERS (14)

TV Announcer

Orpheus (**or** fee us)

Calliope (ka **lie** oh pee);

Apollo (a **pol** oh)

Eurydice (you **rid** i see)

Hymen (**high** men)

Hermes (**her** meez)

Charon (**ka** ron)

Cerberus (**sir** ber us)

Tantalus (**tan** ta lus)

Sisyphus (**sis** i fus)

Daughters of King Danaus (**dan** a us)

Hades (**hay** deez)

Persephone (per **sef** oh nee)

**TV ANNOUNCER:** *(Energetically.)* Today on *Meet the Myth Makers,* we interview the characters in the Greek myth of Orpheus and Eurydice, the story of a young man, Orpheus, who goes down to the underworld, the land of the dead. Orpheus, that was pretty scary thing to do. Why would you do this?

**ORPHEUS:** It began when I was a baby, and my mother Calliope gave me the gift of an extraordinary singing voice.

**TV ANNOUNCER:** Calliope, how could you GIVE your son the gift of an extraordinary singing voice?

**CALLIOPE:** I'm the muse of the beautiful voice, and my role is to inspire some people with extraordinary voices. Naturally I wanted my son, Orpheus, to have the most wonderful voice of all.

**ORPHEUS:** And my father is Apollo, god of music and light. When I was a young man, he gave me a lyre.

**APOLLO:** I gave him a lyre to strum to make his music as bright and scintillating as the sun.

**TV ANNOUNCER:** But Orpheus what does your gift of music have to do with your trip to the underworld?

**ORPHEUS:** My music got so good that people would stop whatever they were doing to listen. Men stopped digging. Women stopped gathering grapes, and children stopped skipping and tossing balls.

**CALLIOPE:** My son's music was so exciting that animals stopped their activities too and froze in their tracks to listen.

**APOLLO:** Yes, and brooks babbled happily. Oak trees wrenched themselves up by the roots. And rocks rolled over to him and hummed.

**TV ANNOUNCER:** Pretty astounding!

**ORPHEUS:** But most importantly, my music attracted the wood nymph Eurydice to me.

**TV ANNOUNCER:** Eurydice, how did Orpheus's music affect you?

**EURYDICE:** One day, I was dancing among the trees when I heard the most magical music, and I danced toward it. From then on, I always followed Orpheus and his music wherever he went.

**ORPHEUS:** The day I saw Eurydice I knew we belonged together.

**TV ANNOUNCER:** So you got married?

**EURYDICE:** We planned a wonderful wedding, and we invited Hymen, the god of marriage to perform the ceremony.

**TV ANNOUNCER:** Hymen, was it a wonderful wedding?

**HYMEN:** NO. I thought it would be. But for some reason, I could not smile or bless the wedding, and the flame of my wedding torch would not light.

**TV ANNOUNCER:** That sounds as if there's a disaster in the wind.

**EURYDICE:** Yes. The next day while I was skipping through the forest a vicious serpent bit my ankle. I died to this world, the land of the living, and was taken to live in the world of the dead.

**TV ANNOUNCER:** Hermes, you are the messenger god, who escorts dead souls to the underworld.

**HERMES:** Yes, and I gently closed Eurydice's eyes and took her to the Elysian fields, the place in the underworld where the good and virtuous people go.

**TV ANNOUNCER:** Orpheus, what was your reaction to the death of your bride?

**ORPHEUS:** This was the most painful thing that could happen. It seemed impossible that such a gentle and innocent person as Eurydice should be taken at so young an age to the land of the dead. I put down my lyre. I was unable to make music anymore.

**TV ANNOUNCER:** What did you do to cope with your profound loss?

**ORPHEUS:** I decided to do what NO person had ever done before. I decided to go down to the land of the dead and beg King Hades to let me bring my bride back to the land of the living.

**TV ANNOUNCER:** How did you find your way down there?

**ORPHEUS:** The trees pointed the way—first down a cave that goes to the River Styx that divides the land of the living from the land of the dead. There I met Charon the boatman.

**TV ANNOUNCER:** Charon, you only ferry dead souls across the River Styx to the underworld. Why did you let Orpheus, a living soul, go across in your boat?

**CHARON:** At first I refused. Orpheus CERTAINLY was NOT DEAD, and he did not have the required coin under his tongue to pay me for the trip. But then he picked up his lyre and played the most magical boating song, and I told him to jump in the boat and took him immediately across.

**TV ANNOUNCER:** Orpheus, did that get you to the land of the dead?

**ORPHEUS:** First I had to get past Cerberus, the vicious, three-headed dog, who guards the entrance gate to the underworld.

**TV ANNOUNCER:** Cerberus, tell us about it.

**CERBERUS:** When I saw Orpheus, I gnashed every tooth in my three heads. I bared my claws and growled fiercely. I was just about to tear him apart, when suddenly he played the most soothing lullaby. I was transfixed and fell asleep immediately.

The Myth of Orpheus and Eurydice or Descent into the Underworld

**TV ANNOUNCER:** Orpheus, did you meet any more big obstacles on your way to find King Hades?

**ORPHEUS:** On the journey through Tartarus, the darkest pit of the underworld, where the most evil souls reside, I met the most miserable sinners imaginable. First there was Tantalus.

**TV ANNOUNCER:** Tantalus, what was your sin?

**TANTALUS:** I wanted to impress the gods, and so I invited all of the gods to dine with me. Then, I boiled parts of my son and served them at the meal.

**TV ANNOUNCER:** Horrible! Tantalus, what was your punishment?

**TANTALUS:** I'm condemned to be continually tantalized by extreme hunger and thirst. I stand in a pool of water. Above me is a vine with juicy grapes. I'm dying of hunger and dying of thirst, but every time I lean over to drink some water, the pool recedes. Each time I reach to grasp the grapes, the vine jumps away.

**TV ANNOUNCER:** Orpheus, who else did you pass?

**ORPHEUS:** The next sinner was Sisyphus.

**TV ANNOUNCER:** Sisyphus, what was your crime?

**SISYPHUS:** I deceived Zeus, the king of the gods, by telling one of his secrets.

**TV ANNOUNCER:** And your punishment?

**SISYPHUS:** I must roll a huge boulder up a hill only to have it roll right down again— and I must do this forever and ever without ever stopping.

**TV ANNOUNCER:** Were there any more sinners?

**ORPHEUS:** The last were the depressed daughters of King Danaus.

**TV ANNOUNCER:** Eldest daughter of King Danaus, what did you and your sisters do?

**ELDEST DAUGHTER:** We each killed our husbands on our wedding nights, and our punishment is to carry water in containers that have no bottoms.

**ORPHEUS:** At last I arrived at the throne of Hades, king and god of the underworld, and his wife, Queen Persephone. I begged Hades to let me bring my wife, Eurydice, back to the world of the living.

**TV ANNOUNCER:** Hades, how did you respond?

**HADES:** At first I refused adamantly. NO dead person had ever been allowed to return to the land of the living, but then Orpheus played the most lyrical love song on his lyre.

**PERSEPHONE:** I wept and begged my husband to let Eurydice return to the world above with her husband, Orpheus, and Hades changed his mind.

**HADES:** Yes, the music and the tears of my wife moved me. I told Orpheus that Eurydice could return with him to the land of the living. But she must follow behind him, and he must NOT turn and look at her until they BOTH reached the world above.

**ORPHEUS:** It seemed an easy thing to do.

**TV ANNOUNCER:** Was it easy?

**ORPHEUS:** At first, I was confident that Eurydice was following me. But just as I stepped into the land of the living, I wanted to make sure she was there. I turned for one look, but it was too early, and she slipped away and vanished from me.

**EURYDICE:** I felt as if I was being pulled back by a hundred hands, and all I could say was, "Farewell."

**ORPHEUS:** I was now sadder than I'd ever been before. I tried to return to the land of the dead to get Eurydice, but I could not. I laid aside my lyre forever. I put my head down and died in hope of reuniting with my bride in the land of the dead.

**HERMES:** Now that Orpheus was dead, I closed his eyes and escorted him to his bride in the Elysian fields. There they were reunited.

**TV ANNOUNCER:** That was quite a story. At last the couple were able to be together in the Elysian fields where the good and virtuous dead souls live in joy and harmony forever more.

# ACTING EXERCISES

Use the following exercises to involve all students in dramatizing and to let every-one experience playing all of the characters. The exercises also develop stage speech and acting skills.

## *Developing Effective Stage Speech Using the Script*

**Goal:** To develop stage-speaking skills and to prepare to act the script.

**Procedure:** First, discuss and practice the four stage-speaking skills. (See chapter 1, "The Four Stage-speaking Principles.") Then, recite each line of the following introduction modeling the good speaking skills and using gestures. Next have the students recite it with you. (This is a good vocal warm-up to use before any rehearsal or recite opening dialogue from the scene you are rehearsing.)

> *(Waving and very energetically.)* Good morning students, adults too.

> *(Pointing on "you.")* Today we'll act a myth for you.

> *(Hands go down on "old," and up on "new.")* From Greece and Rome, it's old yet new.

> *(Opening arms up and out colorfully.)* We'll make it come alive for you.

> *(Gesturing to audience.)* So watch this myth as it's unfurled

> *(Lowering arms dramatically on "underworld.")* Of Orpheus and Eurydice in the underworld.

## *Developing Majestic Bearing*

**Goal:** To use stance to convey majesty.

**Acting Principles:** Belief, Movement.

**Materials:** Drum (optional).

**Procedure:** Tell students that gods and goddesses, kings, queens, and heroes and hero-ines have a royal bearing. Explain that they sit and stand erectly with excellent posture. Model poor posture. First, slouch, then lean on one foot, shift from one foot to another, put your hands in your pockets. As you do each of these, ask "What was wrong with my posture to convey royal stance?" Finally, stand with a royal bearing.

- Then, have them do the following majestic bearing activity.

- Sit with head up, shoulders back, feet together and firmly on the ground.

- Place your hands on each side of the chair to help lift you. Then keeping head up, press hands on chair to help lift you and slowly rise.

- Walk slowly with head up, shoulders back and hands by sides perhaps to the accompaniment of steady majestic drumbeat.

- Finally, stand with feet planted firmly on the floor, hands by sides, shoulders back and head looking slightly up to the back wall of the auditorium. Lift arms up and out in a gesture showing you are ready to lead your people. Let your soul rise out of your chest.

## Becoming the Characters and Integrating Sound Effects

**Goal:** To experience the characters' actions and to coordinate acting with sound effects.

**Acting Principles:** Belief, Control, Voice, and Movement.

**Materials:** Bell; a copy of this exercise for the sound crew only and the instruments they will use in the play.

**Procedure:** Tell students they will do characters' actions from the play and speak their dialogue expressively. Tell the sound crew they will play sound effects to help the actors do their actions. All students (except the sound crew) perform the following scenarios. Read each scenario through once to familiarize students with it. Then, ring a bell. Read it again and coach them through it. All traveling actions are done in place. Girls act female roles and boys, male roles. Both act animals and inanimate object. (Perhaps dramatize ten or so of these and do the rest another day.)

- Become the goddess muse Calliope. Rock baby Orpheus rhythmically. *(SOUND CREW 2, 4, and 5 shake jingle bells.)* Then, lift him up to infuse his soul with a wonderful voice. Freeze.

- Become the sun god Apollo. Rise majestically. *(SOUND CREW 4 and 5 shakes wind chimes.)* Gesture to the sun. Hand lyre ceremoniously to Orpheus. Freeze.

- Become Orpheus. Bow in gratitude for the lyre. Sling lyre over your shoulder, strum. *(SOUND CREW 6 strums tone bells low to high.)* Freeze.

- Become People digging. *(SOUND CREW 3 strikes wood block.)* Hear Orpheus strum. *(SOUND CREW 6 strums tone bells low to high.)* Freeze.

- Become people gathering grapes. *(SOUND CREW 1, 3, 4, and 5 shake rattles.)* Hear Orpheus strum. *(SOUND CREW 6 strums tone bells low to high.)* Freeze.

- Become children skipping. *(SOUND CREW 2, 4, and 5 shake jingle bells.)* Hear Orpheus strum. *(SOUND CREW 6 strums tone bells low to high.)* Freeze.

- Become frolicking lambs. *(SOUND CREW 5 shakes wind chimes.)* Hear Orpheus strum. *(SOUND CREW 6 strums tone bells low to high.)* Freeze.

- Become prancing deer. *(SOUND CREW 3 strikes wood block.)* Hear Orpheus strum. *(SOUND CREW 6 strums tone bells low to high.)* Freeze.

- Become soaring birds. *(SOUND CREW 2, 4, and 5 shake jingle bells.)* Hear Orpheus strum. *(SOUND CREW 6 strums tone bells low to high.)* Freeze.

- Become rippling brooks. Hear Orpheus strum. *(SOUND CREW 6 strums tone bells low to high.)* Babble joyously. *(SOUND CREW 2, 4, and 5 shake jingle bells.)* Freeze.

- Become oak trees. Hear Orpheus strum. *(SOUND CREW 6 strums tone bells low to high.)* Jump and wrench up your two taproots, spin, and freeze. *(SOUND CREW 2 strikes drum twice as each taproot is wrenched and then strikes drum rapidly as trees spin.)*

- Become a huge rock. Hear Orpheus strum. *(SOUND CREW 6 strums tone bells low to high.)* HUMMMMM! harmoniously. Freeze.

- Become Eurydice. Hear Orpheus strum. *(SOUND CREW 6 strums tone bells low to high three times.)* Twirl gracefully. Freeze.

- Become Hymen. Try three times to light the wedding torch and fail. *(SOUND CREW 6 strikes guiro three times.)* Frown and freeze.

- Become the slithering serpent. *(SOUND CREW 6 strikes guiro three times.)* HISSSS venomously. Strike with your fangs. Freeze.

- Become Eurydice. Feel the fangs of the snake bite your ankle. *(SOUND CREW 6 strikes guiro three times.)* Sink slowly to the ground to a count of five. *(SOUND CREW 3 strikes wood block five times.)* Say, "Oh no," and die. Freeze.

- Become Hermes. Fly "in place" on winged feet to Eurydice. *(SOUND CREW 2, 4, and 5 shake jingle bells.)* Motion Eurydice to rise. Reach forward to lead her to the underworld. Freeze.

- Become swirling mist. Swirl slowly to a count of five. *(SOUND CREW 5 shakes wind chimes.)* Freeze.

- Become Orpheus. See Eurydice disappear into the underworld. *(SOUND CREW 1 strikes triangle.)* Look desperately, for her. Freeze.

- Become trees pointing with branches to the underworld five times, to help Orpheus find the entrance. *(SOUND CREW 3 strikes wood block five times.)* Freeze.

- Become Charon. Pole your boat. *(SOUND CREW 2 strikes drum five times.)* Freeze. Scowl and shake a fist at Orpheus. Look to see if he has a coin under his tongue to pay his fare. Freeze.

- Use your hands and head to become the three-headed dog, Cerberus, growling to protect your gates. Reach out a paw in attack. *(SOUND CREW 5 strikes guiro.)* Freeze.

- Become juicy grapes on a vine. See Tantalus reach to grasp you. Jump away. *(SOUND CREW 1 strikes triangle rapidly.)* Freeze.

- Become Tantalus dying of thirst. Lean forward to lap water from a pool. See the pool move away. *(SOUND CREW 2, 4, and 5 shake jingle bells.)* Freeze. Say, "I am SO thirsty."

- Become Sisyphus straining to push a huge boulder up a hill. *(SOUND CREW 2 strikes drum.)* Watch it roll down. *(SOUND CREW 2 strikes drum rapidly.)* Shake head and say, "Not AGAIN!" Freeze.

- Become one of the depressed daughters of King Danaus. Droop drearily. Watch the water in your container run through the bottom again. Freeze. Sigh, shake your head and say, drearily, "Oh no, oh woe." *(SOUND CREW 6 strikes two low notes after "Oh no" and "Oh, woe.")*

- Become King Hades. Rise majestically from your throne to take command. *(SOUND CREW 2 strikes drum three times.)* Look sternly at Orpheus. Freeze.

- Become Orpheus. Bow graciously to King Hades and Queen Persephone. Strum your lyre three times to persuade Hades to help you. *(SOUND CREW 6 strums tone bells low to high three times.)* Freeze.

- Become Persephone. Bow your head in grief at Orpheus's beautiful sad song. *(SOUND CREW 6 strums tone bells low to high three times.)* Freeze.

- Become Eurydice. Limp because of the painful snake-bite wound. *(SOUND CREW 2 strikes wood block three times.)* Freeze.

- Become Orpheus at the entrance to the cave. Turn and look back for Eurydice. *(SOUND CREW 1 strikes triangle on "turned.")* Freeze. See her disappear. Call, "Eurydice!"

The Myth of Orpheus and Eurydice or Descent into the Underworld  213

- Become Eurydice at the cave entrance as Hermes is about to lead you back to the underworld. Call, "Farewell." *(SOUND CREW 2, 4, and 5 shake jingle bells.)* Freeze.

- Become Orpheus strumming his lyre or Eurydice dancing, in their scene of joyful reuniting in the Elysian fields. *(SOUND CREW 6 strums tone bells low to high three times.)* Freeze.

# THE MYTH OF ORPHEUS AND EURYDICE or
# DESCENT INTO THE UNDERWORLD
Adapted from a version by Ovid by Louise Thistle

CAST OF CHARACTERS (In order of appearance.)

CHORUS 1 Leader, very responsible, strong voice

CHORUS 2, 3, 4 Strong voices, ability to follow and pick up cues

CALLIOPE (ka **lie** oh pee) Elegant, majestic

APOLLO (a **pol** lo) Forceful, majestic

ORPHEUS (**or** fee us) Romantic hero; leading role; strong voice; requires line memorization

PEOPLE AND CHILDREN (as many as desired)

LAMBS (1 or as many as desired)

DEER (1 or as many as desired)

BIRDS (2 or as many as desired)

TREES (3 or 4)

WILLOW TREE

BROOK (2)

ROCKS (3 or 4)

EURYDICE (you **rid** i see) Graceful, spirited; leading role; some line memorization

HYMEN (**high** men) Dignified

WEDDING GUESTS also play SOULS IN ELYSIAN (e **leez** i an ) FIELDS (as many as desired)

RED BIRD

SERPENT (venomous)

HERMES (**her** meez) Agile

MIST (2 or 3)

CAVE (2)

CHARON (**ka** ron) Old, cranky

RIVER STYX (sticks) (2)

CERBERUS (**sir** ber us) Vicious

ENTRANCE GATES (2)

BLACK VAPORS (3)

TANTALUS (**tan** ta lus) Famished and thirsty

POOL (2)

DANGLING GRAPES (2)

SISYPHUS (**sis** i fus) Weary, over-burdened

SISYPHUS'S BOULDER

DAUGHTERS OF KING DANAUS (**dan** a us) (3) Depressed

DAUGHTERS' POOL (2)

SHIMMERING GOLD (2 to 4)

PROPS (2)

PERSEPHONE (per **sef** oh nee) Kind, majestic

HADES ( **hay** deez) Powerful, strong, assertive

LYRE

*Sound Crew*

| | |
|---|---|
| SOUND CREW 1 | triangle, rattle, jingle bells |
| SOUND CREW 2 | jingle bells, drum, |
| SOUND CREW 3 | wood block, rattle |
| SOUND CREW 4 | tambourine, wind chimes, jingle bells, rattle |
| SOUND CREW 5 | wind chimes, handbell, gong, guiro, jingle bells, rattles |
| SOUND CREW 6 | tone bells, handbell |

## Basic Stage Setup

The actors sit in chairs arranged in a semicircle in view of the audience. Two Chorus members stand on each side of the stage. Costumes and props are stored under the actors' chairs. The Chorus and characters wearing tunics throughout the play wear their tunics.

The Sound Crew sits with instruments on a table or two to the right or left of the stage area and in view of the audience. Tables are set so that the crew can see the stage action.

## Stage Setup

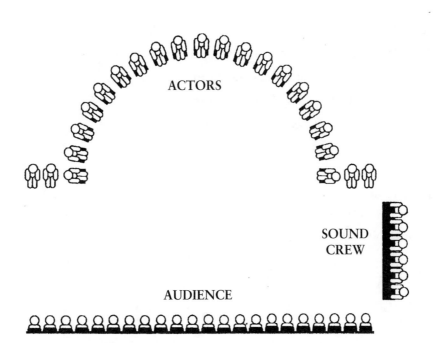

ACTORS

SOUND
CREW

AUDIENCE

*The play might begin with a Greek dance. See chapter 5 for dance instructions and music suggestions.*

# PROLOGUE

> *(SOUND CREW 1 strikes triangle three times slowly to signal the play will begin.)*

**CHORUS 1:** *(Very energetically.)* Welcome audience, and yas sas or to your health too.

> *("Yas sas" is Greek for "to your health" and is used for both "hello" and "good-bye.")*

**CHORUS 2:** *(Pointing on "you.")* Today we'll act a myth for you.

**CHORUS 3:** *(Raising hands up on "new.")* From Greece and Rome, it's old yet new

**CHORUS 4:** *(Opening arms up and out colorfully.)* We'll make it come alive for you.

**CHORUS 1:** *(Gesturing to audience.)* So watch our myth as it's unfurled

**CHORUS 2:** Of Orpheus and Eurydice in the underworld.

**CHORUS 3:** *The Myth of Orpheus and Eurydice*

> *(SOUND CREW 1 strikes triangle.)*

**CHORUS 4:** Or *The Descent to the Underworld*

> *(SOUND CREW 1 strikes triangle.)*

**CHORUS 1:** An ancient Greek myth based on a version by the Roman poet Ovid from the 8th century A.D.

> *(SOUND CREW 1 strikes triangle.)*

# SCENE ONE:
## *The Birth of Orpheus and His Musical Gifts*

> *Characters:* Chorus, Calliope, Apollo, Orpheus, Men, Women, Children, Lamb, Deer, Birds, Brook, Trees, Rocks

**CHORUS 2:** Orpheus was the most magical musician the world has ever known.

**CHORUS 3:** His mother was Calliope, muse of the beautiful voice.

> *(SOUND CREW 1 strikes triangle to accompany CALLIOPE walking majestically center.)*

**CALLIOPE:** I make the world rejoice *(Lifting arms up.)* with a beautiful voice.

> *(SOUND CREW 1 strikes triangle three times.)*

**CHORUS 4:** Naturally, Calliope wanted her son, Orpheus, to have the most wonderful voice of all. So, when Orpheus was a baby, she rocked him rhythmically.

*(PROP PERSON hands blanket bundled like a baby to CALLIOPE who rocks him as SOUND CREW 2, 4, and 5 shake jingle bells.)*

**CHORUS 1:** She lifted him up and spoke these words to infuse his soul with a beautiful voice.

*(SOUND CREW 1 strikes triangle three times as CALLIOPE slowly lifts BABY.)*

**CALLIOPE:** *(Inspiringly.)* Orpheus, my son,

> May your voice be the one
>
> That enchants every soul,
>
> And makes your life whole.

*(PROP PERSON takes baby from CALLIOPE.)*

**CHORUS 2:** Orpheus's father was Apollo, god of light and music.

*(SOUND CREW 4 and 5 shake wind chimes and SOUND CREW 6 shakes hand bell as APOLLO wearing lyre over shoulder strides regally next to CALLIOPE.)*

**APOLLO:** *(Dramatically gesturing to the sun.)* I make the world bright with music and light.

*(SOUND CREW 4 and 5 shake wind chimes and SOUND CREW 2 shakes jingle bells.)*

**CHORUS 3:** When Orpheus was a young man, Apollo gave his son a lyre.

*(SOUND CREW 1 strikes triangle three times.)*

**APOLLO:** *(Taking off lyre and showing it to ORPEHUS.)* I give you this lyre my son. Play it with your whole heart and soul.

> And create words for your songs.
>
> *(Shaking head.)* Never ponderous or long.
>
> But quick, light and free
>
> And always sprightly.

**CHORUS 4:** Orpheus thanked his mother and father for their gifts of music.

**ORPHEUS:** Thank you mother and father for bestowing on me

> Your great gifts of music and bright poetry.

*(ORPHEUS slings lyre over shoulder.)*

**CHORUS 1:** Apollo and Calliope touched Orpheus gently on the shoulders and told him they would always be with him and his music.

**APOLLO:** *(Touching ORPHEUS on one shoulder.)* We will always be with you

*(SOUND CREW 1 strikes triangle as APOLLO touches ORPHEUS on one shoulder.)*

**CALLIOPE:** *(Touching ORPHEUS on other shoulder.)* and your music.

*(SOUND CREW 1 strikes triangle as CALLIOPE touches ORPHEUS on other shoulder. APOLLO and CALLIOPE regally return to their chairs.)*

The Myth of Orpheus and Eurydice or Descent into the Underworld 219

**CHORUS 2:** Orpheus loved strumming his lyre and creating poetry.

(*ORPHEUS mimes strumming as SOUND CREW 6 sweeps tone bells three times.*)

**CHORUS 3:** He practiced and practiced and played and played. So, Orpheus became the most magical musician that the world has ever known.

**CHORUS 4:** People stopped whatever they were doing to listen. Men stopped digging.

(*SOUND CREW 3 strikes wood block three times as MEN stand, step forward, and dig three times. SOUND CREW 6 sweeps tone bells as ORPHEUS strums. MEN freeze).*

**CHORUS 1:** Women stopped gathering grapes.

(*SOUND CREW 1, 4, and 5 shake rattles as WOMEN stand, reach for three bunches of grapes—one after the other. SOUND CREW 6 sweeps tone bells as ORPHEUS strums. WOMEN freeze.*)

**CHORUS 2:** Children stopped skipping.

(*SOUND CREW 1, 2, and 5 shake jingle bells as CHILDREN make three skips. SOUND CREW 6 sweeps tone bells as ORPHEUS strums. CHILDREN freeze. ALL PEOPLE return to chairs.*)

**CHORUS 3:** Animals stopped their activities too. Lambs stopped frolicking.

(*SOUND CREW 4 and 5 shake wind chimes as LAMB makes three skips. SOUND CREW 6 strums tone bells as ORPHEUS strums. LAMB freezes.*)

**CHORUS 4:** Deer stopped prancing.

(*SOUND CREW 5 strikes wood block three times as DEER prances three times. SOUND CREW 6 strums tone bells as ORPHEUS strums. DEER freezes.*)

**CHORUS 1:** Birds stopped soaring, and cocked their heads.

(*SOUND CREW 1, 2, and 4 shake jingle bells as BIRDS fly and flap wings three times. SOUND CREW 6 sweeps tone bells as ORPHEUS strums. BIRDS freeze with cocked heads listening. LAMB, DEER, and BIRDS return to their chairs.*)

**CHORUS 2:** Nature responded musically too. Brooks babbled lyrically.

(*ORPHEUS strums. SOUND CREW 6 sweeps tone bells. BROOK ripples fabric and "babbles" slowly for count of three and SOUND CREW 1, 2, and 4 shake jingle bells. BROOK freezes.*)

**CHORUS 3:** Trees wrenched themselves up by their roots and spun into a circle around Orpheus.

(*ORPHEUS strums. SOUND CREW 6 sweeps tone bells. SOUND CREW 2 strikes drum lightly but emphatically as TREES jump up wrenching one then another taproot. Then SOUND CREW 2 strikes drum lightly and rapidly as TREES spin into a circle around ORPHEUS and freeze*)

**CHORUS 4:** Rocks hummed harmoniously.

(*ORPHEUS strums. SOUND CREW 6 sweeps tone bells.*)

**ROCKS:** *(Loudly and deeply.)* HUMMMMM.

> *(ROCKS and actors in chairs: HUMMMMM.)*

> *(BROOK and ROCKS return to chairs. TREES remain on stage. )*

# SCENE TWO
## *The Meeting and Marriage of Orpheus and Eurydice*

> *Characters:* Chorus, Orpheus, Eurydice, Wedding Guests, Hymen

**CHORUS 4:** The day Orpheus saw the wood nymph, Eurydice, dancing among the trees his music became more magical than ever.

> *(ORPHEUS strums. SOUND CREW 6 sweeps tone bells slowly three times as EURYDICE skips and dances around TREES.)*

**CHORUS 1:** Eurydice felt the power of Orpheus's music and danced toward it.

> *(ORPHEUS strums. SOUND CREW 6 sweeps tone bells several times as EURYDICE continues to dance.)*

**EURYDICE:** *(Joyfully.)* Your music enchants me.

> It sets my heart free.
>
> Your music inspires me
>
> And makes me happy!

**CHORUS 2:** From that day on, Eurydice and Orpheus were never apart.

**ORPHEUS:** *(Strumming.)* My music—

> *(SOUND CREW 6 sweeps tone bells.)*

**EURYDICE:** *(Spinning.)* And my dancing—

**ORPHEUS and EURYDICE:** were in complete harmony.

> *(ORPHEUS strums. SOUND CREW 6 sweeps tone bells as ORPHEUS strums and bows low, and EURYDICE spins and curtsies.)*

**CHORUS 3:** They planned a wedding of wondrous delight.

**ORPHEUS:** *(Excitedly.)* Let's make our wedding a wondrous delight.

**EURYDICE:** *(More excitedly.)* We'll invite all our friends and dance through the night.

**CHORUS 4:** Guests came early to the wedding and danced around the couple to celebrate the event.

> *(SOUND CREW 1 plays taped music and guests dance to Greek dance. See chapter 5 for suggested dance and music.)*

**CHORUS 1:** They invited Hymen, the god of marriage, to perform the ceremony.

> *(SOUND CREW 2 strikes drum ceremoniously as HYMEN carrying wedding torch walks with dignified authority center stage.)*

**ORPHEUS:** *(Bowing head.)* Hymen, please perform our wedding rite.

**EURYDICE:** And make it shine with your radiant light.

**HYMEN:** *(Enthusiastically.)* Yes, I'll perform your wedding rite and will make it shine with my radiant light.

**CHORUS 2:** But when Hymen tried to light his wedding torch it would not burn.

> *(SOUND CREW 5 scrapes guiro three times as HYMEN frowning is unable to light torch.)*

**HYMEN:** *(Frowning.)* What's the matter?

> Where's the blame?

> My wedding torch will not take flame.

**CHORUS 3:** The people gasped knowing something was wrong.

> *(PEOPLE lean forward in chairs and gasp.)*

**CHORUS 4:** Hymen left the ceremony quickly.

> *(SOUND CREW 3 strikes wood block to accompany quick departure.)*

**ORPHEUS:** This seems to be a very bad sign

**EURYDICE:** I'm sure everything soon will be fine.

# SCENE THREE
## *The Death of Eurydice*

> *Characters:* Chorus, Eurydice, Orpheus, Bird, Snake, Mist, Hermes

**CHORUS 1:** But the next day while Eurydice was skipping through the grass on light feet, she paused to listen to a bird.

> *(SOUND CREW 1, 2, and 4 shake jingle bells as TREE and BIRD form. SOUND CREW whistles. EURYDICE skips and then freezes listening. ORPHEUS observes from a distance.)*

**EURYDICE:** Listen to that bird.

**CHORUS 2:** A venomous snake hissed and slithered toward Eurydice.

**SNAKE:** *(Slithering toward Eurydice.)* HISSSSSSSSSS!

> *(SOUND CREW 5 scrapes guiro as SNAKE hisses and slithers. TREE and BIRD return to chair.)*

**CHORUS 3:** The snake sank its fangs into her ankle.

> *(SOUND CREW 5 scrapes guiro three times harshly as SNAKE sinks fangs into EURYDICE'S ankle. EURYDICE grasps ankle.)*

**EURYDICE:** *(Grasping ankle and sinking slowly.)* Orpheus, my husband.

> Oh no, oh no.

> From this world I now must go.

**CHORUS 4:** Eurydice DIED of this world.

*(SOUND CREW 3 strikes five soft slow wood blocks as EURYDICE sinks slowly to ground.)*

**ORPHEUS:** *(Desperately.)* Oh great misery. This just cannot be!

**CHORUS 1:** Mists swirled around Eurydice.

*(SOUND CREW 4 and 5 shake wind chimes to a slow count of five as MIST places white nylon netting over EURYDICE. MIST return to their chairs.)*

**CHORUS 2:** Hermes, the winged messenger god who delivers souls to the land of the dead, flew to Eurydice and magically motioned her to rise.

*(SOUND CREW 1, 2, and 5 shake jingle bells as HERMES flies to EURYDICE.)*

**HERMES:** *(Slowly gesturing Eurydice to rise.)* In this world you cannot stay.

I will lead you now away.

But do not fear. Do not dread.

As I guide you gently to the land of the dead.

**CHORUS 3:** Hermes led Eurydice through a cave down to the underworld.

*(CAVE forms. SOUND CREW 1, 2, and 5 shake jingle bells as HERMES leads EURYDICE through CAVE entrance. CAVE and HERMES return to their chairs.)*

# SCENE FOUR
## Descent into the Underworld

*Characters:* Chorus, Orpheus, Tree, River Styx, Charon, Cerberus

**ORPHEUS:** *(Calling frantically.)* Eurydice. Eurydice. Oh, no. Oh, no. From this world you CANNOT go.

**CHORUS 1:** But Eurydice had vanished.

*(SOUND CREW 2 strikes drum once firmly on "vanished." EURYDICE and CAVE return to chairs.)*

**CHORUS 2:** With bowed head, Orpheus wandered to a tree. He laid aside his lyre.

*(SOUND CREW 3 strikes wood block as one TREE goes center and ORPHEUS walks to it and hangs lyre on TREE—perhaps on the hand, or if the lyre is light enough on the thumb, of TREE ACTOR.)*

**ORPHEUS:** *(Sitting despondently under TREE.)* I have no desire to play. My gift of music has gone away.

**CHORUS 3:** But then, the leaves of the tree shimmered as if dropping tears to soothe him.

*(SOUND CREW 4 shakes tambourine lightly as TREE shakes branches lightly.)*

**CHORUS 4:** He knew what he must do.

**ORPHEUS:** *(Rising and assertively.)* I must DO what all men dread.

> I must go below to the land of the dead.
>
> And beg King Hades my wife to set free.
>
> *(Touching heart.)* And so to relieve my great misery.

**CHORUS 1:** The journey gave Orpheus hope. He wanted to play his lyre.

**ORPHEUS:** *(Taking lyre off tree branch and say affirmatively.)* My lyre now I want to play.

> *(Strumming lyre.)* My gift of music has NOT gone away.
>
> *(SOUND CREW 6 sweeps tone bells as ORPHEUS strums.)*

**CHORUS 2:** The tree pointed to the cave to the underworld.

> *(SOUND CREW 3 strikes wood block five times as TREE points and CAVE forms.)*

**CHORUS 3:** Orpheus went through the cave toward the land of the dead.

> *(SOUND CREW 3 strikes wood block for walking.)*

**CHORUS 4:** *(Gesturing toward STYX as it forms.)* He reached the River Styx that separates the land of the living from the land of the dead.

> *(SOUND CREW 6 strikes four low tone bell keys continually and slowly to create ominous underworld effect as RIVER STYX forms downstage holding fabric vertically taut so that CHARON can mime ferrying behind it.)*

**CHORUS 1:** The cranky boatman Charon who ferries dead souls into the underworld came poling along.

> *(SOUND CREW 2 strikes drum imitating poling strokes as CHARON poles from behind fabric going from stage left to stage right where ORPHEUS waits.)*

**CHORUS 2:** Charon scowled and shook a fist at Orpheus suspecting that he was not dead. Charon demanded that Orpheus lift up his tongue and show him his coin to pay for the boat ride.

**CHARON:** *(Aggressively, pointing at ORPHEUS.)* Lift up your tongue. Let me see the coin to pay for your boat ride.

**CHORUS 3:** Orpheus begged Charon to let him in the boat with no coin so he could go to the land of the dead to retrieve Eurydice.

**ORPHEUS:** *(Pleading.)* Please, Charon I have no coin with which to pay

> But I MUST go to King Hades with no delay.
>
> My wife Eurydice he MUST set free.
>
> And so relieve my great misery.

**CHORUS 4:** Charon put up a hand motioning him to go away.

**CHARON:** *(Angrily.)* GO AWAY! Only DEAD souls are allowed on my boat.

**CHORUS 1:** Then, Orpheus picked up his lyre and played a magical boating song.

**ORPHEUS:** *(Lullingly.)* The waters are lulling. Tiny wavelets they toss.

*(SOUND CREW 6 sweeps tone bells.)*

**CHORUS 2:** Charon stared enchanted by the song. He beckoned Orpheus into the boat.

**CHARON:** *(Trancelike.)* Get in the boat, Orpheus. I will ferry you across.

*(ORPHEUS steps in boat. CHARON poles the boat with ORPHEUS now also behind the fabric going from stage right back to stage left. ORPHEUS strums and SOUND CREW 6 sweeps tone bells.)*

**ORPHEUS:** The waters are lulling. Tiny wavelets they toss.

*(SOUND CREW 6 sweeps tone bells.)*

**ORPHEUS:** As Charon the boatman, takes Orpheus across.

*(SOUND CREW 6 sweeps tone bells.)*

**CHORUS 3:** They arrived at the entrance gate to the world of the dead.

*(SOUND CREW 5 strikes gong twice—as each side of ENTRANCE GATE raises an arm to create sides of the gate.)*

**CHORUS 4:** Orpheus stepped off the boat. From the shadows lunged the three-headed, guard dog, Cerberus.

*(ORPHEUS steps off. CHARON and RIVER return to chairs. SOUND CREW 4 shakes tambourine vigorously and slaps in center as THE THREE HEADS OF CERBERUS—creating one body and showing a paw on each end with other hands behind back—lunges forward, bearing teeth and snarling.)*

**CHORUS 1:** Each of Cerberus's three heads growled fiercely.

**HEAD 1:** *(Loudly.)* **Growl.**

*(SOUND CREW 5 scrapes guiro.)*

**HEAD 2:** *(Louder.)* **Growl.**

*(SOUND CREW 5 scrapes guiro more intensely.)*

**HEAD 3:** *(Loudest.)* **Growl.**

*(SOUND CREW 5 scrapes guiro most intensely.)*

**CHORUS 2:** Each head snarled viciously.

**HEAD 1:** *(Loudly.)* **Snarl.**

*(SOUND CREW 6 scrapes guiro as HEAD 1 raises paw in attack.)*

**HEAD 2:** *(Louder.)* **Snarl!**

*(SOUND CREW 5 scrapes guiro more vigorously).*

**HEAD 3:** *(Loudest.)* **Snarl!**

*(SOUND CREW 5 scrapes guiro most vigorously as HEAD 3 raises other paw in attack.)*

**CHORUS 3:** Cerberus got ready to pounce and tear Orpheus apart. But Orpheus played a lilting lullaby.

*(CERBERUS pulls back to pounce, all heads snarling together and then freezes.)*

ORPHEUS: *(Smiling.)* The doggie's so gentle. The doggie's so sweet.

When I strum my lyre, he drops at my feet.

*(SOUND CREW 6 sweeps tone bells up and down.)*

CHORUS 4: Cerberus sighed and curled up at Orpheus's feet.

ALL HEADS: *(Smiling.)* S————-I————G————-H!

CHORUS 1: Orpheus opened the gate and continued down the path toward King Hades.

*(SOUND CREW 5 strikes gong twice—once for each side of the GATE opening. CERBERUS and GATE return to chairs.)*

# SCENE FIVE
## *Tartarus and Its Sinners*

*Characters:* Chorus, Vapors, Tantalus, Pools, Sisyphus, Boulder, and the Daughters of King Danaus

CHORUS 2: Suddenly the air was filled with mournful moans. Black vapors swirled.

*(ACTORS IN CHAIRS moan. SOUND CREW 4 shakes tambourine vigorously as VAPORS take different stage areas and swirl up, down, and all around creating a mysterious menace. Take time for this effect. Finally, SOUND CREW 4 strikes tambourine emphatically in the center. VAPORS freeze and return to chairs.)*

CHORUS 3: Orpheus was in Tartarus where dwell the most evil souls of the underworld.

CHORUS 4: The first sinner he saw was Tantalus standing in a rippling pool of water.

*(SOUND CREW 2, 4, and 5 shake jingle bells as TANTALUS comes center and stands behind POOL who kneel, ripple, and freeze.)*

CHORUS 1: Above Tantalus's head dangled succulent grapes.

*(SOUND CREW 1 strikes triangle three times as GRAPES form on each side of TANTALUS and wiggle fingers creating grapes above his head. Grapes freeze.)*

CHORUS 2: Tantalus was always hungry and thirsty. But every time Tantalus leaned over to drink from the pool, the water receded.

*(TANTALUS leans forward to drink. SOUND CREW 2, 4, and 5 shake jingle bells as POOL moves away.)*

CHORUS 3: And when Tantalus reached to grasp grapes, the vine jumped away.

*(TANTALUS reaches up. SOUND CREW 1 strikes triangle rapidly as GRAPES put arms behind back as TANTALUS tries to grasp them.)*

CHORUS 4: Tormented Tantalus told this tirade.

TANTALUS: I am so hungry.

> (SOUND CREW 3 and 5 shake rattles as TANTALUS reaches again for GRAPES that move away.)

TANTALUS: I am so thirsty.

> (SOUND CREW 1, 2, and 4 shake jingle bells as TANTALUS leans to drink and POOL recedes).

TANTALUS: I am so hungry.

> (SOUND CREW 3 and 5 shake rattles as TANTALUS reaches again for GRAPES that move away.)

TANTALUS: I am so thirsty.

> (SOUND CREW 1, 2, and 4 shake jingle bells as TANTALUS leans to drink and POOL recedes.)

CHORUS 1: Orpheus asked Tantalus his crime.

ORPHEUS: I don't have much time. But what was your crime?

TANTALUS: (Chanting heavily.) I invited the gods to dine.

> (SOUND CREW 3 strikes wood block.)

TANTALUS: I wanted to make a meal sublime.

> (SOUND CREW 3 strikes wood block.)

TANTALUS: I boiled up parts of my son.

> (SOUND CREW 3 strikes wood block.)

TANTALUS: And served them to eat, just for the fun.

> (SOUND CREW 3 strikes wood block.)

TANTALUS: Now, the gods have made me a fool.

> (SOUND CREW 3 strikes wood block.)

TANTALUS: All day I stand in this pool

> (SOUND CREW 1, 2, and 4 shake jingle bells.)

TANTALUS: I'm dying of hunger.

> (SOUND CREW 3 and 5 shake rattles as TANTALUS reaches to grasp. GRAPES move arms away.)

TANTALUS: I'm dying of thirst.

> (SOUND CREW 1, 2, and 4 shake jingle bells as TANTALUS leans over for water and POOL moves away.)

TANTALUS: I get no RELIEF, what can be WORSE!

> (SOUND CREW 3 strikes wood block twice. POOL and GRAPES return to their chairs.)

CHORUS 2: Tantalus withdrew licking his lips and rubbing his belly and reciting his tortured tirade.

TANTALUS: (Returning to chair.) I am so hungry.

The Myth of Orpheus and Eurydice or Descent into the Underworld 229

*(SOUND CREW 3 and 5 shake rattles.)*

**TANTALUS:** I am so thirsty.

*(SOUND CREW 1, 2, and 4 shake jingle bells.)*

**TANTALUS:** I am so hungry.

*(SOUND CREW 3 and 5 shake rattles.)*

**TANTALUS:** I am so thirsty.

*(SOUND CREW 1, 2, and 4 shake jingle bells.)*

**CHORUS 3:** The next sinner who stumbled into view was Sisyphus struggling with a huge boulder.

*(SOUND CREW 2 strikes slow steady drum beat as SISYPHUS pants and strains, pushing BOULDER ACTOR stooped over creating BOULDER shape, downstage to upstage.)*

**CHORUS 4:** Orpheus stared at Sisyphus and asked him his crime.

**ORPHEUS:** I don't have much time. But what was your crime?

**SISYPHUS:** *(Heavily, powerfully.)* I deceived the great god Zeus.

*(SOUND CREW 2 strikes large drum.)*

**SISYPHUS:** *(Gesturing to BOULDER.)* And from THIS TASK I can't get loose.

*(SOUND CREW 2 strikes drum.)*

**SISYPHUS:** *(Pointing at boulder.)* I must roll this boulder up a hill.

*(SOUND CREW 2 strikes drum as SISYPHUS pushes BOULDER upstage. BOULDER stoops as low as possible, and as he or she rolls in spinning fashion upstage, rises slowly to give the effect of going uphill.)*

**SISYPHUS:** I must roll it NOW against my will.

*(SOUND CREW 2 strikes drum.)*

**SISYPHUS:** *(Pointing up.)* But when I get it to the top,

*(SOUND CREW 2 strikes drum.)*

**SISYPHUS:** It rolls back down and will not stop.

*(SOUND CREW 2 strikes drum rapidly as BOULDER standing spins from upstage to stooped low position as it spins downstage.)*

**SISYPHUS:** *(Gesturing wearily.)* I must do this on and on.

*(SOUND CREW 2 strikes drum.)*

**SISYPHUS:** *(Pointing to BOULDER.)* This task from me is never gone.

*(SOUND CREW 2 strikes drum firmly.)*

**CHORUS 1:** Orpheus watched Sisyphus go struggling with the boulder and repeating his suffering soliloquy.

**SISYPHUS:** *(Stooping wearily and moving with BOULDER toward their chairs.)* I deceived the great god Zeus.

*(SOUND CREW 2 strikes large drum.)*

**SISYPHUS:** *(Gesturing to BOULDER.)* And from this task I can't get loose.

*(SOUND CREW 2 strikes drum.)*

**SISYPHUS:** *(Pointing to BOULDER.)* I must roll this boulder up a hill.

*(SOUND CREW 2 strikes drum.)*

**SISYPHUS:** I must roll it NOW against my will.

*(SOUND CREW 2 strikes drum.)*

**SISYPHUS:** But when I get it to the top,

*(SOUND CREW 2 strikes drum.)*

**SISYPHUS:** It rolls back down and will not stop.

*(SOUND CREW 2 strikes drum rapidly as BOULDER rolls into chair and SISYPHUS returns to his chair.)*

**CHORUS 2:** Finally, three depressive damsels, the daughters of King Danaus drooped into view.

*(SOUND CREW 3 strikes wood block to accompany slow, depressive walk of DAUGHTERS stage center.)*

**CHORUS 3:** The daughters peered into empty containers and droned this depressive dirge.

**DAUGHTER #1:** *(Very woefully.)* Oh there goes the water,

**DAUGHTER #2:** Oh no, oh woe.

*(SOUND CREW 6 strikes two low notes after "Oh no" and "Oh woe.")*

**DAUGHTER #3:** Oh there goes the water,

**ALL DAUGHTERS:** Oh no, oh woe.

*(SOUND CREW 6 strikes two low notes after "Oh no" and "Oh woe.")*

**CHORUS 4:** Orpheus asked their crime.

**ORPHEUS:** I haven't much time. But what was your crime?

**DAUGHTER #1:** *(Gesturing to all the DAUGHTERS.)* We each were to marry the very same night.

**DAUGHTER # 2:** But all of our husbands filled us with fright.

*(SOUND CREW 4 shakes tambourine.)*

**DAUGHTER #3:** So we decided our husbands to kill.

*(SOUND CREW 4 shakes tambourine.)*

**DAUGHTER #1:** And we did it at midnight.

**DAUGHTER #1, 2, and 3:** With a hearty good will.

*(SOUND CREW 4 shakes tambourine and slaps it in the center.)*

**CHORUS 1:** Orpheus stared at the girls in horror.

**DAUGHTER #1:** The gods have made us this rule.

*(SOUND CREW 3 strikes wood block.)*

**DAUGHTER #2:** We must go every day to this pool.

*(SOUND CREW 3 strikes wood block as POOL forms and DAUGHTERS go to it.)*

**DAUGHTER #3:** To fill our containers,

*(DAUGHTERS fill containers. SOUND CREW 3 strikes wood block.)*

**DAUGHTER #1:** But the water

**DAUGHTER #2:** Runs through

*(SOUND CREW 3, 4, and 5 shake rattles.)*

**DAUGHTER #3:** For they have no firm bottoms

**ALL:** What can we do?

*(SOUND CREW 3 strikes wood block.)*

**CHORUS 2:** Orpheus shook his head as the daughters withdrew peering into their bottomless containers.

**ORPHEUS:** *(Gesturing toward all the sinners.)* For their dire crime, these sinners pay and pay. Their punishment will NOT go away.

**DAUGHTER #1:** *(Returning to chair.)* Oh there goes the water,

**DAUGHTER #2:** *(Returning to chair.)* Oh no, oh woe.

**DAUGHTER #3:** *(Returning to chair.)* Oh there goes the water,

**ALL DAUGHTERS:** *(Sitting in chairs.)* Oh no, oh woe.

# SCENE SIX
## *Orpheus Encounters Hades and Persephone and His Request Is Fulfilled*

*Characters:* Chorus, Orpheus, Props, Hades, Persephone, Eurydice

**CHORUS 3:** Suddenly, there was a CLASH and a RUMBLE. Orpheus had arrived in the kingdom of King Hades and Queen Persephone. Two majestic thrones appeared.

*(SOUND CREW 5 strikes gong after "Clash." SOUND CREW 2 rumbles drum for "Rumble." Then, SOUND CREW 2 strikes slow majestic drum beats as PROPS regally carry two chairs representing thrones center.)*

**CHORUS 4:** Presently the great god and king of the underworld, Hades, and his wife Queen Persephone appeared and sat on the thrones.

*(SOUND CREW 1 strikes drum ceremoniously to accompany HADES and PERSEPHONE majestically walking side by side and sitting on thrones.)*

**CHORUS 1:** Orpheus kneeled. Hades sternly questioned Orpheus seeing he was not dead.

**HADES:** *(Rising, strongly and sternly.)* Orpheus what are YOU, a living person, doing in my land of the dead?

**ORPHEUS:** I come here King Hades to your land of the dead.

>In great misery, in great fear and dread.

>Oh, please King Hades set Eurydice free

>And so relieve my great misery.

**CHORUS 2:** Hades scowled at this impossible request.

**HADES:** *(Scornfully, hands on hips.)* Your request is IMPOSSIBLE! No dead person has EVER been allowed to return to the land of the living. Why should I allow YOU to bring YOUR wife back?

**ORPHEUS:** *(Rising.)* Great ruler no one will deny

>Every living soul must die.

>But Eurydice was so young and so free

>And my bride for one day when taken from me.

**CHORUS 3:** Hades sat, frowned, and turned away.

**CHORUS 4:** Then, Orpheus picked up his lyre and spoke.

**ORPHEUS:** On joy's nimble feet, she came dancing to me.

>*(SOUND CREW 6 sweeps tone bells from low to high.)*

**ORPHEUS:** Her heart was so lively. Her spirit so free.

>*(SOUND CREW 6 sweeps tone bells from low to high.)*

**ORPHEUS:** But now that she's gone, I am full of despair

>*(SOUND CREW 6 sweeps tone bells from low to high.)*

**ORPHEUS:** Without my young bride so gentle and fair.

>*(SOUND CREW 6 sweeps tone bells from low to high.)*

**CHORUS 1:** Orpheus's song was so magical that Persephone bowed her head. Then, she rose and implored Hades to let Eurydice return to the world above with Orpheus.

**PERSEPHONE:** Hades, my husband, please grant Orpheus's request. Please let Eurydice return to the land of the living with her husband.

**HADES:** *(Rising.)* Orpheus your song has moved us. I will grant your request, but on ONE condition.

**ORPHEUS:** *(Dropping to knees.)* Anything! I will do anything to get back Eurydice.

**HADES:** The condition is this! Eurydice must FOLLOW you. And you must NOT turn and look back at her until BOTH of you arrive in the world above.

**ORPHEUS:** *(Rising joyfully.)* Oh thank you great king. My heart is full of joy. We will sing and dance in praise of your kindness when WE return to the world above.

**CHORUS 2:** Hades gestured Orpheus to turn his back.

**HADES:** Turn around Orpheus.

>*(SOUND CREW 1 strikes triangle as ORPHEUS turns.)*

The Myth of Orpheus and Eurydice or Descent into the Underworld 233

**CHORUS 3:** Then Queen Persephone beckoned Eurydice to come and follow behind Orpheus.

**PERSEPHONE:** *(Gesturing to Eurydice.)* Come Eurydice and follow your husband.

*(SOUND CREW 1 strikes triangle as EURYDICE rises by her chair.)*

**CHORUS 4:** Eurydice came slowly because of a limp suffered from the snakebite.

*(SOUND CREW 2 strikes wood block to accompany EURYDICE's limp, which should be done gracefully.)*

**CHORUS 1:** King Hades and Queen Persephone stood ready to withdraw. But Hades raised an arm with a final warning.

**HADES:** *(Raising arm.)* Remember Orpheus, DON'T TURN and LOOK BACK at Eurydice until you BOTH reach the land of the living.

**PERSEPHONE:** Fare thee well, Orpheus and Eurydice. May you soon always be together again.

**CHORUS 2:** The king and queen withdrew.

*(SOUND CREW 1 strikes triangle ceremoniously as HADES and PERSEPHONE return to their chairs, and PROPS remove thrones.)*

# SCENE SEVEN
## *Orpheus Loses Eurydice a Second Time*

*Characters:* Chorus, Orpheus, Eurydice, Cave, Mist, Hermes, Willow Tree

**CHORUS 3:** Eurydice followed Orpheus through Tartarus with its swirling black vapors.

*(SOUND CREW 4 shakes tambourine to count of five and slaps it in the center as VAPORS swirl, freeze, and then return to chairs.)*

**CHORUS 4:** At first, Orpheus could hear Eurydice's footsteps and was sure she was there.

*(SOUND CREW 3 strikes wood block to accompany footsteps.)*

**CHORUS 1:** Finally Orpheus arrived at the cave entrance to the land of the living and went through.

*(SOUND CREW 1 strikes triangle three times as CAVE forms and ORPHEUS goes through and freezes.)*

**CHORUS 2:** But just then, he wanted to make sure that Eurydice was behind him. He turned. Mists swirled. Eurydice had NOT stepped out of the underworld.

*(SOUND CREW 1 strikes triangle emphatically on "turned." SOUND CREW 6 strikes two high tone bells successively for count of five as MIST swirls fabric, then drapes it over EURYDICE and then return to their chairs.)*

**CHORUS 3:** Hermes flew to Eurydice and led her back to the underworld. Eurydice vanished. All Orpheus could hear was the misty echoing of Eurydice's "Farewell."

*(SOUND CREW 2, 4, and 5 shake jingle bells as HERMES leads EURY-DICE back to her chair. CAVE returns to chairs.)*

**EURYDICE:** *(Mistily.)* Farewell.

**ALL ACTORS IN CHAIRS:** *(Mistily.)* Farewell, farewell, farewell.

**ORPHEUS:** *(Desperately calling.)* Eurydice! Eurydice!

**CHORUS 4:** Orpheus bowed his head in grief. Now, he knew he would NEVER get his wife into the land of the living.

**CHORUS 1:** Orpheus sat under a willow tree.

*(WILLOW TREE forms and ORPHEUS sits under it.)*

**CHORUS 2:** The tree bowed its head in grief.

*(SOUND CREW 4 shakes tambourine lightly as branches hang over OR-PHEUS.)*

**CHORUS 3:** Orpheus died to this world.

*(ORPHEUS still sitting, leans forward and bows head in stylized death. TREE branches shimmer as SOUND CREW 4 shakes tambourine lightly and mournfully.)*

**CHORUS 4:** Hermes flew to Orpheus.

*(SOUND CREW 2, 4, and 5 shake jingle bells as HERMES flies to OR-PHEUS.)*

**HERMES:** *(Motioning Orpheus to rise.)* Rise Orpheus, from this world you'll go. I'll lead you now to your wife below.

*(SOUND CREW 1 strikes triangle three times as ORPHEUS slowly gets up.)*

# SCENE EIGHT
## *Orpheus and Eurydice Unite Forever*

*Characters:* Chorus, Orpheus, Hermes, Eurydice, Prop People, Lyre, Star

**CHORUS 1:** Hermes guided Orpheus to the underworld.

*(SOUND CREW 5 and 6 shake hand bells as HERMES leads ORPHEUS down center.)*

**CHORUS 2:** There, Orpheus and Eurydice were reunited in the Elysian fields, a golden place, full of pleasure and joy.

*(EURYDICE walks to ORPHEUS. They face each other as SOUND CREW 1, 2, and 4 shake jingle bells and SHIMMERING GOLD flutters over and around them)*

**CHORUS 3:** Orpheus and Eurydice shared his song.

**ORPHEUS:** On joy's nimble feet, she came dancing to me.

*(SOUND CREW 6 sweeps tone bells as EURYDICE skips in big circle around ORPHEUS.)*

EURYDICE: My heart feels so lively, my spirit so free.

> (SOUND CREW 6 sweeps tone bells as EURYDICE twirls downstage right.)

ORPHEUS: And now that she's here, my heart feels no care.

> (SOUND CREW 6 sweeps tone bells as EURYDICE twirls stage left.)

ORPHEUS and EURYDICE: For being together is gentle and fair.

> (SOUND CREW 6 sweeps tone bells as EURYDICE bows to ORPHEUS who bows to her.)

CHORUS 4: Orpheus and Eurydice were truly united forever. And all the happy souls in the Elysian fields danced joyfully too.

> (SOUND CREW 4 shakes tambourine as ORPHEUS and EURYDICE lead ELYSIAN SOULS in the Greek dance done at the beginning of the play.)

CHORUS 1: In the world above, it is said that Orpheus's lyre floated into the sky and became the constellation Lira.

> (PROP PEOPLE place two chairs center. LYRE stands on one chair and holds LYRE at an angle to represent a constellation. STAR holds STAR to the side to highlight the lyre.)

CHORUS 2: And the people there still look up at it reminding them of the love of Orpheus and Eurydice.

> (SOUND CREW 1 strikes triangle three times. On the third triangle strike, ALL ACTORS stand and following CHORUS ONE'S lead lift their arms up first toward Lira and then toward ORPHEUS and EURYDICE. SOUND CREW 1 strikes triangle again to release the freeze and ACTORS and SOUND CREW sit.)

> (ALL CHORUS members go center stage for the finale. They should memorize this part.)

CHORUS 1: "Efharisto," friends and thank you too.

> ("Efharisto," pronounced Ef ha **ree** stoh, is Greek for thank you and literally means good graces and joy.)

CHORUS 2: For watching so kindly our myth for you

CHORUS 3: From Greece and Rome, it's old yet new.

CHORUS 4: We hope it came alive for you.

CHORUS 1: (Pointing to audience.) And here's a last tip from the chorus your friends.

CHORUS 2: (Holding up book.) Read a book of these myths from beginning to end.

CHORUS 3: And study Greece and Rome with their great majesty.

CHORUS 4: (Making big circular gesture.) For the more that you know, the more you'll be free.

> (CHORUS Return to their respective sides of stage to introduce the cast and crew.)

> (To end the performance, CHORUS 1–4 introduce the performers, having them stand and say their names loudly and clearly. When all are standing,

*CHORUS 1–4 thank the audience and then turn toward ACTORS and raise arms. Everyone follows, raising their arms and bringing them down together for a group bow. Performers then sit for the audience performance discussion.)*

**CHORUS 1:** The actors are . . .

*(SOUND CREW 6 strikes one high tone bell after each cast member stands, and introduces her or himself. CAST and CREW remain standing after they are introduced.)*

**CHORUS 2:** The Sound Crew is . . .

**CHORUS 3:** The Chorus is . . .

# PRODUCTION NOTES

## *Costume Suggestions*

For narrative mime presentations students wear all black clothing—black shirts and black shorts, pants, or skirts—with individual character costumes worn as additional pieces to the all-black attire. If actors play characters wearing tunics throughout the play, they need not wear black clothes as long as the clothes underneath aren't visible under the tunic. If possible, students should perform the play barefoot.

**Chorus:** Use pattern for simple, knee-length, choral robe. (See chapter 4, "Creating Costumes, Props and Scenery.") Make it from a cotton-polyester blend or similar fabric. The robe might be purple, dark blue, burgundy, dark green, off-white, or any dignified but not overpowering color. You could use similar or different colors for each chorus member. Tie with a black cord. Use gold, store-bought, laurel-leaf headpieces, or make headpieces with foliage from a floral-supply store.

**Calliope:** Long yellow tunic; white or gold belt; white and yellow, floral headband worn in the Greek style around the forehead.

**Apollo:** Gold or bright yellow, knee-length tunic; wide, gold belt. Tall, gold, tagboard crown, or oval, sun-shape headdress with points resembling the sun. (See chapter 4, "Creating Costumes, Props and Scenery," for headpiece design.)

**Orpheus:** White, knee-length tunic; lightweight, red fabric draped around shoulders, or red cloak; gold, store-bought, laurel wreath.

**Men, Women, Children in Wedding:** Red headbands for men; blue headbands for women; yellow or pastel-colored headbands for children.

**Lamb:** White or black, furry hat with felt, floppy ears attached, perhaps with pink felt inside.

**Deer:** Brown or beige, baseball cap with tall, pointed, tagboard ears—or attach small, tree branches as antlers.

**Birds:** Yellow, orange, or other beak-colored, baseball caps with felt eyes glued on the sides.

**Oak Trees:** Branches of autumn leaves from floral-supply shops.

**Olive Tree:** Branches with small, dark green leaves from floral-supply store

**Brook:** Narrow piece of lightweight, blue fabric to resemble a brook.

**Rocks:** No costume other than black clothing is needed. Actors use their bodies to form the shapes of rocks.

**Eurydice:** Long, pink tunic; pink or white sash or belt tied around the waist; pink or white headband with all white, or pink and white flowers. Eurydice might carry a filmy scarf of white, pink, or pastel color to help create graceful dancing.

**Serpent:** Black sock with red fangs, and a big, yellow eye with red, felt pupil.

**Hymen:** Saffron-colored, knee-length tunic; tall dignified headpiece.

**Mist:** White, nylon netting that is draped around Eurydice.

**Hermes:** Knee-length tunic of lamé or similar metallic fabric; silver belt; three-inch wide, black, tagboard headband with cardboard or tagboard wings covered with aluminum foil attached.

**Charon:** Black, hooded sweatshirt with no logos.

**River Styx:** Five or six yards of black, lightweight fabric that doesn't ravel.

**Cerberus:** Three, matching baseball caps with fierce, pointed, tall ears. The two dogs on both ends each wear one black glove to create a paw on each end, and the student in middle puts hands behind back. Or one student might play the dog wearing a cap with ears for one head and using puppets with dog heads on both hands.

**Entrance Gate:** No costume other than black clothing is necessary. Arms create the entrance gate.

**Black Vapors:** Streamers of black lightweight fabric, crepe paper, or other material attached to a dowel. (Each student has two dowels.) Or drape students in black netting to become vapors.

**Tantalus:** Dark, grape-purple, knee-length, tunic tied with black cord; black, two-inch headband with black laurel leaves with green glitter attached.

**Tantalas's Pool:** Piece of lightweight, deep blue or aqua fabric.

**Grapes:** Purple gloves used to wiggle like grapes bobbing.

**Sisyphus:** Gray or brown, knee-length tunic tied with rope; gray or brown sweatband.

**Boulder:** Black, watch cap or knit cap pulled down to eye level. Body creates boulder.

The Myth of Orpheus and Eurydice or Descent into the Underworld  239

**Daughters of King Danaus:** Small, black, tagboard tiaras with silver glitter and with black netting, representing funeral veils, attached. They should hang around shoulders but not cover faces.

**Daughters' Pool:** Lightweight, blue or aqua fabric, different than that of brook or Tantalus's pool.

**Hades:** Tall, spiked, black crown of tagboard with red glitter on points; black shiny cloak.

**Persephone:** Long, lavender tunic tied with gold cord; gold crown.

**Olive Tree:** Plastic greenery with small leaves from floral-supply store.

**Silver Star:** Black dowel with three- or four-inch, silver star attached to fish line.

## Props

**Calliope:** Lightweight, white, small bath towel bundled to resemble a blanket with a baby inside.

**Lyre:** Use simple lyre design. (See chapter 4, "Creating Costumes, Props, and Scenery" for lyre design.)

**Eurydice's Wedding Bouquet:** (optional) Bouquet of white, plastic flowers from floral-supply store.

**Hymen's Torch:** Use simple torch design. (See chapter 4, "Creating Costumes, Props, and Scenery" for creating a torch.)

**Bird Red:** Red glove, manipulated like bird or a hand puppet.

**Charon's Pole:** Broomstick or other pole.

**Daughters of King Danaus's Containers:** Gallon, bleach bottles, or other lightweight containers with bottoms cut out.

# STORY QUESTIONS, WRITING, ART, AND CLASSICAL CONNECTIONS (DEVELOPING LANGUAGE)

The following questions are listed scene by scene. Interpretive questions are indicated by an asterisk (*). A separate list of general and personal response questions are at the end of the section as well as a Classical Connections section with questions on words from the myths that have entered our vocabulary.

SCENE ONE: *THE BIRTH OF ORPHEUS AND HIS MUSICAL GIFTS*

1. What power does the muse Calliope have? In what way does she help develop Orpheus' musical gifts when he is a baby?
2. Who is Apollo? How does he help Orpheus to develop his musical gifts?
3. How do you know Orpheus loved to play music?
4. Name two extraordinary things that happened when Orpheus played his music that showed he had extraordinary musical powers.

SCENE TWO: *THE MEETING AND MARRIAGE OF ORPHEUS AND EURYDICE*

1. Who is Eurydice, and what causes her to follow Orpheus?
2. What do Eurydice and Orpheus have in common?
3. What did Orpheus, Eurydice, and their wedding guests do at the wedding to celebrate? Why was it particularly appropriate for this couple to celebrate that way?
4. Who performed the wedding rite, and why was it appropriate he perform it?
5. What disastrous event occurred during the wedding? Why do you think this was considered so devastating?

SCENE THREE: *THE DEATH OF EURYDICE*

1. When did Eurydice die? How did she die?
2. How did Orpheus react at first to the death of his bride?
3. Who took Eurydice to the underworld, and why is it appropriate that this character took her?
4. What action did Orpheus decide to take, and why did the decision give him hope?
5. Who was Orpheus going to seek to help him get back his wife?
6. Who in the story has the power to release Eurydice from the underworld? Why might he have this power?

The Myth of Orpheus and Eurydice or Descent into the Underworld  241

## SCENE FOUR: *DESCENT INTO THE UNDERWORLD*

1. How did Orpheus get into the underworld?
2. Why must Orpheus first get across the River Styx?
3. Who is Charon?
4. *Why do you think Charon is so cranky?
5. Why did Charon first refuse to take Orpheus across the river?
6. Why did Charon change his mind and take Orpheus across?
7. What obstacle did Orpheus meet when he arrived at the entrance gates?
8. What is unusual about the dog Cerberus?
9. How did Cerberus react when Orpheus tried to get through the entrance gates?
10. How did Orpheus get past Cerberus?
11. To what character in this scene does the famous quote "Music has charms to soothe a savage beast" most apply? In what way does it apply?

## SCENE FIVE: *TARTARUS AND ITS SINNERS*

1. What kind of people live in Tartarus?
2. What was Tantalus's crime and punishment?
3. What was Sisyphus's crime and punishment?
4. What were the crimes and punishments of the daughters of King Danaus?

## SCENE SIX: *ORPHEUS ENCOUNTERS WITH HADES AND PERSEPHONE AND HIS REQUEST IS FULFILLED*

1. What was Hades reaction when Orpheus first asked him to let Eurydice return to the land of the living?
2. How did Orpheus try to convince King Hades to allow Eurydice to return to the land of the living?
3. Who helped Orpheus get his wish and why did she help?
4. What condition did Hades impose on Orpheus when he brought his wife back to the land of the living?
5. What did Queen Persephone tell Orpheus to do before Eurydice began to follow him out of the underworld?
6. Why did Eurydice limp when she followed Orpheus out of the underworld?

## SCENE SEVEN: *ORPHEUS LOSES EURYDICE A SECOND TIME*

1. Which requirement of Hades did Orpheus neglect to follow as he left the underworld with Eurydice?
2. What disastrous event occurred from Orpheus's disobedience?

3. *Why did Orpheus look back?

4. What was Orpheus's reaction when he lost Eurydice for the second time?

5. Why did Orpheus want to die?

## SCENE EIGHT: *ORPHEUS AND EURYDICE UNITE FOREVER*

1. In what similar way do Orpheus and Eurydice go into the underworld when they die?

2. Hermes guides Orpheus to the Elysian Fields where Eurydice already dwells. What are the Elysian Fields? Why did Eurydice and Orpheus end up in that part of the underworld?

3. What was the first thing Orpheus and Eurydice did when they were reunited?

4. What does the constellation *lira* have to do with the myth of Orpheus and Eurydice?

5. *Is this a happy story? Explain.

## GENERAL INTERPRETIVE QUESTIONS

1. Orpheus strums a lyre when he recites poetry. In what way are the words of a song like the words in a poem?

2. In Greek mythology, everyone who dies goes to the underworld. There are areas for good and bad and people in between. For example, the most wicked souls go to Tartarus and are condemned to eternal punishment. The good go to the Elysian fields, a place of pleasure and joy. Knowing that the underworld is not just for wicked people, would you like to live or visit there? Explain.

3. The punishment of Tantalus, Sisyphus, and the Daughters of King Danaus is eternal and so goes on forever. Do you think it's fair that the punishment will never end? Explain.

4. What does Orpheus do that makes him a hero?

5. Orpheus is considered a sensitive hero. Describe something Orpheus says or does that shows he's sensitive.

6. Orpheus is considered the world's greatest musician, and in the story, his music enchants everyone. Some say that music is the most emotionally powerful of all of the arts. What is it about music that can help create a mood? What type of music do young children, teens, and your parents or grandparents like? What is it about these different types of music that make these different groups of people like that kind of music?

7. In what way does the famous quote from Shakespeare's play *Twelfth Night*, "If music be the food of love, play on" apply to this play?

8. Greek myths include every kind of human situation—there is good and bad, kind and cruel, tragic and amusing. Give an example of characters or situations that are good, bad, cruel, amusing, and tragic.

9. What is the saddest part of this myth? The happiest? The funniest?

10. Orpheus faced painful, upsetting, and frightening trials in his story. What do you think was the worst trial Orpheus faced in the story? Explain why you think that was the worst one.

11. What other myth in this book has the character Persephone? How is Persephone different in this myth than in the other one?

## Writing

1. Write a three or four sentence description of each of the two major characters—Orpheus and Eurydice. You may refer to the script to support your answer.

2. Orpheus was born with a great gift of music. There is a belief that everyone is born with some special abilities. Some people might excel in sports. Others in car mechanics, drawing, science, art, writing, acting, dancing, math, or languages. Which subjects, sports, or artistic activity do you like to do most? Choose one and list three things that you might do to help develop your special interest?

3. *Write a story about your new pet, Cerberus, and how you tamed him. Or, write a story about what happened when you brought Cerberus home as a pet and how you got the family to appreciate him.

## Research

1. Research other myths or stories in which someone is forbidden from doing one thing but does it anyhow with disastrous results.

2. Research other myths in which someone is warned not to look back but does and is severely punished.

3. The god Hermes appears in every myth in this book. Read the other myths in this book and describe what he does.

## Developing Language: Classical Connections

The following are questions on words in the myth that have entered the English language. Use the Glossary to answer these questions.

1. Calliope is the muse of the beautiful voice. What other powers does she have? Who are the other muses, and what are their powers?

2. Apollo is the god of music and light. What other powers does he have? What kind of person is an Apollonian?

3. Why is it fitting that the god Hermes and not another god escorted Eurydice and Orpheus to the underworld?

4. What does the word *tantalize* mean? Why is it a fitting word to derive from the figure of Tantalus?

5. What is a Sisphean task? In what way is it a fitting word to derive from Sisyphus?

6. How is the Greek underworld different from our concept of hell?


## Art

- Draw your favorite character or scene from the myth of Orpheus and Eurydice.

# Writing a Narrative Mime Script and TV Interview

Your choice of stories is not limited to the scripts in this book. Many myths or stories can be adapted into plays. Use the following techniques to help students adapt a story or a myth into a narrative mime script.

Find a simple picture book of the story. Even for older students picture books are a good starting point since they emphasize action and break the myth into manageable bits of information. Their vivid, and often dramatic, illustrations help students visualize the characters and the setting. They also give ideas on costuming and action.

Research collections of myths that have the stories condensed and written in a page or two. *Classic Myths to Read Aloud* by William E. Russell, *Adventures of the Greek Heroes* by Mollie McClean and Anne Wiseman, and *Earth's Daughters* by Betty Bonham Lies (all listed in the Bibliography) are good collections. You might also try the fables in my book *Dramatizing Aesop's Fables* that have the fables written for acting but they are not in a script form. (All of the above books are listed in the Bibliography.)

The essence of a narrative, mime script is action. Help students identify action moments in the story, and show them how to add action verbs to give actors something specific to do. For example, students might change "Arachne was known throughout her Greek village as a wonderful weaver" to "Every morning, Arachne picked up her needle and hummed to herself as she wove beautiful cloth on her loom."

Pare down the story to its essential action. Eliminate unnecessary adjectives, adverbs, and description—or find a way to make description active. For example, "The children went outside on a beautiful spring morning" might be changed to "The children opened the door, and skipped across the green meadow."

Use vivid verbs. *Spied, peered, scowled, glared,* or *squinted* are more specific and easier to act than *looked.* This exercise also, of course, develops vocabulary, and tests comprehension by showing if students can accurately act the verb.

Read the first page of a picture book, and ask students what action words might be added to give the actors something to do.

Try to have the lines of the chorus give the characters cues for what to say, as in the following example.

**CHORUS:** From Chaos sprang Ge, the Earth.

**GE:** I am Ge, goddess of the Earth.

**CHORUS:** Ge commanded Uranus, the sky god, to come forth.

**GE:** Come forth Uranus and create a sky to cover my Earth.

- *Repeat key plot information one or two times. So if the audience doesn't get the information the first time, they will get it the second or third time, as in the following example:*

    **CHORUS:** Only Atlas could calm the dragon with his soothing song.

    **ATLAS:** Only I can calm the dragon with my soothing song.

    **HERCULES:** Atlas, if I hold up the sky for awhile, will you calm the dragon with your soothing song?

- *Include roles for animals and inanimate objects, and when possible, give them things to do.*

- *Include sound effects, both vocalized and those that can be made by rhythm instruments.*

- *Use at least one chorus member, and not more than four.*

- *Have students examine this story that is first written in straight narration, and then it is rewritten into a narrative, mime script. After reading the dramatized version, ask them to point out what action words were added, what inanimate objects were included, how sound effects were added, and how the chorus gave characters cues on what to say.*

# Hercules and the Wagoner
## (Narrative Version)

A farmer was driving a wagon when one wheel got stuck fast in the mud, and the horse could not get it out. The farmer got off the wagon and prayed that the god Hercules would come and help him. Hercules appeared and said, "Don't pray to me, lazybones. Put your shoulder to the wheel, and pull the wagon out of the mud yourself. The gods help those who help themselves."

## (Narrative Mime Script)

CHARACTERS
  CHORUS
  FARMER
  HORSE
  HERCULES
  ROCK
  Sound Crew
  Sound Effects: triangle, wood block, tambourine, rattles

**CHORUS:** *Hercules and the Wagoner*

*(SOUND CREW strikes triangle.)*

**CHORUS:** A fable by Aesop

*(SOUND CREW strikes triangle.)*

**CHORUS:** A farmer was walking beside his wagon pulled by is horse, which trotted along.

*(SOUND CREW strikes wood block.)*

**CHORUS:** The horse stumbled, and the wagon turned over.

*(SOUND CREW shakes tambourine and slaps it in the center as HORSE stumbles and the WAGON turns over.)*

**CHORUS:** The horse neighed, then tugged to pull the wagon out, but he could not.

*(HORSE neighs. SOUND CREW shakes rattles vigorously for tugging.)*

**CHORUS:** The farmer got down on his hands and knees and begged Hercules to come help him.

FARMER: Oh, great god Hercules, please come and help me.

(*SOUND CREW strikes triangle.*)

CHORUS: Hercules sprang from behind a rock.

(*SOUND CREw strikes wood block as HERCULES springs from behind ROCK.*)

CHORUS: Hercules pointed at the farmer accusing him of being a lazybones.

HERCULES: Farmer, you are a lazybones.

CHORUS: The farmer hung his head and grumbled that he was no lazybones.

FARMER: I'm no lazybones.

CHORUS: But Hercules told him not to hang his head, but to put his shoulder to the wheel and pull the wagon out himself.

HERCULES: Don't hang your head, man. Put your shoulder to the wheel and pull the wagon out yourself.

CHORUS: The horse whinnied, impatient for the farmer to be moving along. Hercules raised an arm giving the farmer this final wise advice: The gods help those who help themselves.

HERCULES: (*Raising arm.*) The gods help those who help themselves.

(*SOUND CREW strikes triangle.*)

CHORUS: Then Hercules majestically disappeared behind the rock.

(*SOUND CREW strikes triangle.*)


## Working in Groups

The following explains how to divide the students into groups to develop and perform their own narrative mime script.

- Choose several picture books or short myths from a collection for students to dramatize.

- Divide the class into groups, one for each myth. Have each group choose a secretary. Students in each group work together to develop chorus, narration, and character dialogue for their scene. The secretary records the information in script form. Students then add sound effects and possibly add more object parts to the script as necessary.

- Students practice acting the story in their groups, testing for what works and what does not. They might decide on more sound effects as they go along. If there are not enough instruments to use with every group, encourage students to improvise using objects around the room or give each group one or two instruments to use.

- Students share their performances with the class. The class comments, first mentioning what was good about the performance and then suggesting additions to enhance it.

- Students return to their groups and run through their scenes again, incorporating the suggestions. Again students share their performances with the class and any final adaptations are made.

- Students bring in their own costumes or create their own costumes, scenery, props, and sound effects. They might perform their stories to other classes as "traveling troupes."

## *Writing a TV Interview*

You or the students might also write TV Interviews based on stories or novels. To write an interview, make a cast list including the TV Announcer and all significant characters in the story. Begin the interview with the TV Announcer summarizing the plot, while introducing the characters in the order of their appearance in the story. The characters step forward when introduced. The TV Announcer then interviews each character in the sequence in which they appear in the story. The TV Announcer asks questions about their part in the plot. Study the TV Interviews with each of the five scripts in this book for samples.

## *Writing a Parody*

Students might also write a modern parody of one of the scenes they have performed in this book. The following is a scene from *The Odyssey*. The author was a sixth-grade student—Elliott Spore from Dana Middle School in San Diego, California. Students might enjoy reading and dramatizing the parody.

# Odysseus and His Copilots Land on the Island of the Witch Circe

*By Elliott Spore*

CHARACTERS:
- NARRATORS
- ODYSSEUS
- COPILOTS
- ROBOTS
- CIRCE
- ANGEL

**NARRATOR 1:** Odysseus and his Copilots Land on the Island of the Witch Circe

**NARRATOR 2:** Odysseus and his copilots have been bound to an airplane with an unlimited supply of gas for ten years.

**NARRATOR 3:** They shift into landing gear and prepare for touchdown.

**ODYSSEUS:** O.K., crew, landing in 10, 9, 8 . . . *(Continues to count down, fading into the background.)*

**NARRATOR 4:** Little did they know that this was the island of the witch Circe.

**ODYSSEUS:** Landing now! We can fuel up here. Why don't you guys go explore.

**NARRATOR 1:** The copilots followed the leader through the woods.

**NARRATOR 2:** They came to a clearing. In it was a rough cement house.

**NARRATOR 3:** A robot, obviously broken, stood on the path.

**NARRATOR 4:** From inside came the sound of melodious music.

**NARRATOR 1:** A beautiful woman was playing a piano.

**NARRATOR 2:** The copilots called . . .

**COPILOTS:** Good morning, lady!

**NARRATOR 3:** The lady opened the door and gestured them inside.

**CIRCE:** Welcome. I am Circe, the evil enchan—I mean—lady of these halls. You look thirsty. Let me make you my special, carbonated drink.

**NARRATOR 1:** She put in an evil potion, stirring it well.

**CIRCE:** Drink my evil pot—I mean—carbonated drink.

**NARRATOR 2:** She took a wand and struck the drowsy copilots.

**NARRATOR 3:** The copilots stiffened and became mindless robots.

COPILOTS: *(Now robots.)* Ready to take your orders.

NARRATOR 4: Meanwhile, Odysseus sensed something was wrong.

ODYSSEUS: I'm done fueling. I should go check on them.

NARRATOR 1: Suddenly an angelic figure appeared on the path.

ANGEL: Odysseus, Circe will turn you into a mindless robot. Eat this magic strawberry to prevent the effects of her potion. Say "OOBAHGOOBAH" and she will say, "What?" Then raise your arms and she will bow to you.

NARRATOR 2: The angelic figure flew off. Odysseus walked to the house.

CIRCE: Come into my house. I will make you a carbonated drink.

ODYSSEUS: Thank you.

NARRATOR 3: Circe made her poisoned drink.

ODYSSEUS: This is very good.

CIRCE: Thank you.

ODYSSEUS: OOBAHGOOBAH!

CIRCE: What?

NARRATOR 4: Odysseus raised his arms, and Circe bowed to him.

CIRCE: You must be Odysseus. I am Circe.

ODYSSEUS: I already knew that.

CIRCE: O.K. Well. I won't hurt you anymore. Let me return your copilots.

NARRATOR 2: Circe tapped the mindless robots with her wand, and they turned into humans.

COPILOTS: Thank you Odysseus.

NARRATOR 2: Odysseus and Circe went online and ordered FedEx to bring delicious food and drinks.

NARRATOR 3: And that is the adventure of Odysseus on the island of Circe.

# GLOSSARY OF GREEK MYTHOLOGY
# AND DRAMA TERMS

This glossary of drama and literature terminology includes an explanation of words and phrases from Greek mythology that have entered our English vocabulary. Allusions to Greek mythology are found in literature, newspapers and magazines, ordinary conversation, songs, sermons, ads, and brand names. Teachers might copy the glossary for students to use when answering the questions on these words in the Critical-Thinking Questions section given with each script under the category, Classical Connections. They might also research brand names and names of companies derived from Greek mythology.

**actor:** a performer in a play. In the sixth century B.C., the Greek Thespis (from which we get the synonym for actor, *thespian*) introduced the first actor onto the stage. Prior to this, performances used a chorus of actors. The playwright Aeschylus introduced the use of a second actor, and Sophocles introduced the use of a third actor.

**Amazons (am** uh zonz): strong female warriors who were believed to live in the Black Sea region of southeastern Europe. Some believe the Amazon River was named by a Spanish explorer in the 1400s when he saw the females there fighting along with males. *Amazonian* means as strong as a man.

**ambrosia (am bro** zuh): the food of the gods. It was thought by the ancient Greeks to make those who consumed it live forever. *Ambrosia* today means any food that tastes delicious. The dessert, ambrosia, is made of oranges and shredded coconut. (See *nectar.*)

**Apollo (a pol** oh): the Greek and Roman god of intelligence, music, poetry, and the Sun. The oracle that gave prophecies at Apollo's shrine at Delphi had great influence on matters of state, religion, and law and order. (See *Delphi* and *oracle.*) Apollo was known for his physical beauty; an *Apollo* today means a handsome young man. An *Apollonian* has a love for beautiful artistic things. His Roman name is Phoebus.

**Artemis (are** tuh mis): goddess of the hunt, wildlife, and the moon. She is the sister of Apollo. She is often depicted with a bow and arrow. Her Roman name is Diana.

**articulation:** precise pronunciation of words and syllables using the articulators—jaw, lips, tongue, teeth, and soft palate.

**aside:** short speech delivered by one character and not meant to be heard by the other characters on stage. Asides express what the character is thinking or something that the character knows that the others don't know. Asides are frequently used in classical Greek drama.

**Athena** (a **thee** nuh): goddess of wisdom, the arts, and of war and peace. She was the favorite daughter of Zeus. Her symbols are the owl and the olive tree. Athens, the capital of Greece and a great city of culture and power, is named for Athena. The Parthenon Temple on the Acropolis in Athens is dedicated to her. Any city considered a center of culture and learning might be called an Athens. For example, Boston, Massachusetts, is considered the Athens of America. An *athenaeum* is a literary or scientific club. Her Roman name is Minerva.

**Atlas** (**at** lus): the best known Titan god. Atlas was punished by Zeus for waging war against the Olympian gods and given the task of holding up the sky. The Greek word *atlas* means "to support." *Atlantean* means strong. The Atlantic Ocean refers to Atlas. A book of maps is called an atlas because a picture of Atlas supporting the world on his shoulders appeared in the book of a mapmaker in the 16th century. The Atlas is a powerful ballistic missile.

**King Augeas** (aw **jee** us): King Augeas had 3,000 cattle, the largest herd in Greece, and had neglected to clean his stables for thirty years. One of Hercules' labors was to clean the filthy stables of King Augeas. Hercules diverted the flow of two rivers through the stables and cleansed them.

**Augean stables** (aw **jee** an): an Augean stable is a condition of filth and corruption. "Cleaning the Augean stables" means getting rid of noxious rubbish, whether physical, moral, or legal.

**Birds of Stymphalis** (stim **faa** lus): one of Hercules tasks was to destroy the birds of Stymphalis who shot people with their brass feathers.

**blocking**: coordination of actor's movement on stage. The director usually plans blocking with input from the actors. To "block" a play means to plan and work out the movement of the performers in the play.

**Calliope** (kah **lie** uh pee): mother of Orpheus, and the muse of epic poetry, song, and eloquence. Her name comes from two Greek words meaning "beauty" and "voice." A circus organ consisting of a set of steam whistles is called a *calliope*.

**Celeus** (**see** lee us): king of Eleusis (ee **loo** sis) and husband of Queen Metaneira, who befriended Demeter in *The Myth of Demeter and Persephone*.

**Cerberus** (**sir** ber rus): three-headed, guard dog in the underworld. His job was to keep anyone who was alive from entering the underworld and to prevent anyone already dead from leaving it. Cerberus was frightening, but he could be soothed by music or food. Orpheus got past Cerberus and into the underworld by playing his lyre. Hercules' most difficult and last labor was to bring Cerberus from the underworld to the land of the living. A **Cerberus** is a surly keeper or dog.

**chaos** (**kay** os): according to the ancient Greeks, chaos was an open gulf in which everything existed in a kind of swirling and transparent vapor. Modern scientists think the universe originally really existed like this. Chaos now refers to utter confusion or disorder. The Earth goddess, Ge, emerged from Chaos.

**character actor**: actor specializing in imitating idiosyncratic types, like the cranky boatman Charon; the cruel slave driver, Eurystheus; and the power-hungry Cronus. These roles might be played by character actors.

**Charon** (**ker** on): ferryman who transports dead souls across the River Styx into the underworld. Charon allows only dead souls on his boat, and he must be bribed with a coin. Thus, the ancient custom of the Greeks and other cultures of placing a coin under the tongue or on the eyelids of the dead.

 **Charybdis** (kuh **rib** dis): a dangerous whirlpool off the coast of Sicily. Odysseus had to sail through a narrow pass with Charybdis on one side and the sea monster Scylla on the other. A Charybdis is a serious danger. Between Scylla and Charybdis means making a choice between equal dangers. (See *Scylla*.)

**chorus**: in ancient Greek theater, a group of actors who commented on the action, gave advice to the central characters, and provided background on preceding events.

**Circe** (**sir** see): a beguiling enchantress who turned Odysseus's sailors into pigs. When Odysseus subdued her, she transformed his sailors back to humans and then helped him. A *Circe* is a dangerously fascinating woman. *Circean*, or resembling Circe, refers to anything that appears attractive but that can make people act like beasts. Drugs and alcohol can be Circean.

**colorization**: creating the mood of the language through varying tonal quality, pitch, and gesture.

**Cronus** (**crow** nus): son of the Earth goddess, Ge, and the sky god, Uranus. He was the most crafty and power-hungry Titan. To assure he'd always be the supreme leader, he swallowed his children, the baby Olympian gods. His son Zeus overthrew him. Cronus was connected with Father Time. Words derived from Cronus are *chronology* (an arrangement of events in order of their occurrence); *chronic* (something that occurs over a period of time); and *chronicler* (one who records a series of events in the order in which they occur).

**cue**: final line or word of one performer's speech signaling the next performer that it is now her or his turn to speak.

**Cyclops** (**sigh** klops), the plural is Cyclopes (sigh **klow** peez): one-eyed giants and sons of the Earth goddess Ge and the sky god Uranus. The word *Cyclops* comes from two Greek words meaning "circle" and "eye." The Cyclopes were said to have built gigantic walls ("Cyclopean walls") found in the ancient ruins of Greece. *Cyclopean* means gigantic.

**Daughters of King Danaus** (**dan** a us): the fifty daughters of King Danaus who feared their husbands and so killed them on their wedding nights.

**Daughters of Oceanus** (oh **see** an nus): daughters of the god of rivers of the world and of the ocean. They were the playmates of Persephone.

**Deer of Cerynea** (ser ee **nee** ah): magical, golden-horned deer of extraordinary speed who dwelled on a mountain in Arcadia. One of Hercules' labors was to capture this deer for the goddess Artemis.

**Delphi** (**del** feye): the most sacred and the oldest shrine in ancient Greece. It was the temple of the god, Apollo. Objects found there date back to 1600 B.C. Located on the remote slopes of Mount Parnassus, the ruins of Apollo's temple may still be seen. The Delphic Oracle often assigned difficult tasks to do or gave obscure responses. The oracle told Hercules to serve the cruel King Eurystheus for twelve years.

**Demeter** (de **mee** tur): goddess of ripe grain, vegetation, and agriculture. She was the mother of Persephone. Demeter became tormented with grief when Hades seized Persephone and took her to the underground. She let the food crops die until her daughter was returned to her. Her Roman name is Ceres (**see** reez). From Ceres we get the word *cereal* meaning grasses—such as wheat, barley, and oats—that are cultivated as edible grain.

**dialogue**: speech exchanged by characters. It can also be the speech of one character.

**director**: person responsible for the overall staging of a production. The director coordinates costuming, setting, lighting, music, and sound effects although these are usually executed by experts. Directors direct the actors and interpret the script.

**drama**: from the Greek word *dran*, "to do or to act." *Drama* means a composition to be acted on the stage.

**Dionysus** (die oh **nigh** sus): god of vegetation and wine. He is also the god of the theater. The theater in Athens stood within the sanctuary of Dionysus and was called the Theater of Dionysus.

**Eleusis** (ee **loo** sis): town west of Athens where Demeter found shelter and that is the site of a temple dedicated to her. It became the center for the Mysteries of Demeter, a religious rite open only to special initiates who agreed never to reveal what took place during the rites.

**Elysian** (e **liz** ian) fields or Elysium (e **liz** i um): happy, golden place in the underworld where the good and virtuous go when they die. *Champs Elysees,* the French word for Elysian fields, is the name given to a beautiful boulevard in Paris.

**emphasis:** stress on important words (usually verbs or nouns) achieved through variation in volume, pitch, pause, gesture, and facial expression.

**ensemble acting:** the performance of the group rather than one or two individual central characters is emphasized.

**epic:** long, dignified story poem that tells the adventures of a hero who represents the values of that civilization. *The Iliad* and *The Odyssey* were epics used to teach Greek values.

**epilogue:** a speech usually in verse delivered at the end of a play.

**Eurydice** (you **rid** ih see): beautiful nymph of the woods and dancer who married the great musician Orpheus. She was bitten by a serpent and taken to the underworld the day after the wedding. (See *Orpheus.*)

**Eurystheus** (you **ris** the us): cruel taskmaster who gave Hercules twelve, difficult, dangerous labors to do.

**Ge** (**gee** ): great mother goddess of the Earth, Ge was born out of Chaos and created Uranus, the sky god. The words *geography* (description of the Earth); *geology* (science of the Earth); and *geometry* (measurement of the Earth) come from Ge. Her Roman name is Terra.

**gesture:** any movement of the body, arm, head, or face that expresses or emphasizes an idea or emotion. Examples: a threatening or beckoning gesture; a gesture of acceptance or rejection; gestures of joy or gloom. Gestures help performers achieve complete communication and intensify meaning.

**The Great Bow:** bow that Odysseus used to shoot an arrow through the rings of six axes. Odysseus accomplished this test of "the great bow," thus triumphing over the suitors who had been harassing his wife, Penelope, to marry them.

**Hades** (**hay** deez): king and god of the underworld and husband of Persephone. The word *Hades* also means the underworld itself (where ancient Greeks believed both good and bad souls went at death). The name has spawned such expressions as "go to Hades" and "hot as Hades." His Roman name is Pluto.

**Hecate** (**hek** a tee): goddess of the dark moon and witches.

**Hecatonchire** (hek a ton **keye** ree): hundred-handed offspring of the Earth goddess Ge and sky god Uranus.

**Helios** (**hee** lee os): the first Sun god prior to Apollo. Helios is usually depicted as a charioteer who drives the Sun across the Earth from east to west each day. *Heliocentric* describes the theory that the Sun is the center of the solar system. The heliotrope flower turns toward the Sun. His Roman name is Helius.

**Hera** (**hair** a): queen of the gods and wife of Zeus. Hera is the protector of women, children, and marriage. Often depicted with a peacock whose tail with many "eyes" watch out and report people's doings to her. Her Roman name is Juno, giving us the name of the month June, considered the most suitable for marriage.

**Hercules** (**her** cue leez): roman name most commonly used for the Greek hero Heracles (**hair** ah kleez). With superhuman strength, Hercules is known for the twelve difficult dangerous labors he accomplished. Because of his bravery and perseverance, he was elevated to Mt. Olympus and made a god. A *Hercules* is a man of extraordinary strength. A *Herculean task* is something of extreme difficulty, or requiring superhuman strength. *Herculite* is an explosive. The constellation Hercules contains the brightest cluster of stars in the northern hemisphere.

**Hermes** (**her** meez): the winged messenger god and the god of luck, business, and wealth. Exceptionally swift, Hermes is usually seen with wings on his sandals and hat. His name means "mediator" in Greek, and he "mediates" or brings dead souls to the underworld. A *Hermetic seal* keeps vessels airtight, and when a jar is hermetically sealed, no air can get inside. His Roman name is Mercury. *Mercurial* means flighty and changeable.

**Hesiod** (**Hee** siod): one of the earliest writers of Greek myths. *The Creation and Birth of the Olympian Gods,* in this book is based on the version by Hesiod who wrote the most complete account of the beginning of the universe and ascent of the Olympian gods.

**The Golden Tree of the Hesperides** (hes **per** ih deez): one of Hercules' labors was to take golden apples from this tree located in the west of Greece near the Atlas Mountains and guarded by a dragon.

**Hestia** (**hes** tee uh): goddess of the hearth and home and the very first Olympian god. Her Roman name is Vesta.

**Hippolyta** (hi **pol** i tuh): queen of the Amazons. (See *Amazons.)* One of Hercules' labors was to bring back the precious belt of Hippolyta. The character of Hippolyta, the Amazon Queen, is in Shakespeare's *A Midsummer Night's Dream.*

**Homer** (**hoh** mer): believed to be the author of the great epic poems, *The Iliad* and *The Odyssey.* The Greeks thought he was a blind scholar living in the 8 B.C. who came from the island of Chios. Deeply revered by the Greeks, Homer's works were studied for their wisdom and often quoted. *Homeric* means sublime or majestic.

**hospitality**: a principal Greek virtue and considered a necessary quality of every citizen. Greeks believe even strangers should be treated with special respect and kindness, given food and other comforts, and welcomed to spend the night in their homes. Those who don't practice hospitality are considered rude. The most inhospitable are seen as obnoxious, and sometimes evil.

**hubris** (**hugh** bris): excessive pride, recklessness, or arrogance. People who are hubristic set themselves up as equal to, or superior to, the gods. Their arrogance and excessive disregard for limits always leads to intense suffering. The behavior of General Odysseus allowing his sailors to ransack Troy of its treasures after the Trojan War was an act of hubris.

**Hymen** (**high** men): god of marriage.

**Hydra** (**high** druh): a many-headed snake, living in the swamps of Lerna (**ler** nuh) a district in the eastern Peloponnesus. One of Hercules' labors was to get rid of the hydra, a seemingly impossible task because when one head was cut off, it re-grew. Hercules solved the problem by cauterizing each head with a burning branch. A *hydra* is a problem difficult to overcome and frequently with many issues to resolve. The difficulty of creating world peace is a hydra.

*The Iliad* (**ill** ee ud): the story by the great poet Homer of the war fought on the plains outside the city of Troy between the people of Troy and an alliance of Greek kings. The Greeks started the battle to avenge the insult suffered by King Menelaus of Greece when Paris, prince of Troy, ran off with the King Menelaus's beautiful wife, Helen.

**inflection**: vocal technique in which the voice rises or falls. Rising inflection carries the thought and ideas forward. A falling inflection indicates the end of a thought or idea.

**Iris** (**eye** ris): goddess of the rainbow and a messenger goddess, especially for Zeus. The colored part of the eye is called the iris. *Iridescent* or *iridescence* is a rainbow-like display of colors.

**Ithaca** (**ith** uh kuh): island kingdom of Odysseus in the Ionian Sea off the west coast of Greece. Odysseus spent ten years after the Trojan War trying to sail back to his home in Ithaca.

**lyre**: ancient stringed instrument, somewhat like a guitar without a neck. The most popular lyre had a tortoise-shell sounding board. Lyric poetry was poetry sung to a lyre. Lyric poetry now means poems expressing feelings and emotions. The lyrics are the words of a song.

*The Metamorphosis* (met a mor **phoe** sis): a book of fifteen poetic myths by the Roman writer Ovid (43 B.C.–17 A.D.). It is considered, after Homer, the most important source for classical mythology. The book treats all kinds of love—love of a man for a woman, of father and son, of a daughter and father, of a brother and sister, of gods for humans, of old people for each other, and of the love of the self. The play of *The Myth of Orpheus and Eurydice or Descent into the Underworld* in this book is adapted from the version in *The Metamorphosis*.

**Metaneira** (**met** uh neh ra): wife of King Celeus. She befriended Demeter and gave Demeter her son to care for.

**Metis** (**me** tis): goddess of trickery.

**Muses** (**mew** zez): nine female patrons of the arts, who danced at festivals on Mt. Olympus and who inspired artists. They are Calliope, muse of epic poetry and eloquence; Clio, history; Euterpe, flute playing; Terpsichore, dance; Erato, love poetry; Melpomene, tragedy; Thalia, comedy; Polymnia, mime; and Urania, astronomy. A museum originally was a temple to the muses and a center of learning where scientists and inventors worked. The word *music* comes from *muses*. A muse is a female power who inspires people in their creative work. The verb *to muse* means "to think or meditate on something."

**myth**: the Greek word *mythos* means "a tale or story." Now it refers to stories that use fantastic images to express ideas about life that can't be expressed in realistic terms. Myths endure because they tell of experiences that we all have.

**Narcissus** (nar **sis** us): a beautiful young man who fell in love with his own reflection and died turning into a flower. A family of flowers, including jonquils and daffodils, is called narcissus. Hades seized Persephone as she picked a narcissus.

**nectar** (**nek** tar): drink of the gods, believed to give immortality to any who drank it. A smooth-skinned peach is called nectarine for its sweet taste. The sugary fluid used by bees to make honey is nectar. (See *ambrosia*.)

**Nymphs**: beautiful young females who personify rivers, trees, and mountains and who love music and dancing.

**Odysseus** (oo **dis** se us): one of the most famous characters in literature and hero of *The Odyssey*. He is clever, humane, resourceful. He uses intelligence rather than brute force to get out of predicaments. Like everyone, he is also imperfect and has some human flaws. A great Greek general in the Trojan war, he planned the building of the hollow wooden horse that concealed his soldiers, enabling them to overcome the Trojans. He was made to sail the seas for ten years before he could return home to his wife Penelope and their son Telemachus.

*The Odyssey* (**od** ih see): epic poem by Homer composed in the 8th century B.C. This great masterpiece of western civilization tells the story of the ten-year adventure of the Greek General Odysseus as he made his sea voyage home from the Trojan war. An *odyssey* is a complicated journey or a long wandering. An *Odysseus* is an adventurer.

**Olympians** (oh **lim** pee anz): the gods and goddesses who live atop Mount Olympus. Originally six in number, they were later joined by six more, their offspring. They control natural forces; they are immortal and all powerful. It was considered wise to treat them with careful consideration. They were given presents and bribes to control the elements or for a special favor. For example, they might be asked to send rain or to control the sea.

**Olympus** (oh **lim** pus): mountain range in northern Greece. Its highest peak is Mount Olympus about 96,000 feet. Mount Olympus was the home of the gods and goddesses—but at a height above the visible mountain.

**oracle** (or a **kal**): derived from a Greek word meaning "to pray," the oracle has three meanings: first, a holy place where people went to consult a god or goddess; the priest or priestess who spoke on behalf of the deity; and finally the actual message of the deity. The most famous oracle is at the temple of Apollo in Delphi.

**Orpheus** (**or** fee uss): poet and a great musician who charmed even beasts when he played on his lyre. He was the son of Apollo, who gave him a lyre, and the muse, Calliope, who endowed him with a wonderful voice. He married the wood nymph, Eurydice, who died the following day of a snakebite. Orpheus pursued her into the underworld, but he lost her when he disobeyed Hades and looked back to see if she was following him.

**pantomime**: acting without speaking using facial expression and gesture only.

**Penelope** (pe **nel** oh pee): beautiful wife of Odysseus who remained faithful to him for ten years even though she was besieged by suitors wanting to marry her. The name *Penelope* means faithfulness and patience.

**Persephone** (per **seff** uh nee): goddess of the spring and the daughter of Demeter. She was seized by Hades and taken into the underworld where she became his queen and wife. Her Roman name is Prosperina.

**Pitch**: how high or low the voice is. Professional actors usually play parts in their normal range—extending the pitch as much as three octaves when the character, mood, or intensity of the scene requires it.

 **pomegranate** (**pomm**-uh-gran-et): thick-skinned fruit containing a great many juicy seeds. The pomegranate tree grows in Mediterranean countries, and in other areas that have hot, dry climates. Persephone ate four seeds of a pomegranate while in the underworld and was thus required to spend four months of every year there with Hades.

**Poseidon** (po **sigh** don): brother of Zeus and god of the sea, horses, and the creator of earthquakes. Often depicted astride a dolphin or a horse, Poseidon's symbol is the three-tined trident. A powerful submarine-launched ballistic missile is named Poseidon. His Roman name is Neptune.

**presentational theater**: acknowledgment by the actors that the audience is "present." In presentational theater, actors sometimes look at the audience and may even interact with them. Presentational theater differs from realism in which the actors pretend they are carrying on in their own world and that the audience doesn't exist.

**prologue** (**pro** log): In Greek drama, the "prologos" was the introduction of the play. The prologue is often in verse and calls attention to the theme of the play.

**prompter**: the one who tells forgetful actors their lines.

**protagonist** (pro **tag** on ist): the actor in Greek drama who took the leading role. For example, the actors playing Hercules or Demeter would be considered the protagonists.

**rate**: speed of delivery—for example, in scenes with quickening hoofbeats, quicken the pace. In death scenes or dreamy pensive states, slow it down.

**rhapsode** or **rhapsodist** (**rap** so dist): at first a wandering singer who recited his own poem stories, but later any singer of tales. In Homer's day, Homer and others visited villages and sang tales such as *The Odyssey* that combines history, religion, fantasy, and humor.

**Rhea** (**ree** uh): goddess of the earth and fertility. She was the mother of the first six Olympian Gods: Zeus, Hades, Poseidon, Hestia, Hera, and Demeter.

**River Styx** (sticks): chief river of the underworld that divides the land of the living from the land of the dead. Dead souls were ferried across the river by Charon, the cranky boatman. (See *Charon*.) *Stygian* means hellish or gloomy.

**script**: the text of a play or other spoken performance.

**Scylla** (sil uh): monster with six, serpent heads and three rows of teeth, who emits ferocious barks. Thought to exist in a narrow pass off Sicily and opposite the whirlpool, Charybdis. Odysseus had the difficult task of trying to steer between Scylla and Charybdis and not get destroyed. "Between Scylla and Charybdis" means to be in a situation in which both alternatives are unsatisfactory. (See *Charybdis*.)

**Sirens** (**sigh** rens): beautiful destructive women who lure men to their deaths with their enticing song. Odysseus made his sailors plug their ears with beeswax, and he had himself bound to the ship's mast to resist being lured to the Siren's island. A siren is an alluring woman determined to make men who fall in love with her miserable. A siren song is a dangerously enticing offer. A siren is also a loud, warning sound on such things as an ambulance, police car, fire engine.

**Sisyphus** (**sis** ih fus): a Greek king who was punished by Zeus for telling one of Zeus's secrets. His punishment in the underworld is to continually roll up a hill a heavy boulder that immediately comes rolling down and must be rolled up again. *Sisyphean* means a fruitless task.

**stage**: platform on which actors perform in a theater. From the Latin verb *staticum*, "a standing place."

**tableau**: a picture presented by motionless actors, especially at the end of an act or scene. In the nineteenth century, many plays ended acts in a tableau.

**Tantalus** (**tan** tuh lus): Greek king who committed the horrible sin of serving up his son as a meal at a banquet for the gods. He was punished in the underworld by forever being tantalized by water and fruit just beyond his reach. *To tantalize* is to offer or show something that evokes desire but is withheld.

**Tartarus** (**tar** tuh rus): gloomiest place in the underworld where the most terrible sinners are punished eternally.

**Telemachus** (te **lem** a kus): son of Odysseus and Penelope. He searched throughout Greece to find his father and then helped him overcome the boorish suitors who were trying to usurp his father's wife and throne.

**tempo**: how fast or slowly you speak.

**theater:** derived from a Greek word meaning "a seeing place," a place where plays and other entertainments are performed. Ancient Greek theaters were built into the natural slope of hills and held 14,000 to 15,000 spectators seated on bleachers.

**Thespis (thes** pis): the "Father of the Drama" (about 550–500 B.C.), he created the first actor and the word *thespian* comes from his name.

**Titans (tie** tanz): first Greek gods, existing before the Olympian gods. The Titans were the children of Ge and Uranus and were huge with tremendous strength. Any person of great strength or power may be called a titan or titaness. Titanium is a metallic chemical element used in molten steel. The giant ship reputed to be unsinkable was the *Titanic* that ironically sank after being hit by an iceberg. The dinosaur titanosaurus is also named for the Titans.

**Trojan Horse:** huge wooden horse devised by the Greek General Odysseus and constructed by the Greeks to win the Trojan War. The Trojans thought the horse was a gift from the gods and brought it inside their city gates. The concealed Greek soldiers led by General Odysseus sprang out and defeated the Trojans. A Trojan horse is a concealed danger, such as a spy who makes his way into an organization and then undermines it from within. The expression, "Beware of Greeks bearing gifts," comes from this incident and implies impending treachery.

**the underworld:** also known as Hades, the place in Greek mythology where all dead souls, both good and bad, go. The most evil go to Tartarus, where they are condemned to eternal punishment; the completely good, go to the Elysian fields where everything is joyful and golden; and the not wholly good or bad go to the Asphodel fields, a gray, boring place where souls drift aimlessly in the shade.

**Uranus (you rain** us): god of the sky and husband of Ge, the Earth goddess, who created him. A planet is named Uranus. Uranium is an element used in atomic energy. Uranography, uranometry, and uranology are sciences that deal with the heavens.

**vocal quality:** whether your voice is shrill, nasal, raspy, lilting, simpering, or booming.

**vocal variety:** using as many speaking techniques as needed to convey meaning.

**volume:** loudness or softness of voice. Varying the volume can convey subtle dramatic meanings. For example, recite the first line of line "Double, double toil and trouble," softly and the following line, "Fire burn and cauldron bubble" loudly to create a surprising menace.

**Zeus (zoose):** king of the Olympian gods and the most powerful Greek god. He overcame his father, the Titan god, Cronus, and installed himself and his brothers and sisters as the Olympian gods supreme. Primarily a sky and weather god, the thunderbolt is his emblem. Zeus sired many children including Athena, Apollo, Artemis, and Hermes. They later became Olympians too. His Roman name is Jupiter, the largest planet in our solar system. He is also referred to as Jove spawning the jaunty exclamation, "By Jove!"

# SELECTED BIBLIOGRAPHY

## ACTING AND DIRECTING

Ball, William. *A Sense of Direction: Some Observations on the Art of Directing.* New York: Drama Book Publishers, 1984. Insightful, book with valuable chapters on casting, training actors, and conducting rehearsals.

Busti, Kathryn Michele. *Stage Production Handbook.* Littleton, Colo.: Theatre Things, 1992. A valuable resource for teachers and students producing a play, arranged in a convenient, tabbed, three-ring binder. Includes step-by-step guidelines and checklists that you can copy for students on technical aspects of putting on a show.

Clurman, Harold. *On Directing.* New York: Simon and Schuster, 1997. Entertaining and clearly written book on all aspects of play directing by a master director.

Grote, David. *Play Directing in the School—A Drama Director's Survival Guide.* Colorado Springs, Colo.: Meriwether Publishing Ltd., l997. A helpful book for teachers who want to direct full-scale productions.

Hodge, Francis. *Play Directing: Analysis, Communication and Style*, 4th ed., New York: Prentice Hall, 1994. A thorough account of all aspects of directing a play—of value to the novice and to the advanced director.

Jory, Jon. *Tips: Ideas for Actors.* Lyme N.H.: Smith and Kraus, 2000. An enjoyable book by an expert with useful page-long tips on acting technique, speech, movement, and building a role.

## COSTUMING AND MUSICAL INSTRUMENTS

Brooke, Iris. *Costume in Greek Classical Theatre.* New York: Theatre Arts Books, 1962. An excellent book on ancient Greek costuming by a costume expert. Discusses all aspects of Greek costuming including tunics, headdresses, hairstyles, footwear, jewelry, insignia, cloaks, and belts.

Fiarotta, Noel and Phyllis Fiarotta. *Music Crafts for Kids—The How-To Book of Music Discovery.* New York: Sterling Publishing Company, Inc., 1993. A charming book with a variety of information on music and the creation of simple instruments. Both students and teachers will enjoy this book.

Hope, Thomas. *Costumes of the Greeks and Romans.* New York: Dover Publications, 1962. An invaluable resource of 700 engravings of ancient Greek and Roman costumes taken from ancient Greek vases and statuary. The beautiful engravings are in the public domain.

Sichel, Marion. *Costume of the Classical World.* New York: Chelsea House Publications, 1980. An informative description of ancient Greek costuming and accessories with line drawings. Of interest to students and teachers.

West Music Company, 1212 5th Street., Coralville, Iowa 52241 (1-800-397-9378) A very complete catalogue of reasonably priced instruments. They also have books on teaching music and movement, and other materials helpful for dramatization.

## LITERATURE DRAMATIZATION

Thistle, Louise. *Dramatizing Aesop's Fables.* Lyme, N.H.: Smith and Kraus, Inc., 1993. Aesop's fables dramatized for the classroom or for use on the stage. Includes acting techniques, character warm-ups, dramatizations of eight of Aesop's popular fables, improvisations, and critical-thinking questions.

Thistle, Louise. *Dramatizing Mother Goose.* Lyme, N.H.: Smith and Kraus, Inc., 1998. Seventeen Mother Goose rhymes scripted for dramatization in the classroom and on the stage. Costume and rhythm instrument suggestions, literature questions, and historical background on Mother Goose. Use to perform for younger students and as an introduction to the study of nonsense verse.

Thistle, Louise. *Dramatizing Myths and Tales.* Lyme, N.H.: Smith and Kraus, Inc., 1995. Similar in format to *Dramatizing Greek Mythology*, this book has myths and tales dramatized from five cultures—West African, Mayan, Native American, Japanese, and the British Isles. Includes detailed description of how to cast and direct beginning, acting students in a play.

Thistle, Louise. *Dramatizing Three Classic Tales—The Three Billy Goats Gruff, The Little Red Hen and The Lion and the Mouse.* Lyme, N.H.: Smith and Kraus, Inc., 1999. Three tales dramatized with action pictures and "chant" words to say and act for each sentence. Simultaneously develops language and involves all students in dramatization. Recommended for English- and Spanish-language learners, available in English and Spanish versions. Older students will enjoy performing these for younger students.

## BOOKS ON GREEK MYTHS

Asimov, Isaac. *Words from the Myths.* New York: Houghton Mifflin, 1961. Definitions of English words that have entered our vocabulary from Greek mythology. Includes succinct retellings of the myths. Of interest to middle school and high school students.

Bonham Lies, Betty. *Earth's Daughters—Stories of Women in Classical Mythology.* Golden, Colo.: Fulcrum Publishing, 1999. More than 60 myths with women as the central characters. Divided into such categories as creation stories; stories of pride, beauty and jealousy; and lovers and their beloved. Students might use these to create their own dramatizations.

Daly, Kathleen N. *Greek and Roman Mythology A to Z: A Young Reader's Companion.* New York: Facts on File, 1992. Descriptions in dictionary form of the characters and settings in Greek mythology. Valuable resource for classroom and school libraries.

D'Aulaire, Ingri and Edgar D'Aulaire. *D'Aulaire's Book of Greek Myths.* New York: Doubleday and Company, Inc. 1962. A classic text that captures the magic, wonder, and power of the myths.

Fisher, Leonard Everett. *The Olympians (Great Gods and Goddesses of Ancient Greece).* New York: Holiday House, 1984. Brief sketches of the twelve Olympian gods and goddesses with large, striking, dramatic pictures.

Gibson, Michael. Giovanni Caselli, illustrator. *Gods, Men & Monsters from the Greek.* New York: Schocken Books, 1982. Imaginatively and dramatically illustrated, with intelligent adaptations of major myths.

McLean, Mollie and Anne Wiseman. Witold T. Mars, illustrator. *Adventures of the Greek Heroes.* New York: Houghton Mifflin Company, 1989. Dramatic retellings of the adventures of Hercules, Perseus, Theseus, Orpheus, Meleager, and the Argonauts. Illustrations resemble ancient Greek vase paintings.

Osborne, Mary Pope. Troy Howell, illustrator. *Favorite Greek Myths.* New York: Scholastic, Inc., 1989. Dramatic retellings of myths based on Ovid's *Metamorphosis.* Includes "The Weaving Contest of Arachne and Minerva," "The Story of Echo and Narcissus," and "The Golden Touch."

Russell, William F. *Classic Myths to Read Aloud.* New York: Three Rivers Press, 1989. Major myths of Greece and Rome, grouped according to age-level suitability, to read aloud to students. Includes with each myth, a glossary of words from the myth that have entered our English vocabulary.

## BOOKS ON INDIVIDUAL GREEK MYTHS

Birrer, Cynthia and William Birrer. *Song to Demeter.* New York: Lothrop, Lee, and Shepard, 1987. Dramatic retelling of the story of the goddess of the harvest and her daughter, Persephone. The forceful illustrations are machine-stitched, appliqué and embroidery on fabric. Out of print but available at most libraries.

Fisher, Leonard Everett. *Theseus and the Minotaur.* New York: Holiday House, 1988. A powerful telling of the story in a picture book with stimulating pictures. Students might want to adapt for dramatization.

Lasky, Kathryn. Mark Hess, illustrator. *Hercules, the Man, the Myth, the Hero.* New York: Hyperion Books for Children, 1997. The myth told from Hercules' point of view with big vivid illustrations of his labors.

Lister, Robin. Alan Baker, illustrator. *The Odyssey*. New York: Kingfisher, 1994. Fast-paced telling of the myth with many illustrations.

Loewen, Nancy. *Hercules*. Mankato, Minn.: Capstone, 1999. Informative book about the labors of Hercules. It is illustrated with photographs of ancient Greek painting and statues and of modern paintings and statues. Includes general information on mythology and the classical world.

## BOOKS ON ANCIENT GREEK CULTURE

Gorton, Julia, editor. *Ancient Greece*. New York: Viking, 1992. Clearly written and lavishly illustrated with photos and illustrations that depict ancient, Greek culture.

Millard, Anne. *The Greeks*. New York: Usborne Publishing Ltd., 1990. Succinct reference book, with informative illustrations covering development of Greek civilization and its contributions. Also depicts everyday life, including musical instruments, clothing, and hairstyles.

Rosenberg, Donna and Sorelle Baker. *Mythology and You—Classical Mythology and Its Relevance to Today's World*. New York: National Textbook Company, 1992. Includes retellings of the major myths with background and critical-thinking questions. Helpful resource for teachers.

## SCHOLARLY BOOKS ON GREEK MYTHOLOGY

Fagles, Robert, translator. *The Odyssey—Homer*. New York: Viking, 1996. Down-to-earth translation that still captures the beauty and power of the story.

Fitzgerald, Robert, translator. *The Odyssey*. New York: Doubleday, 1961. Poetic version of the masterpiece, which along with Robert Fagles's translation, is considered the best.

Humphries, Rolfe, translator. *Ovid, the Heart of Love*. Bloomington, Ind.: Indiana University Press, 1957. Considered the best translation of Ovid's *Metamorphosis*.

Morford, Mark P. O. and Robert J. Lenardon. *Classical Mythology*, 6th ed. New York: Longman, 1999. Perhaps the best resource on Greek mythology—scholarly, informative, and highly readable. Includes historical background on the myths, psychological interpretations, color and black-and-white photos of art works depicting the myths, and chapters on mythology in films, paintings, opera, and dance. Highly recommended.

# ACKNOWLEDGMENTS

I want to thank the many people who made this book possible. First, I thank Emily Packer who continues to give me invaluable editorial help and art suggestions. This book in this form would not be possible without her knowledgeable guidance and encouragement.

Several teachers have been instrumental in helping develop these scripts. First, I thank Christy McCabe who directed several of the myths and developed many creative ideas for staging. Joanna Airhart directed *The Myth of Demeter and Persephone*, helped me direct *Hercules*, and gave me invaluable feedback on the critical thinking questions and writing components. Phoebe Levinger, teaching artist at San Diego Junior Theater, gave me several ideas from her imaginative stagings of scenes from *The Odyssey* and *Hercules*.

Sandra Lynn Bennett gave me the opportunity to try out two scripts for the first time. I am grateful to Judy Greenwald for her support and skillful help dramatizing four of the myths with her classes. Kathy Robertson provided creative ideas on ways to use these dramatizations as springboards to other parts of the curriculum. Other teachers who have helped me while dramatizing with their classes are Tish Haake, Kelly Musatti, Cathy Cheshire, Jamie Walsh, Cory Smith, and Cindy Lail. Cindy Lail also gave me the idea for an effective system of nonverbal cues to give students to tell them what is working well and what needs improvement in a rehearsal.

I thank Nick Genovese, chair of the classics department at San Diego State University, for his graciousness giving me important suggestions on sources for the myths, critical-thinking questions, and music. Drama expert Sharon Oppenheimer gave me imaginative ideas for acting activities. Actor Alexandra Aufderheide offered suggestions on dialogue and staging. Actor Guillermo Aviles-Rodrigues gave me valuable knowledgeable information on Greek mythology.

I thank Jo Kilingsworth for her editorial help. I also thank Mary Ann Petteway for her expert editing. I appreciate Kate Wilson's suggestions for literature questions that would interest middle school students. Author-Educator Dianne Tucker-LaPlount gave me ideas on how to use Greek myths to teach reading.

Kit Michelson designed and created imaginative artistic costumes and props that have enriched these productions. Dan Toporski continually and graciously offers me help with my computer needs. Timothy Stepp provided help with illustration suggestions. Norma Slaman and the hosts at the Newbreak Coffee Company in Ocean Beach provide an inviting place to study and meet.

I must thank Heather Reed, Jean Davis, Vanessa Goodman, Joe Miesner, Alice Nodes, and others on the staff of the Ocean Beach branch library for their help with my many book requests. John Vanderby and Evelyn Kooperman of the literature section of the San Diego Library continue to help me with research. Jean Stewart and the staff of the children's section have sent picture books to supplement the dramatization.

The teaching and writing of Sylvan Barnet, my first literature-writing teacher at Tufts University continue to be models for me. His ability to teach and write in a way that honors the complexity of a subject while making it clear and stimulating is remarkable.

Finally, I thank my husband, Charles Francis Dicken, for ideas and suggestions. He read the manuscript and gave me suggestions that improved the writing.

271

## DATE DUE

| DEC 1 8 2002 | |
|---|---|
| | |
| | |
| | |
| | |
| | |
| | |
| | |
| | |
| | |
| | |
| | |
| | |
| | |
| | |
| | |